D1042413

Survival of the Savvy Endorsements

"*Survival of the Savvy* is a critically important book for the new era of business! Leaders need to learn how to win in a world that is both ultra-competitive on the business side and ultra-sensitive to issues involving ethics."

—MARSHALL GOLDSMITH, COAUTHOR OF
THE LEADER OF THE FUTURE

"A refreshing view of the importance of corporate politics. *Survival of the Savvy* isn't about the nonsense of stamping out organizational politics—it's about facing reality and learning how to manage yourself and your team, from the CEO down."

—CAROL BARTZ, CHAIRMAN, CEO, AUTODESK

"Ignore corporate politics and you may find yourself sleeping with the fishes. Organization savvy is a topic that's tough to get your arms around, but *Survival of the Savvy* is tops on my list for its practical and proven approach for navigating through today's rough organizational waters."

—DEB HIMSEL, VICE PRESIDENT, ORGANIZATION
EFFECTIVENESS, AVON PRODUCTS, INC.

"*Survival of the Savvy* assists CEOs to survey their organizations so that they can build relationship bench strength possessing integrity and ethical management while also building a great company culture committed to top performance and loyalty."

—AJIT GIL, PRESIDENT AND CHIEF EXECUTIVE OFFICER, NEKTAR

"Seldman and Brandon are just in time. *Survival of the Savvy* gives us the elite intelligence and powerful tools to ensure personal success and improved business performance during turbulent corporate times. This book is better than an MBA!"

—DENNIS ZELENY, FORMER SENIOR VICE PRESIDENT HUMAN
RESOURCES, E.I. DU PONT DE NEMOURS AND COMPANY

"This book offers indispensable insight into the positive power of politics in an organization. If you can't hire Brandon or Seldman as a personal coach, this book is the next best thing!"

—WENDY BLOOM, SENIOR MANAGER, HUMAN CAPITAL AND
LEADERSHIP, BEST BUY CO., INC.

"You can influence with political wisdom and integrity! Whether you're a CEO, a teacher, or a new employee, you can continually tune your understanding of yourself and of your work environment. *Survival of the Savvy* is an outstanding tool kit."

—JIM KENNEDY, DIRECTOR OF EQUITIES, T. ROWE PRICE ASSOCIATES

"Terrific book that captures the upside and downside of politics in an organization. As you read each chapter, the 'aha's' just keep on coming. Brandon and Seldman have written a true winner, full of proven successful techniques that leaders at all levels will want to practice."

—DEB CAPOLARELLO, SENIOR VICE PRESIDENT HUMAN RESOURCES, CHIEF TALENT OFFICER, METLIFE

"This book delivers a powerful message on leadership. Effective leaders learn early that adapting your leadership style to motivate others is one of the most effective skills any leader can possess. *Survival of the Savvy* shows any individual how to step beyond the comfort zone to become a better leader, parent, or person."

—ERIC FOSS, PRESIDENT, PEPSI BOTTLING GROUP NORTH AMERICA

"*Survival of the Savvy* is invaluable for all business leaders who are seeking to understand the connectivity of emotional intelligence, the application of 'high-integrity' politics in achieving business effectiveness and career success."

—RON PARKER, SENIOR VICE PRESIDENT, HUMAN RESOURCES, FRITO-LAY NORTH AMERICA

"This book is essential for anyone who has ever tried to play a game without knowing the rules. *Survival of the Savvy* offers proven practical strategies, techniques, and rules of the game for anyone who wants to be an MVP in the business world."

—JEAN M. OTTE, FOUNDER AND CEO, WOMEN UNLIMITED, INC., AND AUTHOR OF *CHANGING THE CORPORATE LANDSCAPE: A WOMAN'S GUIDE TO CULTIVATING LEADERSHIP EXCELLENCE*

"*Survival of the Savvy* describes the political landscape inside of organizations. If you want to deftly navigate the political whitewater in your organization, this is the book for you."

—JON PETERS, PRESIDENT, THE INSTITUTE FOR MANAGEMENT STUDIES

"This is a book we all could have used when we were twenty-five years old. It provides perspectives that make so much sense and can be readily applied to any workplace—small or large, public or private. *Survival of the Savvy* can improve almost anyone's personal effectiveness with no compromise on ethics."

—PETE BASSI, CHAIRMAN, YUM RESTAURANTS INTERNATIONAL

"Brandon and Seldman, for the first time, have presented practical strategies for using politics in a positive, ethical fashion. If you work in any organization, whether it be a Fortune 500 company, your local PTA, or your AYSO soccer league, this book will provide invaluable insights to enable you to achieve results in a manner which you can be proud of."

—JOHN MCELROY, SENIOR VICE PRESIDENT, HUMAN RESOURCES AND CORPORATE SERVICES, MITSUBISHI MOTORS NORTH AMERICA, INC.

"This book has provided me with a systemic understanding of the root cause of company politics and how as a leader one can coach the organization to be mature and effective about managing it. As I have always believed, it takes a politically savvy leader to create an environment that is not excessively political. I just learned a lot from this book on how to become one."

—SAM SU, PRESIDENT, GREATER CHINA, YUM GLOBAL RESTAURANTS

"In the crowded field of leadership and business books, Brandon and Seldman have written a watershed resource that is vital for leaders and professionals. Finally, a practical resource for understanding and effectively dealing with politics, ethics, deception, and effectively 'doing the right thing' at high levels of performance!"

—EDWARD BETOF, ED.D., VICE PRESIDENT AND CHIEF LEARNING OFFICER, BECTON, DICKINSON AND COMPANY

"*Survival of the Savvy* is a career-saving 'survival guide' for today's business leaders. Brandon and Seldman have developed a pragmatic tool kit to help managers detect deception and to develop political astuteness in their work environment."

—PETER C. SMITH, EXECUTIVE VICE PRESIDENT AND CHIEF HUMAN RESOURCES OFFICER, BURGER KING CORPORATION

"An extremely insightful perspective on the political world that lies within corporations. While many executives would like to think that their companies are apolitical, this is just not the case and those executives imperil their careers and their companies. This book is like a pocket coach providing practical insights on how to navigate in the 21st Century Corporation."

—MANUEL N. SOUSA, EXECUTIVE VICE PRESIDENT, SAKS FIFTH AVENUE ENTERPRISES

"Two street-smart psychologists with more than a half century's combined experience in performance-improvement coaching and training show that you can be hurt by being overly political or by political blind spots and naïveté. Rather than offer a 'one size fits all' prescription, they help you assess your political style, note your strengths and weaknesses, and then supplement your style with savvy strategies that deliver impact with integrity. Who couldn't use that?"

—ROBERT H. BOLTON, PH.D., AUTHOR OF *PEOPLE SKILLS* AND COAUTHOR OF *PEOPLE STYLES AT WORK*

"The challenge of leadership is much more about *how* to get things done than it is *what* things should get done. This book teaches you the *how* and demonstrates that politics and integrity are not mutually exclusive."

—MICHAEL FEINER, PROFESSOR, COLUMBIA GRADUATE SCHOOL OF BUSINESS

"After reading *Survival of the Savvy* no manager will dare say, 'I'm not political.' Instead, managers will embrace the need to understand what motivates individuals, will know how to detect and handle hidden agendas, and will be able to build a high-integrity culture."

—PETER D. GIBBONS, EXECUTIVE VICE PRESIDENT SUPPLY CHAIN, ICI PAINT

"In the post-Enron era, this is a true practical guide for individuals and leadership teams to navigate the rough waters of corporate integrity."

—JULIE STAUB, DIRECTOR, HUMAN RESOURCES, AUTONATION, INC.

f **P**

Survival of the Savvy

High-Integrity Political Tactics for Career and Company Success

Rick Brandon, Ph.D.
Marty Seldman, Ph.D.

FREE PRESS
New York • London • Toronto • Sydney

FREE PRESS
A Division of Simon & Schuster, Inc.
1230 Avenue of the Americas
New York, NY 10020

This publication contains the opinions and ideas of its authors. It is intended to provide helpful and informative material on the subjects addressed in the publication. It is sold with the understanding that the authors and publisher are not engaged in rendering any kind of personal professional services or advice in the book. If expert assistance is desired, the service of a professional should be sought.

The authors and publisher specifically disclaim all responsibility for any liability, loss or risk, personal or otherwise, which is incurred as a consequence, directly or indirectly, of the use or application of any of the contents of this book.

DESIGNED BY PAUL DIPPOLITO

Manufactured in the United States of America

15 17 19 20 18 16 14

Library of Congress Cataloging-in-Publication Data
Brandon, Rick.
Survival of the savvy: high-integrity political tactics for career and company success / Rick Brandon, Marty Seldman.
p. cm.
Includes index.
1. Office politics. 2. Organizational behavior. 3. Corporate culture. 4. Integrity. 5. Business ethics. I. Seldman, Marty. II. Title.

HF5386.5.B73 2004
650.1'3—dc22 2004056301

ISBN-13: 978-0-7432-6254-5
ISBN-10: 0-7432-6254-9

To our wives, Cheryl and Kelly—your blend of street smarts, integrity, and compassion inspires us each day.

Contents

Survival of the Savvy

Introduction

A Political Wake-Up Call

A Corporate Survival of the Fittest

A corporate survival-of-the-fittest situation *does* exist, especially in tough economic, competitive, and cost-conscious times. Nobody likes to admit that a company has destructive politics or gamesmanship, but good people can become "squirrelly" in any organization given today's pressures. Naïveté and lack of organizational savvy can threaten anyone's influence, organizational impact, career growth, team credibility, and company results. But we will show you how to overcome any potential political disadvantage by employing high-integrity political tactics and strategies.

"High-Integrity" Politics?

For most people, the words *integrity* and *politics* don't mix. When we hear the phrases "Politics as usual" or "He's really political," we think of undesirable behavior such as manipulation, backroom deals, self-serving hidden agendas, bad-mouthing, or compromising values to get things done. Such behavior definitely exists, and in twenty-five years of training and coaching thousands of executives, we've had "unspeakable horrors" whispered to us about the elephant in the room—organizational politics. This elephant has crushed many well-intentioned and capable professionals and leaders.

A major goal of this book is to help you better understand unethical behavior, detect it, and protect yourself and your company culture from it. But we invite you to consider this negative cluster of behaviors as only one type of politics. Here is a broader, more inclusive, and pragmatic definition we recommend.

> **Organizational politics** are informal, unofficial, and sometimes behind-the-scenes efforts to sell ideas, influence an organization, increase power, or achieve other targeted objectives.

Notice that this practical definition is value-free and has nothing to do with partisan politics. It is neither inherently good nor bad, neither vile nor virtuous. Two conditions determine whether organizational politics become constructive or destructive:

1. Whether the *targeted objectives* are for the company's interest or only self-interests; and
2. Whether the *influence efforts* used to achieve those objectives have integrity or not.

If a high level of political prowess resides with individuals of questionable integrity who seek their own personal gain, ambition, or security, then organizational politics harm careers and companies. But political savvy and skill can also help ethical, competent people sell ideas and influence others for the good of organizations. Here's why we've found it more helpful to define politics in this value-free way:

1. *"Don't Throw the Baby Out with the Bathwater."* If you define politics in a narrow, negative way, you may overlook the value of political awareness and skill. If political astuteness is combined with the right values, it can be a win-win situation for you, your team, and your organization.
2. *"Get Off That River in Egypt—De-Nile!"* Negative attitudes toward politics lead to avoidance and denial. At an individual level, this attitude means that you steer clear of the political arena and believe politics shouldn't exist or matter in your career. At a company level, this attitude means that leaders underestimate the

reality of overly political behavior and the rotting effect on careers, the company's reputation, results, and its bottom line.

3. *"Wearing a Target on Your Back."* The costly irony of narrowly defining politics as entirely negative is that under political or apolitical people are even *more vulnerable* to overly political people combining political skill, pure self-interest, and a willingness to do whatever they can get away with to obtain what they want.

Amateur Night

The Apollo Theater in Harlem, New York, is world famous for electrifying performances from star entertainers. Some of these soloists, groups, and comedians got their start at the Apollo's Amateur Night, when novices have a decent chance to win in competition against other amateurs. But there is no "Amateur Night" at the corporation, and the odds are heavily stacked against someone who is a novice in the world of organizational politics. The amateur either defines politics so negatively that he dislikes and avoids it, never developing much political skill, or he denies negative politics altogether, trusting others to do the right thing. When amateurs go up against more politically skillful people, their careers, ideas, and teams are at serious risk. Consider the following real-life examples of the cost paid by defining politics in a rigid manner or limiting one's political savvy.

Amy: Stolen Ideas

Amy is the director of consumer insight for a $3 billion division of a multinational food manufacturing company. Her responsibilities include traditional aspects of market research with particular emphasis on tapping into consumer sentiment. She reports to the senior VP of marketing, who reports to the executive vice president of marketing. Amy is bright, with great technical skills, and can be persistent if she thinks an idea will help the company. Usually, though, she is fairly quiet, polite, modest, and trusting.

The EVP, Sam, is well-known throughout all divisions of the multinational conglomerate. He is charismatic, a great speaker, and perceived to be a true innovator in the company. His personal life contributes to a "rebel" and "maverick" image. He rides a motorcycle, dresses in the style of the MTV generation, and refuses to wear a suit and tie. The senior management team of the parent company ignores his idiosyncrasies because of his results. Senior management across the conglomerate has previously overlooked Sam's reputation for personal indiscretions.

Amy's latest research indicates that consumers want the company to provide larger portions. With this increased perception of value bringing increased sales, Amy feels this strategy will dramatically increase profits. She does not share her excitement about her findings with her immediate boss because he is nearing retirement and she isn't confident that his opinion carries any clout with superiors. Her first two attempts to present her results and strategy to Sam are not successful. In fact, he is impatient and dismissive. Yet, Amy is so sure she is right that she persists and Sam finally agrees to test market her approach. The results are excellent and soon the strategy is rolled out to the entire division. The positive impact on sales and profits is so great that at the end of the year Sam is named Executive of the Year by the conglomerate.

At first, Amy feels tremendous pride and satisfaction that her idea has focused such a dramatic spotlight on the division. At internal meetings Sam credits her research, but Amy starts to notice that Sam often implies that the initial impetus for the research came from him. This becomes even more noticeable after Amy's direct boss, the senior VP of marketing, is transferred to another division. Although somewhat upset, Amy comforts herself with the thought that Sam isn't always precise with words but surely he remembers her insights and persistence. In fact, she expects to be promoted to vice president since she has been director for three years and in several of the other divisions a VP heads her function.

Recently, two events unsettle Amy. One of her peers in another division calls to say he was surprised that at a speech to his division, Sam hadn't mentioned Amy or her research. Jack says that

Sam made it seem the strategy was mostly "intuitive." The second disturbing event is that her new boss says he is too new to evaluate her or recommend her for VP, deferring her appraisal to Sam. Finally, Amy meets with Sam in a disappointing, almost devastating session. The bottom line is that while Sam appreciates her contributions, he cannot at this time recommend her for a promotion. He says that she needs to work on her leadership style and personal intensity. He asserts that she comes across as a "nice woman" but not a leader.

Bart: Misreading the Political Signals

Bart is a senior logistics executive who is heavily recruited to join "Suretain," a transportation company. During the interview process both the executive search firm and the head of human resources tell Bart that his skill set and leadership style are exactly what Suretain needs. They explain that the company is conservative and resistant to change. What they feel is needed is a "change agent" who can bring some new strategies and a sense of urgency and accountability. They use terms such as *create a performance culture* and *remove deadwood.*

When Bart joins Suretain, he finds it relatively easy to add value. Many existing processes can be improved, and Bart moves swiftly to grab the "low-hanging fruit." His early "wins" and positive feedback encourage him to believe he has a mandate for change. After about two months in the new role, Bart is invited to lunch by Kathy, the head of manufacturing. Kathy is an industrial engineer who joined the company after getting her master's degree and worked her way up, over eighteen years, to the top manufacturing role. Over lunch, she compliments Bart on his fast start but gives him a heads-up about the company's culture. She tells Bart that it's important to realize that it has been difficult for people from the outside to be successful and that the company changes slowly, with many key decisions made over longer periods, after many people's input is gathered and consensus emerges. Also, she cautions him that there are several long-standing, close relationships among key executives and suppliers.

Bart gives Kathy time to finish, but his facial expressions and body language are dismissive. Finally he says, "Kathy, thanks for the education, but you have just reinforced my conviction that this place needs to change. In fact, I've been telling my team that we're going to show the company how things should be done. What I've done until now is nothing. I'm going after bigger targets."

Soon, Bart reviews all the major long-term contracts that the company has with suppliers. He decides to focus on the terms for a contract with the "Henozedaman" company. In a series of meetings, he puts pressure on the president of Henozedaman to reverse certain terms or face removal from the approved vendor list. Bart is unaware that the president and the CEO of Suretain are close friends and jointly own resort real estate. In the next month, these events unfold:

- Bart's CEO receives several letters and phone calls from Henozedaman, all of which are critical of Bart.
- The CEO asks the head of human resources to administer some confidential interviews about Bart's behavior and attitude toward people and the company's culture.
- The CEO conducts a feedback session with Bart and tells him that people feel he is too "adversarial," approaches conflicts in a "win-lose" manner, and bad-mouths the company. The CEO concludes by saying, "Bart, I am seriously questioning whether you have the right attitude or approach for Suretain."

Larry: Wounding the King

Larry is a regional vice president for a national retail-store chain. He enjoys considerable respect in the company because of his solid track record and industry knowledge. Starting at age eight, Larry worked in the business, helping his family, who owned a few retail stores. Because of his long experience, he considers himself an expert in all aspects of finding sites, building, and running outlets. Larry is also very willing to state his opinion, with little regard to the audience, since he's a man of principles.

In the fall, there is a market tour in a city where Larry is visiting potential sites for new stores with two senior vice presidents from national headquarters. These executives are from the Development department, responsible for working with regional VPs to locate sites and erect new stores. On the tour, the two execs are fairly insistent that Larry move forward to purchase new sites. At one location, when they advocate an acquisition, Larry challenges their assessment by raising questions about the demographics of the area and the density of competitors, concluding, "We wouldn't meet our profit targets if we put a store here."

The Development executives push harder, emphasizing the need to grow in this region. This annoys Larry, who says, "Listen, I know what you guys are doing. You haven't even run the numbers. You don't care if this site ever makes a dime. All you care about is your bonus, and that is based on how many stores you can get built this year." Larry doesn't budge and soon the market tour ends uncomfortably.

The senior VPs return to headquarters determined to hurt Larry's reputation and block his advancement in the company. They know that Larry is onto their real agenda, and they want to get some "mud" on him. With the annual human resources planning discussions coming soon, they target Larry's boss, the chief operating officer, and the senior VP of human resources. They plant seeds of doubt, saying, "Larry knows the business pretty well, but he is really rigid and not open to new ideas. He's grown up in these mom-and-pop businesses. I don't think he understands the teamwork you need in a big company."

After the planning discussions, Larry's boss meets with him to discuss the outcome of the sessions. He tells Larry, "Your results have been as good as usual, but unfortunately on some other measures you have low marks that will affect your overall rating this year. The general view in headquarters is that you're inflexible, not a team player, and need coaching on your arrogance."

Sondra: Speaking Truth to Power

Sondra is the finance director for a French division of a multinational sportswear company. She has worked for the company for eight years, solely in France. The strongest impression people have of her is that she is conscientious and tends to keep to herself. In meetings, she doesn't talk often, but when she does, her opinions are precise, well reasoned, and display independent thinking.

Recently, Sondra has done an in-depth analysis of the division's sales and marketing agreements. The findings call into question recent forecasts about the division's next quarterly results and may even have negative implications for previously stated results. Normally, she would report this information to the president of the French division and the CFO of the international division. However, Sondra is hesitant to report her troublesome findings because of these recent observations:

- At a recent worldwide meeting of finance directors, the international CFO said that the company was entering a "sensitive" period and that he did not want any "bad news."
- During this meeting as in others at headquarters, Sondra has noticed an absence of debate and "pushback." Normally outspoken people weren't criticizing or challenging ideas, but they were more candid and forthright in conversations outside the meeting sessions.
- Two months ago, a VP of human resources for the Latin American region had a well-publicized difference of opinion with the international CEO. Sondra has just learned that this HR executive has been pushed out of the company.
- The buzz in the company is that the international CEO is highly regarded by the CEO of the parent company. Most people believe he's a likely successor to the top global job.

Sondra decides that the organization has become too political and she has lost respect for the leaders. In the end, she does not present her findings but instead negotiates a severance package. Six months later, the company has to restate earnings, write off $100 million, and suffers a 15 percent decline in its stock price.

An Individual Wake-Up Call

In our executive coaching and training seminars, we see a steady stream of individuals like Amy and Bart, Larry and Sondra, whose careers have been hurt by political blind spots. They suffer from stolen credit and personal agendas, sabotage and power plays, fear of speaking the truth to powerful people, or egos and favoritism. When overly political people do whatever works to get into positions of power, they can damage competent, loyal people or pillage organizational performance. People often sweep politics under the rug or whine "Ain't it awful?" at the watercooler. Some hope that they can find an organization where politics doesn't exist, so they quit and *leave,* only to find the same dynamics at the next company.

Others quit and *stay*—letting their intimidation or resentment about politics drain their time, energy, morale, and performance. For people who define all politics as unethical and a compromise of integrity, two unpalatable choices face them—*lose out* or *sell out*. The political amateur believes that to avoid being burned he must compromise his integrity and "play the game." The good news is that we have proven alternatives for you. *High-integrity political tactics* will help individuals, teams, and companies to survive *and* thrive.

A Leadership Wake-Up Call

Many leaders claim politics aren't important or don't exist. Meanwhile, unhealthy politics stagnate, decay, or destroy their companies. Each day, the newspapers show what happens when low-integrity people with high political skills gain power. They torch finances and reputations, as happened at Enron, Tyco, Global Crossing, WorldCom, the New York Stock Exchange, Arthur Andersen, various mutual fund companies, the New York Times, and others. There *are* less political organizations, but none have repealed the laws of human nature.

This book does more than provide self-help techniques for getting ahead in highly political work settings—we're not merely teaching synchronized swimming in the shark tank! Less political people can *survive* in toxic settings, but they can't truly *thrive* until company leaders wake up and remove their blinders. Top executives have told us they want to ethically gain power, help their teams achieve greater influence and impact, and even take bold steps to rescue the political cultures of their companies. Becoming a steward for your organization's overall political atmosphere is a provocative call to action. This vision of making organizational politics a personal virtue, career management tool, team development vehicle, *and* a cultural asset on the company balance sheet is at the heart of this book.

PART I

THE IMPACT OF POLITICAL STYLES

Chapter 1

Avoid Political Blind Spots

Navigating Smooth and Rough Political Waters

This book is a guide for "navigating the aggravating." Just as ancient mariners used the North Star as a directional marker as they sailed, you hopefully have personal North Star goals that motivate you and keep you on course as you journey through political waters:

- *Influence on the Job*. You want to sell your ideas and receive credit and recognition—for yourself and your team.
- *Business Impact.* Of course, you know you're *not* paid for ideas, don't you? You're paid for ideas that are implemented and succeed—achieving organizational impact. We all seek the fulfillment of seeing our ideas and results make a positive difference for our company.
- *Career Growth*. It's also honorable to want career advancement, promotions, financial reward, and prestige, as long as you don't sell your soul getting them.

The guilt-free good news is that your personal North Star goals also support your company's North Star goals. Your organization needs your good ideas to see the light of day, hopes you can enhance company performance, and wants you to remain a fully engaged part of its future leadership bench strength. It would be counterproductive to your company to allow destructive politics to lead to attrition.

Yet every day, politics can buffet you about. Unless a *Star Trek* captain has beamed you up to a utopian planet, you probably experience these political dangers:

- *Stormy, Changing Weather.* This symbolizes the constantly shifting winds of change—company turbulence, reorganizations, downsizing, new bosses, *being* a new boss, new initiatives and about-face top management agendas—all demanding careful navigation through precarious political waters. You need to predict the weather and rechart your course.
- *Lightning Bolts.* Political jolts include competing agendas, priorities, policies, and programs that strike down your ideas. Besides protecting your ideas, you also pray *you* won't also be hit by the lightning. You need to protect yourself from political surprises.
- *Icebergs.* You can hit unforeseen obstacles, such as frozen perceptions about you or your function. You have a corporate reputation—good or bad "corporate buzz." People sometimes imprison you in a perception based upon a past incident and refuse to update their image even though you've changed. We'll scan the political horizon for these obsolete or accurate icebergs so you can melt them, reshape them, or steer around them.
- *Sharks.* Yes, *Jaws* isn't just a scary Steven Spielberg movie. There *are* predatory people with self-serving agendas. Some take credit for ideas, block good ideas, or sabotage you for personal gain. This seamy side of company life happens, especially in times of fear, economic threat, rampant competition, or the corporate musical chairs of changing jobs.

Political Tip-Offs from Derailed Executives

Executive coaching is sweeping corporate America, but let's be crystal clear about two different emphases within this movement.

In progressive companies that prize professional development, coaching is a perk—an exciting adventure to help talented, high-potential people grow and advance. In physical health, you don't have to be *sick* to get even healthier. Likewise, you don't have to be in trouble to receive developmental executive coaching.

Other executive coaching is required for "fix-it" or even "fix it or else" scenarios. We've worked with many executives who'd hit a ceiling or were on the way out, and our coaching services were the last resort. For years, career-stalled clients were *overly* political—abrasive managers turning people off through alienating, abusive treatment as they clawed their way to the top. Their lack of people skills and disrespectful behavior were now too visible to be ignored.

Now, we're increasingly asked to help *under* political people who treat others with care and respect, but whose careers are endangered due to little organizational impact. These intelligent, technically capable, company-loyal, high-integrity individuals risk being derailed from their career paths. Some are clueless about politics or refuse to enter the political arena, throwing the baby out with the bathwater. Naïve about politics, they lack the organizational savvy and influence to survive in today's fast-paced, high-pressure, downsizing organizations.

The things people say in executive coaching are clues that they have underestimated the role of politics or misread the political climate. How many of the following signals have you experienced, heard about, or seen? The goal of identifying these political tip-offs is to remove any political blinders so that you embrace politics as a fact of organizational life, and to run a reality check.

"I'm Being Underestimated." People bump up against a narrow view of their expertise, talents, potential, or value. They feel pigeonholed or in dead-end positions instead of valued for their broader, strategic strengths. "I just feel like they don't get it. They view me in a very marginalized box instead of treating me like a valued business partner," said one manager. Often, technical or staff people feel like company gofers instead of respected consultants.

"I Got Passed Over." These people are overlooked for promotions—again and again. Their careers plateau or they hit the glass ceiling that many women executives find in male-dominated cultures. There's a corporate jockeying for position and someone else less qualified gets the job nod. The individuals in coaching can't figure out for themselves the hidden success factors. Maybe it's competence. "Sometimes a cigar *is* just a cigar," as Freud observed, but other times it's *not*. Sometimes political factors are at work, factors you've ignored until now.

"I Was a Victim of Downsizing." Some people sigh, "I wish I *had* a job to complain about!" They are shocked victims of a merger, reorganization, downsizing, or cost cutting. Why is it that when the corporate dust settles, some people always seem to land on their feet while others get a severance package? We know a president of a large beverage conglomerate who lost his job a week after receiving the second-highest performance review in company history! Every time someone is let go, it's not necessarily because of political dynamics, but often that plays a critical role in the "Why me?" career speed bump.

"I'm Not Sure of the Scorecard." Sure, there are written criteria for evaluation and clear job objectives. But often people report a gnawing sense of not being tapped into what really matters, a vague uneasiness that they're walking on thin ice. People work hard, so this trial-and-error guessing game about the true success equation is unsettling. The company talks about fairness and meritocracy—it doesn't matter what you look like or whom you know. But some clients helplessly complain, "Bull! The reasons people win and lose are more subjective and I can't figure them out." When managers move higher in their organizations, the scorecard measurement criteria change, just as when a minor league baseball player is called up to the majors. When rising stars are promoted, they're often sobered to learn they've entered a new ball game where the unwritten, unspoken rules may be unclear.

"I'm Not Getting Credit." These people initiated or contributed to a project, but aren't recognized for their efforts or results. Their ideas were successful, but at the end of the day, someone else gets more credit. At an awards ceremony or meeting, others get the kudos and the limelight. Despite being central to achieving targets or forging innovation, they miss out on the rewards.

"I'm Not Able to Sell My Ideas." Often, the person wistfully moans he couldn't get his idea off the ground in the first place. He has ideas that will benefit the company, but is thwarted. He isn't sought out for advice or input, and people don't answer his calls. Sometimes it's a clear "No," but other times the rejection is dragged out through a year of withheld resources. Then at performance review time, he's asked, "So, Jerry, what have you accomplished this year?"

"I've Hurt My Career by Speaking Out." There may not be a manager who doesn't say something like "I want you to know that I encourage healthy conflict. If I'm full of beans on something, don't pull your punch." Phrases like *Challenge Conventional Wisdom* may be printed on laminated posters, but there's a danger in blindly accepting these proclamations as gospel.

The punitive reaction may leak out subtly—awkward silences at a meeting as others watch in hushed amazement, a conveniently forgotten invitation to a key strategic meeting, or an appraisal rating that's lower than anticipated. Other times, the retribution explodes in glaring ways—the person is ostracized or fired on trumped-up claims of cost constraints. Are we advising you to dummy up and become a corporate Stepford wife—a conforming, compliant, silent zombie? No, but we are suggesting you learn political judgment to avoid these pitfalls.

"I'm Not a Part of Key Networks." These people feel like outsiders without advocates. Do you realize that most of the time when people talk about your career, you are not in the room? We call these

unofficial interactions that impact your advancement "impromptu career discussions." Someone makes an offhand comment about you like "Will lacks fire in the belly." "Danielle is really not a team player." "Jamal doesn't have a sense of urgency." "Hank's kind of an empire builder, don't you think?" "Donna's OK, but she lacks intensity. Anyway, what were we talking about?"

That's how quickly career decisions are made about you when you're not around! The off-the-cuff trash talker is often astute enough to use subjective, inferential descriptors that are clear as fog. These labels can't be proven or argued, but they have a way of following you around. We need someone to say, "That really isn't how he is," or, "You have the wrong version of the story," or, "That was three years ago and he's changed a lot." We need a network of allies to let us in on the dirt and to look out for us in informal ways, so we're not at a disadvantage during these impromptu career discussions.

"I Was Sabotaged and I Didn't See It Coming." When this happens, you never forget it. It's like a kick in the stomach. Someone goes after you—often behind your back. This politics tip-off is so distasteful yet critical that it deserves a second look under a magnifying glass.

The Many Faces of Sabotage

In Oliver Stone's chilling *Wall Street,* Gordon Gekko (fashioned after real-life financier Ivan Boesky) shamelessly announces, "Greed . . . is good. Greed is right. Greed works." Many families get along fine until somebody dies. The *Journal of Social Psychology* reports that 45 percent of middle-class families argue about the estate. If brothers and sisters bring in the lawyers over $50,000, imagine what relative strangers may do when millions are at stake in stock options, golden parachutes, and fat salaries. Now mix greed with the drug of *power* and sprinkle in a dash of financial fears, and you have a recipe for political sabotage. There are many faces of sabotage—many types of political lightning that can strike in organizations. The more that corporate leaders allow such behavior, the more toxic the political climate becomes and the greater the erosion of the bottom line.

Behind-the-Scenes Sabotage

Someone indirectly hurts you behind closed doors, often so deftly that you're not even aware it's happening.

Gossip, Rumors, and Bad-Mouthing. Predators secretly spread gossip or trash-talk about you, your results, or your actions. If you're in the way of their ambition, they label you "clueless" or "not fitting the company mold." Too clever to go after you on competence, they use an ambiguous label. If confronted, they claim their words were misinterpreted or taken out of context. Any empty apology is too late because the damage has been done.

Planting Seeds of Doubt. Behind closed doors they subtly block you from receiving a key high-visibility assignment—through a raised eyebrow, a discouraging word whispered in someone's ear, or innocently asking, "Wouldn't Helen be better qualified?" This is always done under the guise of doing what's best for the organization.

Marginalizing. This is a comment that limits you, such as "Barry is such a good salesperson we need his numbers." Barry's now blocked from the headquarters executive vice president job in sales management. Ever had a letter of recommendation that was so bland, so vanilla, that it was actually a nonendorsement? You felt like saying, "Thanks for nothing!"

Out-of-the-Loop Sabotage

Indirect sabotage impedes your power or access to resources, slowing down your contributions or eroding your organizational impact.

Withholding Information. Information is power, so if you're out of the loop, your impact shrinks. A fellow money market sales rep knows something about your client's past financial investment strategies but keeps this under wraps. He may be busy or lazy. Or he *may* be a quiet saboteur trying to stay on top of monthly sales rankings. Maybe you're shut out of a meeting, watching the conference room door close as you're given a polite smile. You know that the meeting will hold the information that makes attendees the "in crowd."

Cutting Physical Resources, Head Count, or Budget. Obstructing routes to essential resources is one way a superior can set you up to fail. It's easy to hide behind a companywide scarcity mind-set, but what if more favored teams don't have to get by with as few resources as you do?

Assignment to Corporate Siberia. A rising star or veteran manager beloved by many is banished from headquarters to a low-visibility job—political quarantine. This scarlet-letter-tainted exile may be geographical or functional. Organizations all have less glamorous places to be trapped. To muffle the voice of an engineer who disagrees with a pet project, an ambitious but threatened midmanager calls in his chits and pulls strings to get the thorn-in-the-side technician reassigned and branded as an untouchable.

Butt-of-the-Joke Humor. Mean-spirited humor cuts deep, eroding your confidence. A saboteur makes a slur that becomes company lore and brands you as a target. Behind your back, the joke is blown out of proportion and trickles throughout the organization, devastating your career. We knew a chief operating officer on track to be the CEO. He had one bad habit—saying "you know" during his presentations. One of his peers influenced several in the audience to make tally marks every time he said "you know." They shared their tick-mark numbers over drinks as he lost credibility and became an outsider.

Out-in-the-Open Sabotage

These next tactics are overt. You know they're happening since they usually happen in meetings. At least these ploys are easier to predict, spot, counter, and defuse through this book's countertactics.

Sarcasm and Insults. This most blatant form of sabotage, open name-calling and disrespect, can come from a bullying boss with trademark abusiveness, a cunning direct report who fancies your job, or an unprofessional colleague. Sarcasm is often sideways anger, so the cutting comment may signal resentment about a valid beef with you. But it's sabotage if there's a pattern, and you need to dance carefully to avoid a blow to your credibility and power base.

Fixing Blame. Your image can shrivel if you're the team whipping post or brunt of garden-variety blame by peers. Sometimes a blamer is negative and vilifies *everyone*. Other times, a saboteur calculates a personal attack because he is covering his tracks and you stand in his way. He may even target you as the preplanned scapegoat at the start of a risky project in case it blows up.

Interrupting, Steamrolling, or Freezing Out. These manipulative tactics are less abrasive, but still discount you and block your influence. The saboteur dominates the discussion so you can't get in a word edgewise. Sometimes she's just a blundering clod at group process skills or her passion for her ideas gets out of control, but other times the lack of a platform for expressing yourself is the product of a slicker, more engineered effort.

Condescending or Patronizing. The sabotage is so sweet you can't feel the knife go in, but the wound inflicts credibility shredability! Someone says, "Teresa, you're new, so you'd have no way of knowing, but our norm for customer visitations to headquarters is (blah, blah) . . ." His voice tone takes on a softer, mock-protective air, like a patient parent helping a faltering child. The saboteur winks at others with a syrupy smile that sends the true message—you're not acclimated or part of the inner circle. You confront him later to find feigned surprise or hurt since he was "only trying to help you."

Testing, Tripping Up, or Exposing. A "friend" ambushes you by publicly asking for help on a thankless, draining task so that you look uncooperative if you decline. He asks you a question to trip you up. You're emotionally loaded on an issue, so he raises the raw-nerve topic to trigger you. A teammate "helps" you with faulty data, equipment, or manpower. He gives you enough rope to hang yourself with a new project he knows you aren't ready to tackle. A peer is conveniently too swamped to help you meet a deadline or keeps mum instead of pointing out a mistake you made.

Are You Cheered Up Yet?

If these accounts of sabotage don't exactly make for nice, light, mellow airplane reading, here are some reassurances about some common reactions to learning these political tip-offs.

- *"Isn't This a Cynical View of Human Nature?"* The previous accounts admittedly portray a crass view of company life. But we're not actually cynical people. We *don't* light up a room just by leaving it! Our goal isn't for you to distrust everyone or read negative motives into every situation. It's just that we don't want you to be naïve. *Savvy* is the operative word here. We want to protect you for the future through awareness, so that you're not at a disadvantage.
- *"I'm Not into Politics, but Sometimes I Sabotage, Too." Overly* political power hoarders are the usual practitioners, but *under* political people may also commit sabotage out of revenge or desperation. Victim-generated sabotage is still counterproductive. Please don't beat yourself up if you've sabotaged others. Even if your mom was a travel agent for guilt trips, we invite you to drop the guilt and just let awareness of your own sabotage lead you to avoid perpetuating the problem.
- *"Do I Have to Become Manipulative?"* Nothing we recommend for entering the arena of organizational politics requires sacrificing your ethical standards. You can choose noble ends to pursue

and moral means to reach them. You can hold on to your self-respect as you gain influence and power. That's what we mean by *high-integrity political tactics.*

A few years ago we realized, "Why wait until people are derailed and need remedial executive coaching to better navigate politics? Let's teach people to be savvy before they run into problems." So we harvested our street-smart concepts for demystifying politics and funneled them into an Organizational Savvy workshop. Participants appreciate the straight talk about a typically taboo topic, welcome their company-endorsed open forum to validate their feelings, and can immediately implement our objective approach to a normally nebulous issue. Now, through this book, which also includes a companywide leadership focus, we'll empower you with nonmanipulative tactics for elevating politics from a dirty word to a character virtue and company asset. The first step is to understand the political styles and mind-sets of different people.

Chapter 2

Two Political Styles, Two Sets of Strengths

Two Different Worldviews

How well do you read people? The oft-quoted words of Lord Philip Chesterfield over two centuries ago are still true: "Learning is acquired by reading books, but the much more necessary learning . . . is only to be acquired by reading men, and studying all the various editions of them." There are many style-typing models for better reading, understanding, influencing, and working with colleagues, direct reports, and managers.

This book pinpoints recognizing *political styles* as the key for unlocking the door to enhanced organizational impact. In life, when a key doesn't fit a keyhole, we try a different key. Yet, in the sphere of organizational politics, we often expect other people to change when we can't easily achieve our goals with them. That's analogous to demanding that the keyhole change! The answer is to search for a different key, to adapt our own political style and behavior. The political style postures and skills you'll now learn add more keys to your key ring for opening doors to enhanced collaboration and organizational influence. This material may at first seem a bit theoretical, but bear with us. It will ultimately provide you a great many insights into your own behavior and that of others.

The two political styles are the *Power of Ideas* style (*Less* Political people on the left side of our Organizational Savvy Continuum) and the *Power of Person* style (*More* Political people on the right side of our Organizational Savvy Continuum). Please remember that being on the right or left side of this continuum has nothing to do with being ideologically to the political right (conservative) or political left (liberal). Also, you can be *more* political without being *overly* political, or *less* political without being *under* political.

Our value-free definition of "organizational politics" says that if you avoid extremes, each political style is positive—with different strengths, motivations, and mind-sets. Each style holds a different set of values on six dimensions that comprise what we call political style. We'll help you optimize your style's strengths and minimize its risks by avoiding the extremes of the following scale.

The Power of Ideas Political Style (Less Political)

Power of Ideas people on the left side of our model are not necessarily apolitical or under political—just less politically driven than their right-side counterparts. These people aren't saints. They just have a different filter for viewing power, politics, ambition, and

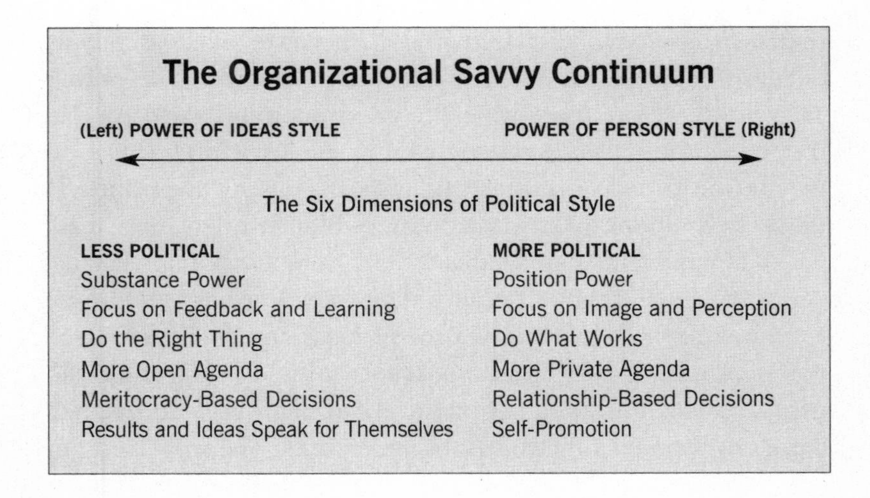

promotion. They evaluate ideas, proposals, and recommendations by asking themselves different questions from their Power of Person colleagues. We celebrate the following *Less Political (LP)* ways of thinking possessed by individuals, teams, and entire companies. These positive mind-sets make up the left-side posture on each of the six dimensions of political style.

Substance Power (LP). The Power of Ideas people view power as residing in their facts, logic, analysis, intuition, creativity, and innovation. They devote more energy, time, and attention to the power derived from substantive and task grounding. They believe true power resides in the work itself being a good job—by their work results being sound and their ideas representing a sound business case scenario. This substance-power focus can be technical and quantitative, or it can be qualitative: artistic, aesthetic, creative, or visionary. So Power of Ideas style people are *not* only technical individuals. They bring a pride in their competence and ideas, and great enthusiasm for their work. Their steadfast work ethic and commitment to quality is critical for start-up modes, pushing on a mission-critical project, getting a new product revision out, or when a college intern knows she must pay her dues with job excellence and proven results.

Focus on Feedback and Learning (LP). Power of Ideas people believe in substantive excellence as the pinnacle of true power. They are therefore more willing to admit their mistakes and that they don't know everything, so that they can learn. No one likes to be told he's made a mistake or craves "constructive criticism" unless he's a monk living in a monastery. But left-siders more readily and genuinely seek feedback and demonstrate intellectual curiosity to "get it right," because they know learning is the route to power as they define it—excellent ideas and results. Revered Power of Ideas leaders also model the attitude of a learner and treat mistakes in others nonpunitively to cultivate feedback-rich work environments that blossom into results. The well-liked former CEO of the Mirage and Bellagio hotels, Steve Wynn, routinely visited new employees six months after they began work to ask how he himself was messing up and what he could do better. Former Southwest Airlines CEO Herb Kelleher once walked onstage before thousands at a companywide meeting and smashed three eggs on his forehead. With egg on his face, he admitted that he'd made a mistake with company strategy and needed the employees' help to overcome the blunder.

Do the Right Thing (LP). Power of Ideas people screen decisions through the question "Do my actions have integrity and are they good for the company?" They place ethics and what's beneficial for the common good over personal success. Less likely to go outside the system or cut corners to achieve their ends, they patiently go within the system, minimizing maverick behavior. They're admired for an unwavering moral compass, spirit of self-sacrifice, and willingness to share credit and power. A Power of Ideas manager promotes a direct report for a great job outside the team even if it means losing valuable talent in order to strengthen the larger organization. He may recommend a new organizational design knowing full well that it might impact his role. Colleagues and bosses endorse left-siders, since their integrity spurs loyalty and inspiration.

New York Stock Exchange chairman Dick Grasso's forced resignation due to outrage over his $187 million pay package left the organization in mayhem. John Reed, the wealthy former CEO of Citibank, came out of retirement to act as interim leader—for a whopping salary of one dollar, a left-side trait. The whistle-blower at Arthur Andersen took a risk in exposing conflict-of-interest practices at Andersen, and heralding ethics auditing at many accounting firms. A pro sports franchise's star player unselfishly agrees to restructure his own contract to allow the team money to sign a desperately needed rookie or free agent. He earns the respect of teammates, catapults his team into play-off contention, and becomes a media darling.

At a company level, customers want relationships with organizations they trust and respect. The Tylenol tainting that caused many deaths led to a textbook example of how to respond with integrity to a corporate crisis. Once the company discovered that its pills were poisoned, it removed all products from shelves worldwide. They launched an investigation that paved the way toward protective packaging from which we all benefit.

More Open Agendas (LP). Power of Ideas people value honesty, saying exactly what's on their minds in a forthright manner. They put their cards on the table, stating their goals openly. In a negotiation, they avoid manipulative maneuvering such as highballing or lowballing their position, instead choosing to "tell it like it is," trusting that a spirit of mutual-benefit bargaining and honest exchange of one another's bottom-line wishes will yield a win-win outcome and ongoing trust. In budget allocation meetings, you can count on the Power of Ideas salesperson to give you a true financial projection rather than secretly sandbagging accounts to make her next performance period a breeze.

Meritocracy-Based Decisions (LP). The Power of Ideas individual has an implicit belief in meritocracy, that good performance will seize the day. He trusts his work will be rewarded and judges others based on competence, *not* whom they know. This purist barometer for advancement sprouts from a deep-seated belief that true power resides in the substantive worth of one's ideas, analysis, creativity, and intuition. A meritocracy criterion for decision-making about employees, vendors, and consultants reaps wonders for companies: a work ethic, reliable and deserving professionals, reduced political maneuvering, less self-serving bragging, and faith in equitable rewards. When people with this meritocracy political-style mind-set populate an organization, the glow of hard work is appreciated and attracts talented applicants to this "land of opportunity."

Results and Ideas Speak for Themselves (LP). An extension of the Power of Ideas belief in meritocracy is this last political-style dimension—the leap of faith that results will speak for themselves and that ideas will be compelling enough for others to see their merit: "I don't need to promote myself or my work because my work stands for itself and will earn me just rewards." What are Power of Ideas people doing? Basically, they have their heads down doing their jobs! Believing in the "soft-sell" approach of letting the results speak, this left-side trust is a career asset in organizations that frown on braggarts and prize humble leaders. This is like the athlete who lets his on-field performance speak instead of hyping himself. In his bestseller *Good to Great,* Jim Collins found model leaders embody a paradoxical mix of personal humility and strong professional will, so the humility side speaks to Power of Ideas people. Collins applauds these leaders not for being "I-centric" or larger-than-life heroes but for exuding modesty.

The Power of Person Political Style (More Political)

We'll now retrace the same six dimensions of political style, but this time focus on the positive mind-set and traits of the Power of Person political style. Remember, right-siders on the Organizational Savvy Continuum are not necessarily *overly* political. Please monitor yourself if you're triggered into derogatory labels that are only accurate for the extremes—*Machiavellian, manipulative,* or *shark.* We hope that this *more* political side of the Continuum doesn't cause a knee-jerk negative reaction since our nonjudgmental definition of organizational politics means that the Power of Person characteristics are admirable ones that even left-siders can emulate. We would not want to be on a team or in a company without the following attributes, talents, and strengths.

Position Power (MP). The major political-style dimension discriminating the Power of Ideas from the Power of Person people is how they define power. Instead of seeing power as linked to substance as their left-side colleagues do, right-side people spend more time thinking about hierarchical position power—who has it, who doesn't, who's up, who's down, who's in, who's out? They are street-smart and practical, and they strive to be on the right side of power. Often well connected, they are good at studying people who are powerful and aligning with them. They quickly and expertly scan the political landscape to assess the official power structure and hierarchy as well as the unofficial, informal power dynamics.

Power of Person people can deftly read between the lines to track power trends, predict power shifts, and anticipate the preferences of movers and shakers. Don't you want someone on your team who can astutely advise the group on how to present a proposal to powerful superiors? They can reality-test ideas through a power-tinted screen: "What will people in power think of this idea? Which powerful people support or oppose what we're going to suggest?" When you need someone to detect booby traps in a politically sensitive minefield, the Power of Person style is your trump card. The Power of Person team leader also protects power, turf, and territory appropriately, nurturing his group's reputation, sticking up for his people, ensuring respect for resources and roles, and protecting departmental headcount and budget.

If this position-power focus of the Power of Person style creates a bitter taste in your mouth, you're thinking of people who abuse power, unethical leaders who use their position to betray people who created their wealth. Yet, it's heartening how many powerful people have used power as a force for good. Think of Abraham Lincoln, Franklin D. Roosevelt, Martin Luther King, Harry Truman, and Gandhi, who used their influence to forge positive social change, proving that power and integrity are not mutually exclusive.

Focus on Image and Perception (MP). While perception may not be reality, Power of Person leaders understand that many important decisions are made based on perceptions. They know that an important source of power is lodged in a realistic and healthy focus on one's image and that of one's team. While left-siders may not even be thinking about impressions or their reputations, right-siders are aware of exactly what perceptions are desirable or not in their organizations, and they know how they are currently viewed in relation to these traits. These realist Power of Person leaders make it a point to strategize ways to improve their reputations—they have a plan to change problematic perceptions.

If you frown on awareness of perceptions and enhancement of your image, then never attend a presentation-skills course and ignore all advice about dressing for success! Impression management includes caring about being a skillful presenter, looking the part, ensuring well-packaged proposals, cultivating self-branding expertise, and acting on survey feedback to alter negative perceptions. At an organizational level, where would we be without the focus on image and perception ushered by our marketing, public relations, and media departments? In the same way that all left-siders are not poor presenters (just a little less comfortable), please do *not* equate all right-siders with being so polished that they lack substance or competence.

Do What Works (MP). Power of Person people show an admirable can-do attitude that translates into steadfastly looking for ways to achieve their ends. When blended with good ethics, this "art of the possible" attitude allows the person to advance to do great things for the organization. This leader is skilled at figuring out "What will work?" It might involve figuring out a manager's agenda, blending an idea with her business objective, being willing to compromise to move a good idea forward, or even sharing credit for an idea with others who have power in order to win approval for a recommendation. In documenting traits of executives who built enduring greatness, Jim Collins includes an unwavering, ferocious resolve and steadfast determination to do whatever needs to be done to achieve greatness.

The left-side Power of Ideas respect for proper channels stems from a "do what's right" mentality and is honorable. But corporations also need flexible, success-minded right-siders willing to deal with the gray zone of influencing. Left-siders may wait until a "decision-making meeting," while right-siders beat them to the punch by influencing stakeholders before the meeting. Corporate agility can be a survival competency, and going outside of usual channels can be done ethically. A zero-tolerance policy makes sense for functions like safety, quality assurance, and regulatory compliance. However, rigidity and refusal to adapt the rules can be a liability in other situations.

Tough choices are sometimes the "price of the dream" if you seek success, impact, and influence in organizations. Joel DeLuca's book *Political Savvy* refers to Abraham Lincoln's caution that we don't learn to deal with ethical dilemmas by totally avoiding them. This judgment call in balancing "what's right" with "what works" to achieve success was expressed at a companywide level during the eighties war for talent that raged between high-tech companies. The siphoning of employees from one company by another was common practice. National Semiconductor didn't want to end up on the short end of the stick, so they rented a recruiting billboard with a toll-free number right across the street from the Dallas headquarters of rival Texas Instruments. Power of Person people skillfully read the unwritten rules about what's OK or not, and they make pragmatic while ethical decisions to avoid being at a disadvantage.

More Private Agendas (MP). Left-side Power of Ideas people value honesty and integrity so highly that they may prematurely blurt out everything on their minds. But not sharing the entire truth is *not* the same as being dishonest. Naïvely revealing everything on your mind can hurt someone's feelings or can give the upper hand to someone you should not trust. There's a difference between honesty and idiocy! The right-side Power of Person style is more prudent, patient, and self-controlled, practicing verbal discipline. This leader is more discerning with information and appropriately strategic with agenda—waiting for the optimal time, place, and method to share critical data, especially if someone can misuse it. This is like a good poker player holding his cards close to his chest to scope out the other players and their reactions to *their* cards.

Relationship-Based Decisions (MP). Unlike the Power of Ideas style that makes hiring, firing, promotion, vendor, and supplier decisions based more exclusively upon competence, the Power of Person style also factors relationships, loyalty, and alliances into the decision-making equation. This can be ethical and efficient as long as honorable right-siders don't heap rewards or advancements on unqualified friends. Relying on trusted partners with proven track records is good business. Loyalty blossoms into sustained performance versus complacency or deadwood. Top executives hire productive assistants from their last company in order to hit the ground running in their next organization. A pro sports coach going to a new team brings along his own staff, who understand his philosophy and system. In business, the integrity issue only arises if an opportunist breaks rules or employs a scorched-earth strategy of pirating away entire teams to leave barren and dry a former employer who had treated him fairly. Just because right-siders make decisions based more on relationships, don't think that left-siders are all tucked away in their cubicles; they may be collaborating with others on ideas.

Self-Promotion (MP). There's an old European curse, "May you be blessed with a great idea and no one to implement it." In business today, promoting yourself and your ideas is a requirement for advancing. Take a moment to think of a friend or co-worker who might have a greater impact by stepping out and promoting herself. Not only salespeople but *everyone* needs to talk about achievements without fearing labels like *conceited* or *pompous.* Power of Person people tout their teams and highlight their contributions at appraisal, bonus, or advancement time. In *Now, Discover Your Strengths,* Marcus Buckingham, formerly of the Gallup organization, appeals for a "strengths revolution" in business. Ben Franklin called wasted strengths "sundials in the shade" so Buckingham helps companies to embolden individuals to highlight their strengths. Traditionally, many women rate self-promotion up there with walking on crushed glass and root canals. Dana Hall, a New York City investment manager, sponsors workshops that teach women in business to "brag" through announcing their accomplishments and results.

The Style Strengths Finder

Vive la différence! Every company needs each political style's perspectives. We invite you not just to tolerate or accept, but to celebrate political-style differences. The Power of Ideas and Power of Person styles offer equally legitimate belief systems and advantages—potent strengths to reach North Star goals of influence, business impact, and career growth. Imagine combining the values of the left-side Power of Ideas style with the skill and drive of the right-side Power of Person style and you will see the benefits of embracing both political postures.

Now please complete the Style Strengths Finder on the next page of this chapter. Checkmark (✓) any trait that describes you. If an item fits you greatly, circle (○) it. If you don't particularly see the item in yourself, leave it blank. For each of the six dimensions of political style, gauge whether you lean more toward the strengths associated with the Power of Ideas or Power of Person style. Depending on how many style traits fit you, estimate how greatly you relate to one style side or the other. You can have strengths on both sides of a dimension, because style qualities are just a matter of degree and these traits aren't mutually exclusive. However, if you think you relate to attributes on each side of a given dimension, challenge yourself further to decide which side's strengths are more natural to you, less of a stretch to access, and more automatic. After all, the goal of this tool is to choose which of the two primary political styles you most resonate with in your values, priorities, and actions.

Honestly assess whether you identify with your political style somewhat, considerably, or greatly, since you will soon place yourself along an Organizational Savvy Continuum that depicts the

Style Strengths Finder

Power of Ideas (Less Political) Left-Side Style	Power of Person (More Political) Right-Side Style
Substance Power	**Position Power**
___ (1) Shows passion and focuses on ideas and results	___ (1) Has street smarts and studies who is powerful
	___ (2) Senses reactions, aligns with power
	___ (3) Uses position power for good
Focus on Feedback and Learning	**Focus on Image and Perception**
___ (2) Genuinely seeks feedback	___ (4) Knows others' perceptions
___ (3) Treats others' mistakes non-punitively	___ (5) Plans strategy to improve reputation
___ (4) Builds feedback-rich environments	___ (6) Excels at presenting and packaging
Do the Right Thing	**Do What Works**
___ (5) Models integrity and unwavering moral compass	___ (7) Strives for the art of the possible with a can-do spirit
___ (6) Puts team and company good over self-interest	___ (8) Compromises as needed
___ (7) Respects proper channels and rules	___ (9) Knows how to work the system
More Open Agendas	**More Private Agendas**
___ (8) Has open, honest, up-front agendas	___ (10) Has strategic, prudent agendas
___ (9) Trusts in others' good faith	___ (11) Exerts verbal discipline and caution
Meritocracy-Based Decisions	**Relationship-Based Decisions**
___ (10) Believes good work will be rewarded	___ (12) Stresses loyalty and strong alliances
___ (11) Promotes others for work reasons versus friendship	
___ (12) Avoids distracting political maneuvering	
Results and Ideas Speak for Themselves	**Self-Promotion**
___ (13) Shows humility and soft-sells strengths	___ (13) Self-confidently shares strengths
___ (14) Keeps head down and does the job	___ (14) Sells ideas and self with boldness

degree to which you believe in and demonstrate your style's qualities. There is no mathematical equation to use, and simply adding up your checkmarks won't lead to the answer, because some traits can carry greater importance. So this is more of an overall feel you're trying to establish for which mind-set best describes you.

Whichever style you align with more closely, the news is great because both styles offer assets for your career, team, and company. Problems emerge only if you embrace either style to the extent that you behave in extremes that create risks and liabilities. The Style Strengths Finder is a helpful directional screening tool for figuring out your political style, but additional clues lie in understanding the political-style risks that are identified in the next chapter.

Chapter 3

Political Style Risks

"OK, Doc, That's the Good News. What's the Bad News?"

Alexandre Dumas wrote in *The Count of Monte Cristo,* "Any virtue carried to the extreme can become a crime." Humor is a terrific icebreaker unless you crack jokes at a quarterly sales meeting where results are dismal: "Well, no place to go but up!" Similarly, from each seed of political style strength can sprout a risk. For instance, overdoing the Power of Ideas strength of "more open agendas" could lead to saying the wrong thing to the wrong person. Overemphasizing the Power of Person tendency to "do what works" could become blind, selfish ambition. Pumping up the volume on any positive trait, pushing it to the extreme, or using it at the wrong time morphs it into a danger to you, your team, or your organization. Whether your political style remains constructive or becomes destructive is purely a matter of degree.

Watch the Political Style Traffic Lights

Using a traffic light metaphor, the More Political (MP) Power of Person style has a green traffic light, so full speed ahead! Your style strengths and mind-set are career and company assets. But driving your MP Power of Person style mind-set too far to the right on the

Organizational Savvy Continuum makes you Overly Political (OP), so imagine a red traffic light to signal yourself to stop such extremes. Likewise, the Less Political (LP) Power of Ideas style strengths deserve an encouraging green traffic light, but can be exaggerated to the point of being Under Political (UP), also requiring a red traffic light. The yellow-light zone on the Continuum means you're in a hazard zone, flirting enough with style risks to warrant proceeding with caution. If you are at a far-right Borderline Overly Political (BOP) style position, you could slip into being Overly Political (OP) and may already be perceived that way. If you are at the far-left Borderline Under Political (BUP) spot, it means you should be careful you aren't seen as being or actually becoming Under Political (UP).

Each Style Has a Fatal Flaw

Each side of the Continuum faces a different fatal flaw, a unique danger running through its characteristic risks. These risks aren't a

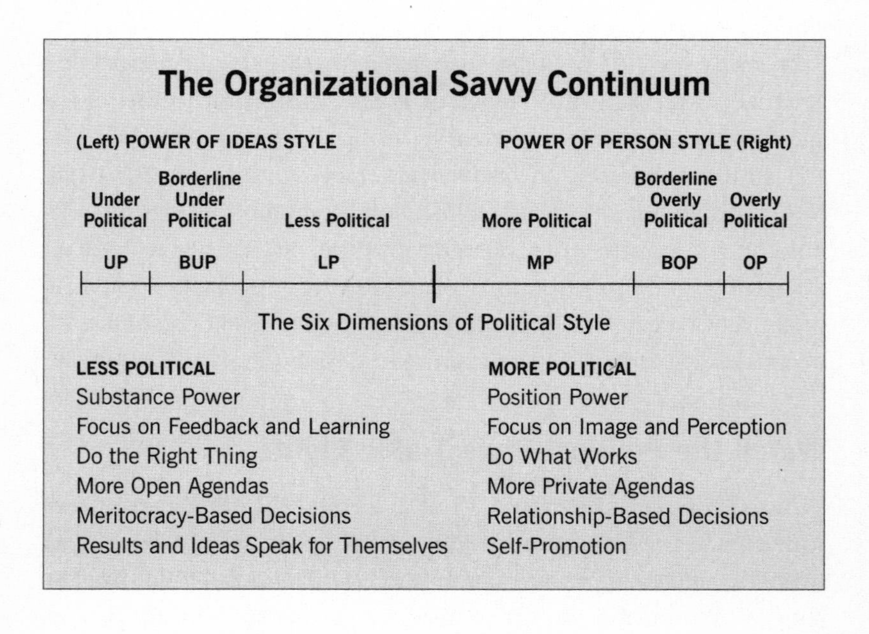

certainty, but ignoring them could seriously harm you, your team, or your company.

- *Power of Ideas* (Less Political) people risk losing out to More Political people because of a "corporate survival of the savvy." They may think, "Well, since my style risks are just a matter of degree, I don't really need to worry, because I can just tone down my left-side characteristics." Unfortunately, you do need to worry and act, because you are vulnerable anytime you face off or even just work with a person who is more political than you. The further left *you* are (Under Political) combined with the further right *others* are (Overly Political), the more you are at a disadvantage when competing for these five areas of political capital: (1) power, (2) credit for results, (3) who receives blame, (4) promotions, and (5) resources. To keep you or your team from getting the short end of the stick in a more political organization or with more political people, you may need to move right on the Continuum to acquire the savvy and skill of the Power of Person style. This does not mean you will become manipulative or Overly Political (OP), just more politically savvy.

- *Power of Person* (More Political) people risk compromising their ethics and values or falling prey to naked self-interest. Let's not get too righteous about such integrity loss, since we aren't talking about a small group of evil people who start out with questionable values. Overly Political people usually start out with a strong set of principles, but power, ambition, pressure, or greed seduces them into compromising their value system. It starts out small and snowballs. They may give in to performance pressure and stress by inventing things for journalistic stories, fudging scientific results, plagiarizing for academic articles, or cheating on tests. Perhaps the lure of power blinds them to self-deception as they do something out of character. The first time that they get away with it and derive benefit starts a pattern of rationalizing the misdeed until they have gradually lost their integrity. This gradual moral erosion can cost you dearly if you lose the trust of others, scar your company, or one day wake up to realize you've won the rat race but have become a rat! You may need to move left on the Continuum to embrace the values and integrity of the Power of Ideas style. It's never too late to reverse the pattern and regain your moral balance point.

The Power of Ideas Risks of Being Under Political (UP)

The glowing report card of strengths in the Power of Ideas style becomes a disadvantage if the Less Political (LP) mind-set snowballs into the following Under Political (UP) risks. Remember that these UP risks have a common thread of being at a disadvantage when competing with MPs, BOPs, and OPs at Amateur Night. But these challenges can be overcome through awareness and by honing some of the savvy tactics we'll prescribe.

Being Underestimated (UP). With their heads down doing their jobs and dutifully believing in the meritocracy, extreme Power of Ideas people lose out to more political people when competing for power, credit, promotions, or resources. Of course, you might say they're not even *in* the competition if they abandon the arena. Under Political people can have a low or passive profile. You tell them to stop apologizing so much and they say, "OK, sorry." The UP takes modesty and self-deprecation to the point of being seen as weak and inconsequential, undeserving of respect.

A UP's lack of self-promotion stems from letting results and ideas speak for themselves, leading to diminished recognition. UPs underestimate how busy seniors are, not realizing what crapshoot odds they have of their boss, or their manager's boss, really understanding their contributions. One company CEO refused to invest in trade shows, believing customer word of mouth was the purest form of business development and should be enough. A branding consultant cautioned him, "You're the industry's best-kept secret! No one's heard of you. Your salespeople feel like Sisyphus climbing the marketing mountain."

Insufficient Network (UP). UPs dislike all politics or equate them with low integrity. Instead of seeing politics as ethical organizational impact, they morally rationalize their insular world. They refuse to network, view corporate functions as a nuisance, and think schmoozing is sleazy. They shy away from sitting with seniors, abandoning that networking opportunity to the more ambitious. Most UPs fail to form enough cross-organizational alliances or join professional affiliations. They suffer lack of exposure and wind up without a seat when the music in the corporate musical-chairs game stops. The UP underestimates loyalty, overlooking how often promotions, hiring, bonus awards, and resource allocations are decided on factors beyond competence. Who is going to get the plum job—someone keeping her head down doing her job or someone who is visible and working the system? It's back to Amateur Night! Myopic UPs with their heads into their own function lack a cross-organizational perspective, suffering inbred ideas and stagnation. This "idea incest" makes them nonstrategic and blocks collaboration.

Blind Spots about Image (UP). UPs relate anything to do with image enhancement to shallow politics and used-car sales. They are often clueless about their reputation and how they come across to others and don't act to shape and limit damaging perceptions. They strike others as having poor executive presence because they don't hone their image, appearance, or presentation skills. A group of molecular scientists at one medical company infuriated their sales colleagues whenever copresenting to potential partners. The UPs consistently rambled on and on about one tiny piece of flawed data, using poor presentation skills and boring the customer while overshadowing and dooming the partnership's big-picture promise. They refused to polish their image because to them it meant selling out and becoming slick salespeople.

Lack of Verbal Discipline (UP). Honesty pushed to an extreme can hurt feelings, bruise egos, or leak information to people who use it against you. Examples are when UPs blindly speak the truth to power without taking into account who the receiver is or considering the potential consequences of failing to be discerning. The UP mistakes idiocy for honesty! At times, UPs commit career-limiting blunders by having too open an agenda, innocently revealing their thoughts and feelings, confronting ulterior motives they detect in others, or being so passionate about their ideas that they state them in ways that the egos of powerful superiors are offended.

False Comfort, Easily Deceived (UP). Like organizational psychologist Jack Gibb, we define true trust as earned trust: Trust = Risk Successfully Survived. If you are continually burned or see others hurt by someone and don't protect yourself, you're a victim of "false comfort." Politically naïve people allow their basic faith in human nature to blind them to the seamier side of organizational life. They trust people who should not be trusted, leaving themselves vulnerable to theft of ideas, blame, and sabotage. If your Less Political mentality makes you an easy target for predatory turf behavior, stolen ideas, scapegoating, or open sabotage, then your left-side strengths have become liabilities.

The desire to do what's right can also lead an Under Political person to excessively place company good over self-interests. It's great to be giving, refusing to be self-*ish* like an Overly Political (OP) person, but if you become self-*less,* you may be the bull's-eye on a target. We know of an Under Political president of a major beverage corporation's USA division who volunteered his division to claim more than its accurate share of losses in order to help the company audit look better. He didn't document his altruistic action, so his team's reputation suffered and he was later fired for underperformance.

The UP's definition of power as residing in the work itself means that he keeps his head down doing his job. So he lacks peripheral vision and is naïve about politics. Now add inherent good-faith trust and the desire to do what's right, and UPs can end up like one who told us, "I know it's a dog-eat-dog world, and I've been wearing Milk-Bone underwear!" UPs automatically assume that others are operating as they are, acting with honesty and sincerity in their hearts. Unfortunately, the saying goes, "An honest, sincere person is easier for people to deceive." The UP takes people at their word and overlooks how some people's idea of sincerity comes from the George Burns quote "Sincerity is everything. If you can fake that, you've got it made." So if you have the Power of Ideas style and are wondering if you've become naïve and under political, take the advice given to novice poker players: "Look around the poker table. If you don't see a chump, you're it!"

Holier-Than-Thou (UP). Other times, radical Power of Ideas people's unwavering integrity becomes inflated into a judgmental holier-than-thou attitude that they wear on their chests as a capital *I* for "integrity." Their moral compass is fine until you don't happen to define what's ethical in the same way as they do. Then their cliquish exclusion is a not-so-distant relative of the Overly Political Good Old Boy Club: "Who has high enough moral fiber to earn membership in my high-integrity club?" This behavior is called *fundamentalist*, but there's nothing "fun" when someone goes "mental" on you as a "fun-da-mentalist" reactionary.

Inflated integrity can mean a refusal to compromise, shooting oneself in the foot, like the sales manager we know who refused to let his people take clients or prospects to lunch. The executive ignored a common business courtesy, set up his sales force to look cheap, and blocked business development. The UP manager's idealism needed to be balanced with practicality, because he was putting his people behind the eight ball and they resented him for it. The naïve UP sometimes has trouble advancing or getting ideas implemented because he wears his integrity on his shirtsleeve to the point of blocking his own success. His drive to do what's right gets perverted into stubbornness. He's like the musician who refuses to play commercial tunes since it compromises his artistic integrity. So now he plays plenty of his own music—while starving on the street corner.

In the movie *The Contender,* a U.S. vice president dies and Joan Allen plays a senator appointed as the replacement, subject to congressional confirmation hearings. Gary Oldman plays an Overly Political villainous congressman who leaks pictures of her sexual escapades. The photos are fake—it's not her! She refuses to address the issue because she feels it would dignify questions that would never be asked of a man. An admirable stance, but being right gets her the booby prize. She loses the confirmation and hurts her career, administration, and country until the savvy president rescues her nomination.

Missed Opportunities (UP). The Under Political can be so into respecting proper channels and doing the right thing that he is seen as a pain-in-the-bottleneck who doesn't get ideas implemented efficiently and suffers low organizational impact. Told that a decision will be discussed at a Friday meeting, many UPs arrive to state their case, only to discover that others have already secured advance approval in private meetings *before* this now token, rubber-stamp meeting. Working the system can certainly be overdone, but it can also be underutilized while others leapfrog past the frustrated UP. Can you think of people with great ideas who miss opportunities for recognition and credit because of a severely low profile or steadfast adherence to protocol that others are willing to appropriately bend?

The Under Political Can Survive

While UP people face these disadvantages, there's no need for doom or gloom since such extreme left-side risks are softened by several conditions. Your far-left style may still fit well if your entire company has an extreme Power of Ideas culture, as in some high-tech, biotech, or think-tank companies where the CEO sets forth a high-integrity, egalitarian, lower-profile set of values. You're less vulnerable in jobs where results are quite measurable, as in sales or accounting. You also thrive with your head down in your work if what you do is mission critical. We remember working with one of the programmers of the code for a giant computer company's operating system. He had no position power, but had job security and status in spite of a UP temperament. You're protected if you work for a powerful right-side Power of Person boss, assuming that he supports you and depends upon your substantive expertise. You bolster his image of knowing what he's talking about and you provide him with grounding in the business while you may ride his pony of position power and image expertise—a practical, symbiotic working relationship. Finally, at lower levels, politics may not matter or you may avoid them. But as you move into management, from midmanagement into executive positions, or from executive to boardroom ranks, more and more political savvy is required. This is especially true if you seek not only to get by, but also to rise through the ranks.

The Power of Person Risks of Being Overly Political (OP)

More Political (MP) people astutely focus on position power, image and perception, doing what works, relationship-based decisions, more private agendas, and self-promotion. This is invaluable for careers and companies until they overdo it and usher in a tsunami of Overly Political (OP) risks. All of the following risks boil down to an epicenter fatal flaw. The OP compromises his principles to get ahead and loses his ethical balance—either along the way or from the outset. Eventually, the answer for OPs will lie in blending right-side political skills with left-side values.

Power Trips (OP). Henry Kissinger called power "the great aphrodisiac." More Political (MP) people define power as position power, but Overly Political (OP) people are power-obsessed, like the Pig in George Orwell's *Animal Farm:* "All animals are equal, but some animals are more equal than others." They seek control *over* people rather than *with* people and don't mind intimidating people. They smugly reassure a peer, "Don't worry. Mike won't cross me." Unlike left-siders, who wonder how your idea might help the company or if it has merit, OPs screen your idea through their power and ego paranoia to the point of feedback freak-out, wondering how your suggestion makes them look for not thinking of it.

OPs can also be turf tyrants, overly protective in hoarding or guarding resources and constantly worried about how your plan affects their power base, while demanding, "What do you mean you hired a consultant?" "Why are you talking to my people?" "We don't need this new task force!" Their preoccupation with power causes name-dropping ad nauseam and ego trips as they boast about a power lunch, whisper who's "in" or "out," or eagerly reveal a senior's nickname or in-joke. A normal amount of positive name-dropping builds credibility, creates commonality, or endorses an idea. But name-dropping is a pain when it's constant, exaggerated, or false.

A Less Political (LP) Power of Ideas person treats everyone with respect, from the president to mailroom clerk. But the ego-trippers' Jekyll-to-Hyde treatment is based on perceived power. You'll catch them kissing up and kicking down. If you lack power or aren't connected, they may dismiss you, ignore your phone calls, or insult you in public. But if you're powerful or wired in, they may laugh at your jokes, dress and talk like you, pat you on the back, and compliment your ideas before turning around to roll their eyes.

Fall from Grace: Distrusted (OP). OPs risk being distrusted by everyone and one day feeling very alone looking in the mirror once they realize that they've been playing for their soul and losing. The Overly Political player pollutes the Power of Person dimension of "do what works" into "do whatever it takes" or even "do whatever you can get away with." Self-interest and getting ahead to do well for yourself and your family is one thing, but if you are motivated by pure self-interest at the expense of others or the company, you have had a fall from grace and sold your soul. In 1887, Lord Acton wrote in a letter, "Power tends to corrupt and absolute power corrupts absolutely."

UPs naïvely reveal agendas too openly, but Overly Political individuals barrel past savvy prudence with selfish agendas. They take *shrewd* to *lewd,* trashing good ideas and pushing bad ones just to advance some hidden agenda for their own gain—financial rewards, a pet project, a bonus or promotion, a favor for a friend, a greedy end. American Airlines secretly gave lucrative compensation packages and retirement plans to the ailing company's top forty-five executives while putting a gun to union heads, warning them to take new contract concessions or see the company crash and burn in bankruptcy. It didn't work. CEO Donald Carty, who himself earned $1.3 million in 2001 along with $6 million in options, was forced to resign as the airline's stock crash-landed and quarterly losses hit over $1 billion.

OPs may dig a moat around their castles of hidden self-interests to create insulated teams that we call *private power pockets.* Outsiders are denied access to the team, intergroup collaboration shrinks, information is kept under wraps, and paranoia reigns. Later in the book, you'll learn to detect private power pockets and weed them out.

The very word *politics* conjures up images of behind-the-scenes politicking, cutting corners, and making special deals in smoke-filled rooms. This type of secret-handshake and chameleon-like behavior means that the OP will do anything to win support for a pet cause, even supporting ideas he actually opposes, just to exchange favors. He'll do whatever it takes to gain power, money, or control, including crossing ethical or legal lines, bribing, or bargaining.

He plots to take credit for your idea so that if a project succeeds, he can convince others *he* invented the wheel, or he may fix blame and distance himself from unsuccessful initiatives. More than just being sleazy or slippery, the more vicious sabotaging sharks won't think twice as they bad-mouth you or try to get rid of *you,* not just your idea. Make sure you're not doing water ballet in the shark tank while OPs come in for the kill.

Pedestals Can Topple (OP). Besides the fall from grace, OPs also risk a fall from power, because pedestals are shaky to stand on. When OPs in high places fall, they fall hard.

- *Being Exposed*. Compliance by fearful underlings is not the same as commitment. Sooner or later, abusive bosses get fingered during exit interviews or "dinged" on survey feedback. Companies are using climate surveys and open feedback systems to make blatant Overly Political behavior more transparent, so extreme right-siders are being ousted. Safeguards like whistle-blower protection and legislation mandating corporate governance mean OPs finally need to watch their backs.
- *Power Shifts or Showdowns*. In the Old West, young gunslingers looked to beat the fastest gun. On the corporate open range, power seekers lurk around the corner gunning for the top dog. A power shift in the boardroom gives an enemy a chance for payback. Power conflicts lead to battles for the spot at the helm and former Goliaths go down in flames.
- *Mutiny and Coups*. Recently, an entire cadre of top executives defected from one major investment firm to another. The Wall Street fiasco was blamed on the power-driven style of the division head, costing the firm negative publicity and sky-high compensation packages to lure the coup ringleaders back. The boss was relegated to a mere figurehead.
- *Silent Sabotage*. The word *sabotage* is storied to be from the

French word for wooden shoe, *sabot,* to recall how French workers threw their shoes into newfangled machinery to foil the efforts of industrial revolution bosses. Today, sabotage slows down even the most vicious of OPs. One such power freak was asked, "How many people do you have working for you?" He knew he'd alienated others as he wryly admitted, "About half of them."

Blindly Obvious Behavior (OP). Amazingly bright people sometimes can't see how obvious their power-tripping, distrustful, and unethical behavior is to others. While many OPs are highly skilled at deception, others let their reckless behavior get so out of hand it's like a neon sign flashing. Meanwhile, their arrogance contorts into such narcissism that they can't see how people can now "play them." We warn any high-level person of "CEO disease," which is the susceptibility to manipulation by other power trippers who know how to feed the runaway ego of a boss. We warn powerful people, "You're probably not as smart, funny, or good-looking as you think you are. You've been receiving a steady diet of flattery, people laughing at your jokes, and raving about your strategy. That guy who you're ticked off at for disagreeing with you is your only real friend." Ironically, it's often radical OPs who contract the most serious cases of CEO disease, because of their gigantic egos that soak up the BS.

Sun Microsystems CEO Scott McNealy expressed "sincerest apologies" for his "imprudent remarks" after insulting the Securities and Exchange Commission as "absolutely wacko." He compared Federal Reserve chairman Alan Greenspan to Chauncey Gardner, the slow-witted Peter Sellers character in *Being There*. In that movie, Capitol Hill treats Gardner as a genius policy adviser, mistaking his simple gardening tips as brilliant economic observations. Investors and analysts assailed McNealy's "brash and contrarian personality" as "not very presidential" and demanded his persona makeover from Sun's board, even putting a full-page open letter in the *Wall Street Journal*.

Cronyism (OP). Appreciative loyalty and proven partnerships descend into good old boy networks as deals and favors are made for complacent pals and improprieties are ignored. OPs hire and promote robots and clones—people who look, think, and vote like them, with many costs to the company. Competent people are excluded from the team to make way for yes-men and friends. Teams lose diversity through a mentality of "you're either with me or you're against me." Companies put projects out to bid to select vendors, but it's a token act and waste of time if OPs already know their palms will be greased and which firm will win.

At times the inequity in pay for "corporate royalty" versus the masses can be obscene, internally divisive, and morally reprehensible to the public. Many CEOs' and chairmen's outrageous pay makes them poster children for greed while their boards of directors condone the questionable compensation package. *The New York Times* observed, "Boards themselves are frequently packed with the chairman's friends and associates, who are unlikely to be rabble-rousers . . . these kinds of sleepy boards are commonplace across the nation."

Disasters Waiting to Happen (OP). OP rulers of corporate dominions can become reckless and cocky. Their fiefdoms are riddled with people fearfully ignoring their towering egos and ruthless behavior. The result can be costly scandals, lawsuits, compliance violations, and acts of greed or graft. Like Icarus flying too close to the sun, these grandiose legends in their own minds may fall prey to mistakes in judgment and ethical lapses that cause their own demise as others marvel at their brashly shortsighted stumbles. The organizational counterpart is the ticking time bomb of companywide hubris. The 2003 *Columbia* Accident Investigation Board's scathing report on the shuttle's tragic explosion lambasted NASA as an "overconfident culture" that engaged in risk-taking and self-deception. The board indicted NASA with blistering descriptions of a "history of ignoring external recommendations" after the 1986

Challenger disaster, a "culture of invincibility," and a discounting of lower managers' concerns.

Lack of Professional Growth (OP). Their ego-driven resistance to constructive feedback causes intense right-siders to limit their expertise, business grounding, and task level knowledge. Plus, they may spend so much time on lunches with the bigwigs, getting their names in the company newsletter, and "working the room" that many lack any real substance or ideas, earning them the description "empty suits." Mark Twain once quipped, "All you need in life is ignorance and confidence, and then success is sure." A workshop attendee's boss told him, "Ties are for people who don't have data." At a group level, an OP team's performance and growth can atrophy.

A Heads-Up to the Overly Political (OP)

Larger-than-life OPs who run amok infect their organizations with disillusionment, snuff out innovation, and poison company pride. Outrageous looting or regulatory misdeeds trigger lawsuits, fines, scandal, or media uproar that pummels the bottom line. There can be public outrage, loss of investor confidence, market loss, profit erosion, and stock devaluation. Our mission is not to help ruthless OPs to survive or thrive. But if you are an OP, we *do* care about your welfare, too. Think of this book as a tough-love intervention. We hope you will consider serious changes, preferably for the right reasons (it's the right thing to do), or if need be, for the "wrong" reasons—because you know you're at greater risk than ever before of being exposed, toppling, having blind spots, or handicapping your organization and your career.

The Style Risk Tracker

Many people can relate to both sides of last chapter's Style Strengths Finder, but they can even more readily differentiate their political style based on style risks. So please review the Style Risk Tracker at the end of this chapter to see which political style's risks fit you more. You probably won't relate to these style recognition clues as much as you did to the items in the Style Strengths Finder, because these style risks characterize style extremes (UP and OP). But some of these tendencies may resonate for you. If the left-side risks sound familiar, you more likely hold the Power of Ideas style. If some of the right-side risks fit more, you are most likely a Power of Person individual. If you can't relate to many of these risks at all (major blind spots), you have a healthy Less Political (LP) or More Political (MP) style. If you relate to a couple of the risk categories on one side but not all you may have a Borderline Under Political (BUP) or Borderline Overly Political (BOP) style.

Overcoming Political Style Risks: Hope for the Extremes

We're not trying to chip away at your self-esteem. Our message is one of hope through awareness, choice, and skills. If you're too far left on the Organizational Savvy Continuum, then retain your values but blend savvy strategies for each risk. Add influence and impact to your existing integrity. A shift from self-sacrifice toward getting your needs met for recognition and advancement, if nothing else, helps your team. We remind Under Politicals (UPs) and Borderline Under Politicals (BUPs) who are afraid of becoming self-*ish,* like Overly Politicals (OPs), that being self-*less* means you're literally without a sense of self. So you can instead be self-*ful*—not "full of yourself," but simply acting in behalf of yourself or your team while still caring about the company. Even the sage Rabbi Hillel is noted for his query "If I am not for myself, who is for me?"

If you are too far right on the Organizational Savvy Continuum, move from being Borderline Overly Political (BOP) or Overly Political (OP) by tempering your political skills with a greater focus on values and morals. Blend company interest with self-interests to protect yourself and your organization. You won't *lose* organizational impact by adding integrity. You'll actually increase your potency, because your power focus will be more trusted and respected. In this spirit, we'll now explore the attributes of the balanced political style we call *Power of Savvy*.

Style Risk Tracker

UNDER POLITICAL RISKS	OVERLY POLITICAL RISKS
Being Underestimated	Power Trips
Insufficient Network	Fall from Grace: Distrusted
Blind Spots about Image	Pedestals Can Topple
Lacks Verbal Discipline	Blindly Obvious Behavior
False Comfort, Easily Deceived	Cronyism
Holier-Than-Thou	Disasters Waiting to Happen
Missed Opportunities	Lack of Professional Growth

SOLUTIONS TO RISKS	SOLUTIONS TO RISKS
Keep Your Values, Add Political Skill	Keep Your Political Skill, Add Values
Move from Self-*less* to Self-*ful*	Move from Self-*ish* to Self-*ful*
Add Influence and Impact to Integrity	Add Integrity to Influence and Impact

Chapter 4

Finding the Vital Balance

The Power of Savvy Political Style

Our goal is to steer you toward the green-light, safe-travel zone of organizational savvy that represents a foolproof third political style we call the Power of Savvy style. It is made up of the style placements we've already called the Less Political (LP) and More Political (MP), with their healthy, valued mind-sets. These people lead with their strengths, avoiding the potential risks of the Borderline Under Political (BUP), Under Political (UP), Borderline Overly Political (BOP), and Overly Political (OP) styles. Regardless of whether they are usually on the right side (More Political) or left side (Less Political) of the Continuum, the Power of Savvy style balances the best of both worlds. They can access the Power of Person specialties of image, influence, and power as well as the Power of Ideas assets of substance, integrity, and protocol. This balanced political style's tagline is "impact with integrity."

As you navigate your job, career, and company ship through political waters toward your North Star goals, your best odds lie in this Power of Savvy style. Savvy leaders blend integrity, task competence, and political skill. Their ethics guide them to do the right thing and what's best for the common welfare. They also gain influence, get things done in their culture, and understand the

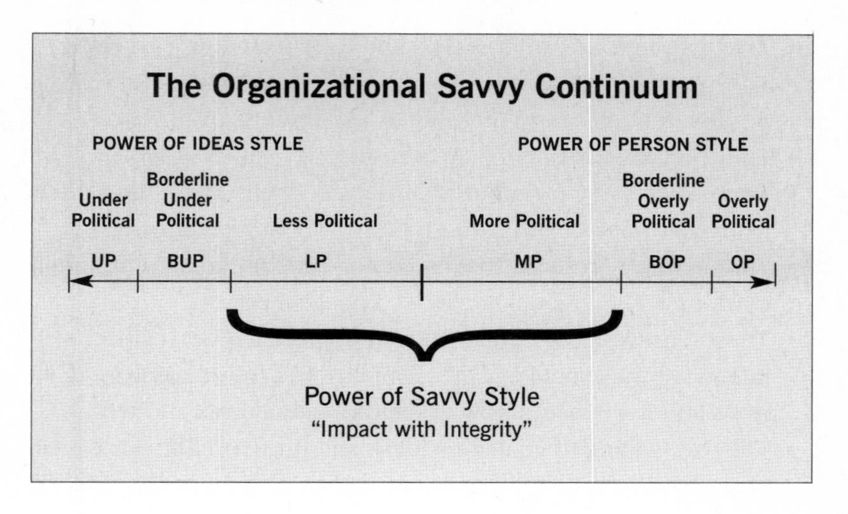

range of political behaviors that occurs in an organization. They're realistic about people's potential for acting with altruism or with self-interest.

Power of Savvy leaders detect deception in the form of misleading information, sabotage, and private power pockets. They use their awareness and skills to make good decisions about internal hires and promotions as well as external vendors and partners. To recognize a Power of Savvy person, look for a surplus of Style Strengths Finder clues and shortage of Style Risk Tracker items. You can also admire their following characteristics and skills, which will be discussed in detail in future chapters.

- They understand different people's attitudes about power and politics and adapt their own approach for optimal influence and protection.
- They are professional in their attitudes about organizational dynamics and willingly enter the political arena to achieve influence, impact, and career growth.
- They read the official and unofficial power networks, corporate priorities, "system," cultural norms, and unwritten rules for success.

- They pay attention to how they and their teams are perceived.
- They strategically plan how to reshape perceptions and build a positive reputation for themselves and their teams.
- They build and maintain key networks.
- They effectively promote themselves, their ideas, and their teams in a showcasing rather than showboating manner.
- They exude a presence that conveys quiet confidence and humility along with personal impact and positive power.
- They sensitively recognize when people exercise political self-interest at the expense of the company, and they make wise decisions about when and how to handle such ulterior motives.
- They are willing to challenge ideas and bring up difficult issues, but they do so skillfully, without alienating others. They blend tact, prudence, and forthrightness with superiors.
- They understand how to get ideas implemented while factoring in timing, setting, conflicting agendas, allies, and advocates to decide which battles can be won now and which to defer with patience and restraint.
- They take responsibility for managing their own political stock while cultivating the political health and savvy of their teams and entire organizations.
- They are not easily manipulated and have keen radar for weeding out deception and naked self-interest.
- They strategically recruit, select, and assemble teams for a blend of results, integrity, and political astuteness.
- They forge healthy, balanced political cultures by teaching organizational savvy, managing teams for "impact with integrity," and creating feedback-rich environments.
- They model ethics with realism by firmly taking a stand on integrity issues without coming across as self-righteous, impractical, or judgmental.

The Payoffs for Adopting a Power of Savvy Style

Besides embodying the above traits, the Power of Savvy individual savvy tactics that are covered in part 2, and the leadership savvy strategies of parts 3 and 4 for building savvy teams and company cultures, will bring these benefits:

- *Avoiding Risks and Flaws.* Avoiding Overly Political or Under Political blind spots heightens career and company success. Embracing the middle range on the Continuum automatically protects you from the last chapter's flaws. Far-left people can adopt the skills we'll prescribe to overcome style risks, and far-right individuals can blend their existing skills with moderation and values to prevent personal, team, or company distress.
- *Balance.* You're in trouble if image obsession threatens results, or if you ignore your image or influence to focus solely on substance. The Organizational Savvy Continuum is like a teeter-totter, so keep your balance by not venturing too far to either side.
- *Choice.* Power of Savvy people are liberated from being victims of habit. They have awareness and "response-*ability*"—the ability to respond since they aren't on autopilot.
- *Style Reach.* The Power of Savvy style can access all points along the Organizational Savvy Continuum since being toward the middle means it's closer to every style placement. It's easier to draw upon the best of both worlds, unlike the more extreme style postures that must stretch to reach all of the other style attributes.
- *Strategic Flexibility.* Power of Savvy people are less stuck and adapt their approach to the situation. They draw on Power of Person gifts to scan for a new boss's unwritten rules or to self-promote at appraisal or bonus time. They adopt a Power of Ideas substance focus if they need to build credibility or if their team is racing to release a new product.

- *Respect and Collaboration*. Political styles have worldviews that can collide as each uses a separate calculus to evaluate ideas. Negative judgments can fly and tensions can flare. The Power of Savvy style nourishes cooperation by genuinely prizing both the Power of Ideas and Power of Person styles. Empathy for both style mind-sets defuses style-based frictions.

Blocks to Adopting a Power of Savvy Style

Given these benefits of moving toward the middle of the Organizational Savvy Continuum, people ask, "Why are some people so uncomfortable budging from their Overly Political or Under Political style extremes?" Many people try to deny the existence of organizational politics, so, of course, feel no need to change their political style. Their utopian belief that organizations are logical systems subject to laws of order ignores that companies are actually human systems desperately struggling to be more rational. Other people's reaction to organizational politics is moral indignance: "I shouldn't have to change because organizations shouldn't be this political." This more emotionally loaded view equates all politics to manipulation, resulting in blind spots and stubborn refusal to adapt one's Under Political style.

Derogatory judgments and stereotypes also keep people blocked from the midrange political-style strengths. The Power of Ideas style is seen as a naïve victim, ostrich, wimp, geek, goody-goody, doormat, bureaucrat, or bottleneck. The Power of Person style also suffers from loaded perceptions as a cutthroat, snake, game-player, power tripper, or empty suit. Rigid people miss the treasure chest of strengths buried in each style. Some Under Political people (UPs) and Overly Political people (OPs) fear overshooting the Power of Savvy style and swinging like a pendulum too far to the other side. The UP worries she'll gather so much momentum, she'll become an obnoxious OP braggart. The OP shudders at the thought of becoming disrespected as a "non" without a shred of visibility.

Finally, some people stay stuck in their style extremes due to general rigidity. As Popeye the Sailor Man says, "I yam what I yam and dat's all dat I yam." Let's face it. Some people don't like to change their habits, take feedback, or modify their beliefs, as evidenced by things they actually say: "You can't teach an old dog new tricks." "What you see is what you get, so sue me!" "You're confusing me with someone who cares." "Thanks, I've had enough personal growth for the century."

"Let Me Be the Person I Am!"

When one of the authors' sons was four years old, he was awakened from a nap to wash his hands and come to dinner. Tired, grumpy, and unhappy about being told it was family time, the sleepy little guy surprised Daddy by tearfully grumbling, "Why can't you let me be the person I *am*?" (Boy, did he ever know just how to guilt-trip a psychologist father.) No one enjoys being told he can't be himself, so we certainly respect you to decide for yourself whether you're comfortable with your political style. Hopefully, you're not resenting our wake-up call to *you* about organizational politics and grousing, "Why can't they just let me be the person I am?" Admittedly, we *are* asking you to make sure that your political style is working for you, your team, and your company. You have a home-base political-style placement where you function most frequently, naturally, and effectively. Just remember you can consciously decide to adopt the Power of Savvy postures of More Political (MP) or Less Political (LP), which provide the best chances for style strengths, impact, influence, integrity, balance, choice, flexibility, and collaboration.

PART II

INDIVIDUAL SAVVY TACTICS

Chapter 5

Map Political Styles

"Basically, We Need the Eggs!"

At the end of Woody Allen's movie *Annie Hall,* the joke is referenced about the guy who frantically goes to a psychiatrist about his crazy brother who's running around clucking and thinks he's a chicken. When the psychiatrist asks the worried family member why he doesn't have his brother committed, the man replies, "I would, but we need the eggs." Similarly, we all put up with all of the absurdity and crazy-making in our companies because, basically, *we* need the eggs! And what Woody Allen implies about personal relationships also holds true in our work relationships—*we* help to create the madness. However, this chapter encourages you to identify people's political styles so that you can make more sense out of company chaos. Through knowledge of political styles you will manage your own style limitations, influence others by predicting their attitudes and behavior, and protect yourself by looking at political styles before leaping into any action.

The Political Style Map

You may wish to spend a few minutes with a blank piece of paper "mapping" the political style placements of individuals and teams you encounter. Draw the Organizational Savvy Continuum with its categories of Less Political (LP), Borderline Under Political (BUP), and Under Political (UP) to the left and More Political (MP), Borderline Overly Political (BOP), and Overly Political (OP) to the right. Then feel free to use the Style Strengths Finder in chapter 2 and the Style Risk Tracker in chapter 3 to judge which placement best fits various people in your work world.

There's no set formula for identifying political style, so just consider all the traits you can to get a directional read. Don't jump to conclusions based on one clue without weighing the majority of signals and considering the circumstances. Even the mildest More Political (MP) or even a Less Political (LP) person might once in a while dabble in one of the far-right flaws, but that doesn't make him Overly Political (OP). Another individual may have quite a few left-side strength or risk clues, but an overshadowing behavior like trashing someone's reputation for personal gain might make him an OP or BOP.

To assess the political style of an entire team or organization, just imagine the overall entity's value system and chemistry while considering, "If this were a single person, where would he or she fall along the Organizational Savvy Continuum?" Obviously, many individuals within the group might not fit the style assessment of the overall team. We often have teams compare their style with other teams' style biases around the six dimensions of political style. When estimating the style of your team or the entire company, whose vantage point are you considering—that of other teams, competitors in the industry, customers, suppliers, or employees? Since political style is a matter of degree, each group's perspective leads it to view your team's style differently. Also, new employees may feel differently from veterans, who may have seen a gradual shift to the right as the company has grown (politics do seem to come with the territory of company growth).

With these guidelines, you might want to consider the following individual and group interdependencies as you map out political styles.

- *Official Power*. Place key bosses and superiors on your style map. Purposely include left-side managers to prove to yourself that this model is more about mind-set than position power.
- *Unofficial Power Influencers*. Place informal power holders and influencers on the map.
- *Emerging Leaders*. Map the "heirs apparent" and rising stars.
- *Yourself*. Place yourself as you are today and as you were at other times in your career.
- *Colleagues and Reports*. Include right-siders who do not possess position power to again show that the Continuum is not all about position.
- *Teams, Departments, and Divisions*. Map the style of your team and various other groups you encounter. Try to include several different placements for your own team, with each one coded to indicate which other team's perspective you're assuming. Each group might view your team differently since political style is all relative.
- *Overall Organization*. Place the culture of the enterprise. Again, use a code for each different perspective you're assuming (for example, employees, competitors, customers, the general public).

Red Alert! It's Not as Easy as It Looks

Style identification is a subjective art and many fluid dynamics blur accurate political style recognition. So develop a working hypothesis about people's style and modify it as you take in new data, adjusting for how well you know them and how characteristic traits are for them. The point isn't to arrive at some objective truth about style placement. Style assessment is intended to be a door opener for understanding yourself and others so that you can better self-manage your weaknesses, influence others, and protect yourself from their (and your) extremes. Still, the more accurate your style estimate, the better the odds for productive and harmonious working relationships. So, here are some tips as you map out political styles.

Political Style Is Not about Position Power. The Organizational Savvy Continuum isn't correlated with position power. It's more about your attitude toward power, your view of politics, your ambition, and what you're willing to do to achieve power. You may run into more right-siders the higher you go in a company, but any job level can be held by a person with the Power of Ideas *or* a Power of Person style. We know many Borderline Under Political top executives and many individual contributors who are Borderline Overly Political or even power-mongering OPs. In the get-rich-quick days before the dot-com crash, many low-level engineers held all the cards, made millions, and were on power trips. Their sense of entitlement and self-importance led them to bully their companies and do whatever they wanted, including not even reporting for work. They weren't phoning in sick. They were phoning in rich!

Political Styles Are Not Static. There's enough stability for the Continuum to be practical, but many factors create style variability and shifting:

- *Period of Life.* People change over time, due to career turns, maturation, or life experience. Some Power of Ideas college grads want to save the world with their ideas and integrity. Others are OPs from Ivy League schools who act like prima donnas. Whatever your style was years ago, it has most likely shifted some, either through conscious choice or natural, gradual evolution.
- *Home versus Work.* A person can be savvy at work but naïve and overly trusting in personal relationships, letting others manipulate or take advantage of her.
- *Greed, Fear, or Ambition.* Even UPs can commit OP heinous acts when greed intoxicates them or power goes to their heads. Threat and fear can change behavior, so watch for style swings during job instability, a regulatory or personal crisis, or impending cutbacks.
- *Job Expectations.* A person changes to survive a boss or a company culture with certain norms. An MP can become demure

with a tyrant superior. One LP said he *had* to act as an OP when he worked for a Washington, D.C., lobbying group.

- *The Stage of a Team or Company.* A start-up mode, delay with a new product release, merger, scandal, or competitive challenge each demands a different political style.

Style Recognition Is Not a Science. The Organizational Savvy Continuum is a road map, just as any theoretical model is meant to be, but no road map is like driving the real road. Road markers disappear, construction causes detours, and weather conditions alter terrain. Similarly, people don't demonstrate every predicted trait like a cookie-cutter version of their political style.

- *We're Generalizing.* Political style shorthand helps us understand different mind-sets about power. But any label oversimplifies. If we ask you to imagine a "tree," you may picture an apple tree when we mean a redwood! Do we have a sapling or two-hundred-foot skyscraper in mind? Is it wet with dew or scorched from fire?
- *Political Style Is Only a Piece of Truth.* You're much more than your political style, so a defensive reaction to feedback might mean you're an image-conscious Borderline Overly Political (BOP). But maybe you're the opposite—a Borderline Under Political (BUP) who suffered a wounded childhood of put-downs, so you get easily bruised.
- *Any Behavior Can Have Different Intents.* It's hard to measure style, since many clues relate more to motivations than to actions. A behavior can be a right-side or left-side clue depending on its intent. Being sent to executive development can be a generous investment if coaching is valued at a company, or an act of sabotage to brand you.
- *Savant Style Traits Exist.* Some developmentally disabled or autistic people have uncanny genius in an isolated skill, such as a child who can name the proper day of the week if you name a year and date. People of one political style may demonstrate a key charac-

teristic from a different style, either due to style range or being an exception to the rule. You'd err by treating people as a caricature of their style. We know two strong Power of Person clients with clear Power of Ideas traits. One is quite ego-free about feedback (the left-side dimension of "focus on feedback and learning"), and the other cherishes his values about diversity and devotes time to three nonprofit agencies that help minorities (the left-side dimension of "do the right thing").

Once you've plotted your own political style and have placed colleagues and associates along the Organizational Savvy Continuum, the practical implications of your assessments come into play. Your political style awareness is a lens through which you will better understand and navigate your work environment. You'll manage your own style drawbacks, influence people more purposefully, and protect yourself from committing political mistakes that ignore others' style-based preferences.

Style Awareness to Manage Weaknesses

In *People Styles at Work,* communications expert Robert H. Bolton illustrates the idea of managing weaknesses with the Greek figure Achilles. The hero's mother dipped him as an infant into a magical river that made him invulnerable, except for the one heel by which she held him. As a man, Achilles protected his heel from arrows by wearing a lead boot over it. Likewise, you won't necessarily get rid of your own style-based Achilles' heels, but you can protect and manage them in these ways.

- *Make the Weakness Irrelevant.* Marcus Buckingham, in *Now, Discover Your Strengths,* suggests that developing one's strengths is more important than fixing weaknesses. His examples include the NBA's Dennis Rodman—a lousy scorer, but his rebounding broke records. Cole Porter's plots bored many, but his music was sheer genius. Which of your style strengths reduce the impact of your style weaknesses? Lean into them.

- *Compensate for Weakness.* Minimize a style weakness by working around it. Delegate or ask for support, or rearrange the situation to reduce weakness. A myopic BUP with inbred ideas can ask someone on his team to visit other groups and share cross-organizational perspectives at staff meetings. An OP can solicit anonymous written feedback if he knows he's prone to defensive, emotional reactions. How can you rearrange tasks, processes, or the environment and have people compensate for your weaknesses?
- *Develop Skills to Grow beyond the Weakness.* If you saw your own shadow while reading about style risks, the rest of the book provides answers through skills. Don't waste time fixing every weakness, since life's too short. But if a critical risk hurts you or burns others, it demands an action plan and resources such as a workshop, books, a mentor, or a coach. A low-impact UP may want to attend a presentation-skills program to work on image. An OP who mistreats less powerful people needs to contract with a mentor to teach him interpersonal sensitivities and skills.
- *Confront Your Demons.* Some style weaknesses are serious character flaws. Obviously, we hope you'll take more drastic action to tackle problems such as cronyism or stealing credit for ideas. For such issues, the action step is simple . . . *stop it!*

Style Awareness to Influence Others

The goal of assessing political style isn't to slap a label on someone, but to understand their preferences regarding the six dimensions informing the Organizational Savvy Continuum. We're not becoming fake chameleons, just building bridges. We want to better collaborate and influence others by taking into account their operating systems. When you lobby for an idea or collaborate, you'll build more rapport and persuasion if you not only consider their business priorities, but also their political preferences. Are they more to the left (a Less Political Power of Ideas mentality) or right (a More Political Power of Person mind-set) on each of the following six style dimensions?

Substance Power ↔ Position Power. When you present an idea, is this person only focused on the soundness of your business case (Less Political), or should you also shop the concept to others and benchmark it with competitors so that you can name-drop powerful supporters or discuss how the team will look by not keeping up with the Joneses (More Political)?

Focus on Feedback and Learning ↔ Focus on Image and Perceptions. Are you on thin ice if you approach the person with improvements to his plan because his ego is so invested (More Political), or does this senior epitomize the spirit of mutual learning, so that you can freely share advice, feedback, and challenges without worrying about face-saving efforts (Less Political)?

Do the Right Thing ↔ Do What Works. Does this person view every protocol step as vital, such as following exact interview procedures for hiring an officer (Less Political), or is he okay with taking "opportunistically reactive" shortcuts around an impractical technicality to avoid losing an incredible talent to the competition (More Political)?

More Open Agenda ↔ More Private Agenda. At budgeting or planning time, does someone openly share data to determine a true stretch goal (Less Political), or does he sandbag by withholding information about a possible huge client he's nearly landed (More Political)? You may be fine with this tactic knowing it's just his style, or perhaps he's just worried about too much stress. Some people at quota-setting times point to the famous planning session dilemma: "Do you want to be a hero for an hour and suffer for a year, or suffer for an hour and be a hero for a year?"

Meritocracy-Based Decisions ↔ Relationship-Based Decisions. Are you wasting time recommending a new vendor to your decision-maker boss who has previous loyalties (More Political)? Perhaps *you're* the new vendor and you learn from your network that a former client has left and that the incoming contact speaks about meritocracy values (Less Political). He might appreciate a gracious letter reviewing your track record of results and a phone call explaining that you don't take the account or his confidence for granted—you intend to earn it through stellar service and results.

Results and Ideas Speak for Themselves ↔ Self-Promotion. Is this a conservative senior who views anything that smacks of "selling" as too flamboyant (Less Political)? You're better off framing achievements as "excitement about what the team has accomplished," or describing promising new findings for the company. Or, does he view promoting achievements as spurring a spirit of celebrating strengths and healthy competition (More Political)?

Style Awareness to Protect Yourself

Reading Individuals' Political Styles. If your hunch is that a person is a Borderline Under Political Power of Ideas individual, protect yourself from his potentially exaggerated focus on learning and continuous improvement by expecting delays in planning. Do extra homework before presenting a proposal since he'll be scrutinizing your substance. If a person is an extreme Power of Person Overly Political player, don't forget his image preoccupation. Be careful not to lower his opinion of your idea with a spontaneous presentation that lacks punch or appears sloppy. Watch for hidden agendas or information that he might filter to keep an upper hand. We'll teach you to not unwittingly threaten his power, ego, or turf. Prevention is better medicine and easier than retracing your steps for damage control after misreading political style.

Reading Teams' Political Styles. Your influence and political safety also depend on reading entire teams' styles and how they view your style or your team's style. Interfacing with a Less Political (LP) group might hit some snags if you are more into taking shortcuts for expediency, but you'll worry less about receiving proper credit for your contribution from that team. On the other hand, documenting contributions and activities might be more prudent with a More Political (MP) group since even without intent they might remember differently from you how project contributions unfolded.

Gauging an organization's style helps you discern the norms for success and how to slant this handbook's savvy strategies. A tactic that's appropriate for one political culture can be too strong or weak in another. Asking others about your corporate buzz might be considered crass in some organizations' cultures. Developing a more prestige-oriented appearance to enhance your power image might be too slick in a more down-to-earth company. As you promote yourself and your accomplishments, if you're in a left-side culture, you may feature your team versus touting your own results. On some teams, ethical lobbying is opportunistic "selling," so you're better off with a more consultative flavor of merely informing and making a softer recommendation if asked.

Maps Point the Way

The political style mapping you've completed is truly valuable. Knowing your style helps you to choose which tactics you need or may already be overusing, such as building your network or honing a power image. You'll need different political skills in varying amounts depending upon the style of your overall organization. Besides, you wouldn't try to travel somewhere without knowing the destination's location and the "you are here" starting point. Now that you know your own style tendencies and the style preferences of key people, you can use this book's individual savvy strategies to find your way without crashing or getting lost. If you're already in a ditch, the coming tactics may help you get back onto the road toward your destination.

Chapter 6

Deactivate Your Political Buttons

The Toughest Person to Influence

Survival of the Savvy's high-integrity political tactics increase the influence you and your team possess, but this chapter hones a special kind of influence. During the past month, how often have you invested time in carefully selecting your words to influence someone else? Most likely, plenty of times. During the past month, how often have you invested time in carefully selecting your words to influence *yourself*? Ah, a trick question. Most people don't consciously strategize the words they use to influence themselves. We'll do that now, using the approach of Self-Talk, a technology researched and applied in brain research, psycho-immunology, sports, performance psychology, and sales training. Here, we'll apply this proven tool to better cope with politics and power in your organization.

Piercing the Emotional Veil

Let's pierce the emotional veil that surrounds power and politics so that you aren't crippled by your emotional reactions. Outrage about politics can prevent you from entering the political arena or hook you into doing something rash. Emotional reactivity to politics is like a time bomb waiting to be detonated at the wrong time, so let's "deactivate your political buttons." The choice certainly remains to be so resentful, shocked, or anxious about politics that you leave your organization, but the grass isn't always greener on the other side of the fence. Besides, your life situation may not allow you to leave an overly political company, and you can't just divorce your company culture. So another choice is to forge street-smart attitudes so that your emotions don't eat up your stomach.

Garbage In, Garbage Out

Whether you're conscious of it or not, you talk to yourself constantly—when you're awake, sleeping, daydreaming—all the time. This ongoing automatic mind chatter programs your brain with views about you, other people, your job, your organization, the world, and life. Our 10 billion brain cells have often been described as a supercomputer, but like all computers, they follow the rule of GIGO: "Garbage in, Garbage out." Whatever junk you program in comes out in a similar fashion. Your brain computer doesn't say, "I know you didn't mean to program me this way. I'll change it around for you." It simply processes the program you put into it. When your head is full of upsetting self-statements, you feel anxious, angry, or intimidated. Your thoughts either sabotage or support how you handle politics, as well as every other facet of your personal and professional life. Do you think of politics as "navigating the aggravating" or as "an opportunity to make a positive impact"?

Athletes use Self-Talk to support and psych themselves up for amazing feats. At the Seoul Olympics in 1988, Greg Louganis cracked his skull on the diving board during the preliminary round of the three-meter springboard competition. Two days later, he was in danger of losing the gold medal to a young Chinese diver who scored a perfect 10. After Greg nailed a 9.6 to win on the toughest dive he'd ever done in competition, he was interviewed about what he was thinking just before his dive, knowing he was in danger of losing the gold. Louganis said he reminded himself that he'd practiced the dive for years and that he knew he could do it at that moment. This Self-Talk created feelings of determination and confidence. He also told himself that even if he didn't win the gold, his mother would still love him and that being the second-best diver in the world is not so terrible! This last Self-Talk generated feelings of calm, relaxation, and perspective that took the pressure off Greg as he dived.

But so much of our Self-Talk is negative and self-sabotaging. Dr. Albert Ellis, founder of Rational Emotive counseling, blames faulty thinking for most emotional upset. We predict awful outcomes like "I'm going to get fired in this downsizing." Maybe . . . maybe not. But now it preoccupies our minds and work so that our performance dips, producing a self-fulfilling prophecy. We use unrealistic and inaccurate language like *always, never,* or *total* ("I never get any good leads from management!" "That SOB customer always gives me a hard time in front of her boss to show me who is boss." "Well, that appointment was a total disaster"). Untrue, exaggerated statements create strong feelings, stress, and lowered performance. Is it really "always" or "never"?

Do you jump to conclusions, mind-reading what a person is thinking even though all you really know is their external behavior? Be careful with your wild, crazy-making Self-Talk—your inferences. The boss yawns during an important presentation. Your Self-Talk could be "Oh, great! He's *totally* bored and hates the proposal. I'm blowing it. There goes my bonus." First off, don't upset yourself with words like *totally* and *hates*. And *is* he bored? What would a camera objectively record? It would show him yawning. The boredom is your inference. Maybe he was up all night with his newborn baby. Instead of making a mountain out of a molehill, just describe the molehill.

If your Self-Talk places unrealistic expectations upon your company, others, and yourself, you're set up for disappointment. Challenge yourself with questions like "Where is it written life should be fair?" "Who says politics shouldn't exist?" We run around "shoulding" all over ourselves: "I *should* have told him what I thought." "I'm idiotic. I *shouldn't* have wimped out at the meeting." When we're done shoulding all over ourselves, we start shoulding on other people: "Lou *should* stick up for our team more with top management. He's a lousy manager." "Marilyn *shouldn't* cop out of her part of the development cycle. I hate her." "Politics *shouldn't* be so pervasive." Part of cleaning up Self-Talk is to stop beating up ourselves and others in our minds.

Fish Didn't Discover Water

Self-Talk is an automatic mental habit, but we can tweak it if it doesn't serve us well. This takes being fully aware of any negative internal messages about power, politics, and promotion. Marshall McLuhan, who coined the famous phrase "The medium is the message," also said, "We don't know who it was that discovered water, but we're pretty sure it wasn't a fish." The fish can't see what's right in front of them. Like fish, we're not always aware of what's surrounding us constantly—in this case, our nonstop Self-Talk that's percolating in our heads.

So let's become aware of any trash talk we lay on ourselves about politics. You may wish to take a few moments to identify your negative Self-Talk. We've hopefully already shifted your thinking about politics, power, and promoting yourself. So rewind your mental videotape to uncover the programming messages you had in your head before you opened this book. Keep yourself honest and surface any negative ingrained Self-Talk you had about the issues we address in this book—politics, building a power base, lobbying for an idea, going through proper channels or jumping through hoops, whatever. Also try to realize any upsetting Self-Talk you habitually have about your job, your company, or even yourself.

Look for self-programming that you know needs to be tweaked and improved because it creates anxiety, resentment, insecurity, anger, or other upsetting emotions. Notice your Self-Talk *about* your negative Self-Talk. Try not to get critical of any dysfunctional Self-Talk you uncover: "There I go again, putting myself down! Darn! I can't believe this. I always use poor Self-Talk. I'm *so* clueless. I'll never get anywhere in business." . . . Now, how's *that* for lousy Self-Talk?

Once you're aware of Self-Talk that needs a tune-up or even a major overhaul, be sure that your Self-Talk is healthy about changing it. Make a leap of faith that you will alter your mental habits. Some people think, "I can't change my Self-Talk. You said it's an automatic habit." How's *that* for self-sabotaging Self-Talk? More self-defeating programming. If you can't change your Self-Talk, who can? The five constructive Self-Talk tools you will use to clean up any problematic Self-Talk are (1) focus on the present, (2) visualize positive politics, (3) reprogram politics and power, (4) reframe politics and power, and (5) keep perspective.

Focus on the Present

Mark Twain wrote, "My life has been a series of terrible misfortunes . . . most of which never happened." We all slip into negatively imagining the future. Actors have dress rehearsals, but poor Self-Talkers have dread rehearsals. Sure, we all get the worry fits, especially about how a political situation might turn out, so it's important to plan as best we can. But then try to keep your thoughts in the present moment, since that's where performance excels. Return your mind to the present instead of being preoccupied with the past or future. Focus on your breathing, imagine your mind is a calculator and hit the CLEAR button, or simply shift your attention to what's happening *now*. Avoid inordinate focus on the future if it creates anxiety, or on the past if it keeps you stuck in resentment. Let this anonymous quote sink in:

The past is history.
The future is a mystery.
This moment is a gift.
That's why they call it "the present."

Visualize Positive Politics

> I never hit a shot, not even in practice, without having a very sharp, in-focus picture of it in my head.
>
> —JACK NICKLAUS, GOLF PRO

See Your Goal Achieved. If your thoughts tend to hang out in the future, at least learn to visualize positive outcomes. Vividly imagine achieving your political goal, seeing in your mind's eye the result, positive outcome, or achievement you seek. After Bruce Jenner lost the 1972 Olympics decathlon, he trained every day for the next four years. He not only rigorously worked out his body, but he also steadfastly trained his mind. He cut out the face on a poster of the actual decathlon winner and replaced it with his own face, so that he could visualize himself each day as the champion. You know who made the Wheaties box in 1976!

Mental Rehearsal. Concert musicians use positive mental movies to mentally practice the perfect performance instead of spinning dread rehearsals. Studies of basketball free-throw shooting showed that supplementing physical practice of free throws with mental rehearsal—imaging the exact arc of the ball—improved the results . . . nothing but net! Made famous in the book *Seabiscuit,* the 1930s' greatest horse-racing jockey, George Woolf, used to imagine every length of every race, producing so much confidence that he earned the name Iceman.

You may have the jitters before delivering a critical top-management presentation. Surveys have placed fear of public speaking as people's number one fear—above death, which one list places at number seven. Comedian Jerry Seinfeld says this means if you're at a funeral, you're better off being in the casket than delivering the eulogy! But people calm themselves about presenting to a large group by learning to visualize. One of your authors was a math major, but the other believes there are three

kinds of people in the world—people who can count and people who can't! People with similar math deficiency or even math anxiety are taught to overcome it by mentally rehearsing a math test-taking situation while deeply relaxing themselves.

How to Do It. To visualize effectively, get into a state of mind where your unconscious mind is susceptible to receiving new images and healthier tapes—relaxing, meditating, or jogging repetitively. See yourself in a targeted performance situation as intensely as you can and experience the exact surroundings, sounds, and sensations. Visualize each exact step of this scenario and envision yourself coping well, delivering a stellar performance. It's helpful to mentally rehearse a problem point. See yourself getting upset, but then observe yourself relaxing and using positive Self-Talk to stay in control. Now you're prepared for real-life speed bumps.

Reprogram Politics and Power

This is the most common Self-Talk tool, the granddaddy technique, in which you recondition your thoughts. Reprogramming gets a bad name from touchy-feely, New Age associations with the term *affirmations.* You may remember this being spoofed on *Saturday Night Live* by Al Franken's character Stuart Smalley. He played a TV-show pop psychologist wimp who was hopelessly insecure but shared his mental secrets for feeling better as he repeatedly said into a mirror, "I'm good enough, I'm smart enough, and doggone it, people like me."

But reprogramming your mind with more realistic or more positive statements has been proven effective in brain research. For instance, if you're programming yourself to believe that all politics is a snaky game, you aren't likely to get involved, even ethically, right? If you're projecting untrue assumptions onto a colleague, you'll probably treat her in ways that get you into hot water, right? Here are tips for reconditioning your thought patterns.

- *It's Not Denial.* People correcting their Self-Talk can be overly positive and Pollyanna-like. You're not pretending bad things never happen. Reprogramming doesn't mean denying that some events and actions by others are truly a hassle, unethical, or bad news. You're just monitoring any inflammatory internal language that produces upset or overly pessimistic mind-sets that don't match reality.
- *Use the Present-Tense Language of Achievement.* If you say to yourself, "I'm going to calm myself about overpolitical power-mongers," your unconscious mind may believe you, but what *century* will this occur? Change your Self-Talk by thinking as if it's already occurred, "I am calm and poised with Overly Political people and I cope well with their unreasonable behavior." That's present-tense language of achievement.
- *Use Repetition.* Changing Self-Talk doesn't mean just occasionally saying a few positive words to yourself about politics. It's an ongoing, disciplined effort to be your own best internal coach, teacher, mentor, and parent. Confucius once said, "The mightiest warrior is he who can conquer himself."
- *No Cop-outs!* We certainly don't want Overly Political people to use Self-Talk to rationalize their inappropriate behavior or be too forgiving of themselves. Use reprogramming only to raise your odds for "impact *with* integrity."

Applying Reprogramming. Let's adapt reprogramming to politics, as one speech attendee wrote us about doing: "The most important lesson that I took away from your seminar was that politics is not a last resort solution that you fall back on when you have exhausted all honorable tactics. Instead, politics is an indispensable element of a successful and honest career. Politics is not a deadly weapon whose use is justified only when survival is at stake. It is a potentially friendly tool that can be and should be used even in times of peace."

How do you trash-talk yourself into distaste, fear, tension, stress, annoyance, or disgust? It might be about politics, power, self-promotion, ambition, ego-tripping peers, your job, yourself, or any other topic. Any aspect of your life causing you angst or fury is a great place to consider a counterconditioning campaign. Otherwise, you'll keep the same counterproductive scripts that may be preventing you from adjusting your political style, implementing a political skill, or achieving the credit your team deserves. The following examples of reprogrammed Self-Talk relate to the political tactics we'll discuss. We'll provide several options for each topic, so don't think you should use them all, since that would be too wordy and canned. Of course, the best alternative is to come up with your own reprogramming to tweak your Self-Talk.

Topic	Negative Self-Talk	Reprogrammed Self-Talk
Nonpolitics Example: Cold-calling or Prospecting	"I hate cold-calling. It's such a waste of time and I feel like I'm prostituting myself or imposing on people. Why can't this company give us qualified leads so we can sell!"	"Prospecting is part of selling. Selling is a percentage game. Every time I pick up the phone, I raise my odds of a sale. Ten percent of my calls end up with a letter sent, and ten percent of those are appointments. And twenty-five percent of my meetings wind up with a sale. It's a game where you win some and lose some." "Cold-calling is really warm-calling since it builds relationships with real people." "I'm not imposing if I approach prospecting in a down-to-earth, friendly way. People know it's a part of business development."

Topic	Negative Self-Talk	Reprogrammed Self-Talk
Politics	"Senior management should eliminate the pain-in-the-butt politics that pollute this place."	"Top management is doing the best it can. Political behavior exists in all organizations." "I've been throwing the baby out with the bathwater since *politics* isn't a dirty word. If political awareness is combined with concern for the company, it is a positive force for influence and impact." "My goal is to use high-integrity political astuteness to help the company, my team, and myself. I can align with other ethical people to create the critical mass of high-integrity political leaders we need."
Networking	"I shouldn't have to schmooze and buddy up to people all over the company to get ahead. I hate playing that game or going to big functions where everyone is working the room and copping out. I'm not comfortable since I like to keep more to myself."	"In a complex, changing organization, good networks provide me with information about corporate strategies and priorities. This is useful for understanding how to get things done, present my team's ideas, and add value." "It's 'networking' and 'relationship building,' not 'schmoozing.' I network across the organization so that I'm a known quantity."

Topic	Negative Self-Talk	Reprogrammed Self-Talk
Pump Up Your Power Image	"I'm not interested in maneuvering for more power since it's corrupt."	"Power is a force for good. I may not seek the top position, but I need to understand power dynamics, positioning, and turf battles so that I can obtain resources for my team and help good ideas come to fruition." "My people depend on me to protect them and achieve power to do great things for the organization."
Promote Yourself with Integrity	"Doing my job and getting good results should be enough to move my career and the team's credibility forward. I shouldn't have to self-promote or talk about my group's accomplishments. That's just shameless boasting. I'd rather take the moral high ground. I'm not going to compromise!"	"People in senior management positions are extremely busy. There is a chance they won't always know what I've done or how impressively I've done it. They might not be aware of the broader implications of my team's most recent success." "Someday management might be making a career call on me and I want them to make an informed decision based on knowledge of who I am, my talent, and my potential."
Respect Ego and Turf	"This executive is a pompous, incompetent idiot. I'm not going to sell out by kissing up and telling people what they want to hear just to get ahead."	"He has an ego. I protect my own and my team's best interests. I use self-control and verbal discipline." "I'm street-smart and choose my timing, setting, and words carefully."

Topic	Negative Self-Talk	Reprogrammed Self-Talk
Ethical Lobbying	"Why should I have to sell this idea over and over? The benefits to the company are obvious, and I'm just not a salesman. Besides, it doesn't matter what I think because it's *their* job to make the decisions. All I can do is present the facts."	"Other people and departments have different perspectives and priorities that block them from understanding the value of an idea that's clear to me. Lobbying ideas is just another name for influencing." "I'm doing the company and my team a disservice if I don't lobby for ideas that I believe are good for the organization and obtain key people's buy-in."
Conversational Aikido to Defuse Sabotage	"Who the hell does he think he is? I'm not going to put up with his bullying. I'll show him he's not my boss and take him down. He wants a fight? He's got one. I just became his worst nightmare."	"I can always play hardball later, but first I can calm the situation down by not taking this personally." "He's out of control. If I lose my cool, it poisons my image and throws me off-balance."

Reframe Politics and Power

This fourth Self-Talk strategy involves viewing the same stimulus or event through a different lens. Any picture can look better with a different frame around it. Any experience has multiple meanings and interpretations. Why not choose a new definition or frame, one that works *for* you instead of against you, by focusing on the situation's potential and promise—one that doesn't repel or depress you? The Chinese word for "crisis" has two characters. One means "danger" and the other "opportunity." That's reframing. We've been reframing politics during the entire book as "strategic influence." Here are some more sample ways to reframe the concepts in this book so that you become your own spin doctor in a positive sense.

Negative Self-Talk	**Reframed Self-Talk**
"Self-Talk is a bunch of psychobabble and New Age fluff."	"Self-Talk is a set of *internal influence tools* to raise my odds for managing my reactions."
"Political game playing . . ."	"Building *impact and influence* . . ."
"Selling out and copping out by kissing up . . ."	"*Protecting* myself and helping seniors to save face so I can influence better for my team."
"Cutthroat, sabotage tactics with evil intent . . ."	"*Survival of the fittest* by someone who has been seriously burned in the past."
"Manipulative and calculating . . ."	"*Savvy and strategic* enough to maneuver effectively and know the ropes."
"Conceited bragging and boasting to grab credit . . ."	"*Decent and bold self-promotion* to gain visibility and deserved credit for myself and my team."

Keep Perspective

During family crises, one of our fathers used to calm the situation by reminding us that "no babies died." One of our seminar instructors regains her perspective by comparing any job bummer to being in bullet-ridden wartime Bosnia: "Let's see, we have my lousy performance-appraisal rating here and we have Bosnia over here. Bosnia . . . appraisal . . . Bosnia . . . appraisal."

One of us was family-vacationing in Paris when his computer, passports, tickets home, and traveler's checks were stolen as he knelt to hug his seven-year-old daughter. That night, with the family forced to stay at a hotel before renewing their passports at the American consulate, Daddy's wise little girl eased the entire family's distress by saying, "Daddy, remember about Self-Talk. You *could* have lost *us*." From the mouths of babes! What helps *you* count *your* blessings or calm down?

The Inner Game of Politics

Damon Runyon, the short story writer, once said, "The race does not always go to the swift, the battle does not always go to the strong. But that's the way to bet." Use the prescribed Self-Talk skills to (1) focus on the present, (2) visualize, (3) reprogram, (4) reframe, and (5) keep perspective. We'll place our bet on leaders who manage their internal environment while they navigate the external one. You've perhaps heard of *The Inner Game of Tennis* or *The Inner Game of Golf*, by Timothy Gallway. Self-Talk is the "inner game of organizational politics," the first one you need to win.

Gandhi knew something about coping with politics, effecting culture change, and exercising self-discipline. He mastered his own emotional reactions in order to maintain internal balance and peace of mind in the midst of chaotic external circumstances. He summarized the promise that Self-Talk holds for increasing your internal and actual power.

> *Your beliefs become your thoughts . . .*
> *Your thoughts become your words . . .*
> *Your words become your actions . . .*
> *Your actions become your values . . .*
> *Your values become your destiny.*
>
> —MAHATMA GANDHI

Chapter 7

Detect Power Dynamics, Agendas, and Unwritten Rules

We've overcome the first hurdle to political savvy—awareness. Perhaps we've simply verified what you knew but haven't verbalized. We hope we're in alignment with you regarding four pillars of political awareness.

- *The Need.* Our individual-level wake-up call linked politics to career and job success. We made an initial leadership wake-up call linking politics and company success, and we'll return to this organization-wide perspective later.
- *Balanced Viewpoint.* We shifted organizational politics away from the old definition of politics—*poly* (many)–*tics* (bloodsucking parasites)—to a value-free concept allowing for ethical means and ends to achieve "impact with integrity."
- *The Organizational Savvy Continuum.* You have a cognitive framework for understanding the beliefs, preferences, strengths, and weaknesses of each political style.
- *Your Reactions.* You're aware of Self-Talk that fuels your helpful or harmful attitudes, emotions, and actions within the political arena.

This is a solid foundation for the internal, mental savvy tactics in these next two chapters and the external street-smart action tactics in remaining chapters just around the bend. But more is needed. Power of Savvy people know how to get things done in an organization, as if they have a sixth sense. You can manage the maze if you (1) read the power dynamics, (2) read the agendas of powerful people, and (3) read your company's system and the unwritten rules.

Read the Power Dynamics

The Power of Savvy person senses where official and unofficial power resides. He is at least a part-time student of power dynamics. Your matriculation into the political student body means paying attention in class, which is *always* taking place! Are you daydreaming?

Official Position Power. Position power and rank, decision-making status, and lines of command form the skeleton of the power structure. This is clear from company organizational charts, approval chains, and sign-off protocols. Identify the current top leaders in as many functions as you can across the enterprise. Be aware of the leaders at as many levels as is practical outside of your narrow slice of the company. Can you name the generals and first lieutenants throughout the line business and other geographical locations, or do you have a reputation for being out of touch or disconnected?

Unofficial Influence Power. Savvy leaders also read the white spaces on the organizational chart. Besides tuning your antennas to official position power, pick up on the informal influencers and power connections. Who is part of the favored inner circle and who are the outcasts? Do you know who's wired in, who has the ear of top management, and who *really* makes the decisions? We love the lead character's reply to his son in the Woody Allen movie *Mighty Aphrodite* when asked who the boss is between daddy and mommy: "Who is the boss? You have to ask that? I'm the boss. Mommy is only the decision maker." Title can be just that—a mere title.

Who holds power by being an indispensable subject-matter

expert, a corporate legend, or having access to the ear of top management? Whose jokes are laughed at, who interrupts whom, and how are different people's agenda items placed in meetings? Who receives favors or gets away with unfairly bending rules? Who sits in power seats at the conference table or nearest the boss? Who has budgetary or resource clout? Who is swayed by someone else's power and influence? Is it out of respect or fear? The savvy know the sticky relationships to avoid, as well as the good and bad blood between seniors so that they aren't caught in the middle.

In a heavy-duty negotiation, the supposed decision-maker nervously checks his notes to be sure he's covered everything, excuses himself to make a quick phone call, and wipes a bead of sweat that tips you off. He's feeling a shadow loom over him, the pressure of the true decision-maker, whom he's afraid to disappoint or anger. Power of Savvy people read between the lines for connections between powerful people—the puppets and puppet masters.

In the smash-hit independent film *My Big Fat Greek Wedding,* Lainie Kazan plays mother to the central character, Toula. The mother and daughter want the bullheaded, proud immigrant father to permit his daughter to work at the aunt's travel agency instead of the family's Greek restaurant. The mother calms her daughter's worries about how the "boss" of that family will respond by reassuring her, "Toula, the man is the head, but the woman is the neck and she can turn the head any way she wants."

Emerging Leaders. Know who is next in line to attain top positions—the heirs apparent in various departments based upon succession plans, career ladders, and the grapevine. Initially, it may appear to be a senior executive, but that person may be a nonrespected lackey whose stock is lowering. Many companies call emerging leaders Hi Po's, for "high potential" managers, and they are often put on a fast track of special training and grooming. This can even begin early in careers when "golden boys and girls" are plucked out of prestigious universities and put into high-visibility rotation programs for rapid advancement. We're not suggesting that you shamelessly woo these rising stars or play up to them, just that you understand the political landscape.

Read the Agendas of Powerful People

Gregory Peck makes a scene from Harper Lee's American epic novel *To Kill a Mockingbird* immortal in the award-winning movie. The wise and patient lawyer-father, Atticus Finch, holds his daughter, Scout, on his knees, rocking on the swing as he explains, "You never really understand a person until you consider things from his point of view . . . till you climb inside of his skin and walk around in it."

Once you know who holds the official, unofficial, and emerging power—your stakeholders—learn what matters to them. You'll later learn to ethically lobby these people so that they are more likely to endorse your ideas, initiatives, and recommendations. As master salespeople and influence connoisseurs testify, the core of persuasion lies in knowing others' needs, goals, and problems so that you can speak their language and blend your ideas with their objectives. Be a savvy leader who gathers intelligence on people's hot buttons, taboos, and values.

Ask trusted people who know the stakeholders—their direct reports, company veterans, and peers who are wired in. Look for clues in published memos, open letters, and presentations by the seniors. Get a copy of top-management presentations and study the buzz phrases, issues, and topics. Speculate about a person's agendas—both public and more private—from changes the organization is facing. If it's a growth period, issues of acquisition or merger appeal may be foremost in a senior's mind. In a hiring freeze, cost containment is the central focus. Interview the stakeholder (a novel, underutilized method . . . ask her!). If the setting and language are appropriate, directly query a senior about her charter, goals, objectives, and personal vision for the organization. In normal conversation, notice what issues grab her attention, what she seems stressed about, or why she cancels a meeting.

Superstar negotiators gather every piece of information they can about the other party—how she thinks and feels, her passions and fears, current-event topics to avoid, and personal preferences such as favorites in food, music, sports, fashion, or entertainment. Where'd she attend school, what's her family like, who is important to her? It's as if you are writing a personal dossier on the stakeholder to identify hooks for getting on her wavelength.

Long before any lobbying situation arises, figure out powerful people's priorities. Anticipate trends that they might start thinking about and guess what they're reading. Size up the players—not just to tailor-present an idea by linking up your agenda, but also so that you can cultivate rapport as you network and avoid political pitfalls during day-to-day interactions.

Read the System and the Unwritten Rules

The Power of Savvy style knows how to get things done in an organization—not just who the formal and informal power brokers are and what matters to them, but also how the organization's system works. He thinks about "sandboxes" and turf, the labyrinth of egos, and different people's constituencies. He knows the procedural errors, the channels for pushing something through, the right person to nudge, where the purse strings lie, the land mines to avoid, when to bend the formal rules, which rules really matter, and the unwritten rules.

Savvy leaders avoid the pendulum swing from impractical rigidity about proper channels to blatant disregard for rules, instead settling on middle ground. They work through the formal system of approval chains and sign-off hoops as appropriate, but they also work *around* the system when necessary and fair for the good of the team or company. They know the ropes and can swing from them without hanging themselves. Compliance, safety, and regulatory rules are indispensable, but resisting commonsense improvisation can perpetuate red tape and waste. Many entrepreneurial leaders who test the limits harbor disrespect or even contempt for unrealistic counterparts who worship the rules. Protocol paranoids are often discounted by others as sheepish, meek followers instead of trailblazers and risk-takers.

Peter Scott-Morgan is an expert at analyzing unwritten rules, and *The Unwritten Rules of the Game* is the title of his insightful book. He says the unwritten rules are obvious if you just ask and observe. He notes how written traffic manuals for merging into a Boston or Paris thoroughfare tell you to slow down, make eye contact with oncoming drivers, courteously wait your turn, and slowly merge into the flow. *Wrong!* Local inhabitants know to avoid eye contact, speed up, and force their way into the flow. Others expect this and know they are liable if they hit someone from behind. Merging drivers may even endanger themselves and others by slowing down.

Organizations have similar off-the-record understandings—unwritten rules and informal behavioral norms for getting things done that are different from those written in handbooks, orientation scripts, values statements, and training protocols.

- *No Return Calls.* One client tipped us off not to expect prompt return phone calls from her company, even though the organization respected and regularly used our workshops. She explained, "The informal norm is to wait for at least three calls from a vendor before returning a call. People believe this unwritten norm helps the company to maintain an upper hand with consultants and leverage a one-up 'we don't need you' stance in price negotiations."
- *P&Ls.* Many companies have a written standard that each team's profit and loss compared to other teams will impact their future budget. Obviously, this can and does lead to unwritten rules such as "Don't share resources or people with other teams since it'll cut into your results" and "Hide any losses in your financials as best you can." If a punitive boss blasts people for previewing bad results, the unwritten rule becomes "Keep shortfalls under wraps until the last minute, hoping you can shore up results in

time." Of course, this leads to lots of crisis management and firefighting.

- *Dress.* A global truck manufacturer's managers and employees tell us that it is the norm to stroll the first-floor lobby and training rooms in shirtsleeves with your tie loosened. But once you get on the elevator, you just *know* to clean up since you'd have to be wearing a straitjacket not to wear your suit jacket.
- *Workload.* One leading company in its field told us that the written rule is "balanced work and family life," but that the unwritten rule is to balance between twelve-hour and sixteen-hour workdays.

To read unwritten rules, first examine the officially written and spoken rules (policies, manuals, job descriptions and processes, business strategies, approval chains, and so on). Then observe top management's behavior in relation to these rules and also notice what behaviors are actually rewarded and acted upon. The unwritten rules aren't documented anywhere, but they form a political subtext that must be read. It's not necessarily unethical to exercise enlightened self-interest and a decent boldness about rules, as long as you play by the same informal rules as others, don't take unfair advantage, and strive for honorable ends.

Unwritten tacit understandings are influenced by the culture of an industry, geographical region, and country, as well as by the current economy, legislation, and work atmosphere. At a large Eastern European bank, a nagging performance problem was branch managers' lack of action on top management's memos. Top managers rarely left their offices, instead churning out long written announcements that lower tiers ignored. The country in general was a nonreading culture. The monologue memos by executives were viewed as burdensome to read, especially given the workload. Since top managers only left their executive enclaves to interact when a crucial item was being overlooked, an unwritten rule evolved: "Don't waste your time by reading management's memos. They'll let you know which ones matter."

Answers to Every Question You'll Ever Ask

In our introduction you met Bart, hired by a conservative, family-founded firm for his leadership style of urgency and powerful accountability. He ended up a corporate casualty because he misread and disrespected company culture and unofficial rules about power and consensus, the proper pace of change, and key relationships between the CEO and suppliers. Even though his numbers were great and he fulfilled his change mandate of removing deadwood, forging a performance-oriented culture, and cutting costs, his failure to read politics, power, and informal rules caused his tumble. You'll avoid such mistakes by detecting power dynamics, the agendas of powerful people, and the informal system's unwritten rules that augment the formal system's written rules. Poor Bart was so intent on achieving results, he wasn't thinking about the other questions to ask—about power, power connections, agendas, cultural norms, and unwritten rules.

Many people arrive at our workshops expecting some sort of handout revealing what the political norms for success are in their organization. Of course, while people like Bart might benefit from such clear guidelines, we *can't* distribute such a universal job aid because the rules differ for every pocket of every company and for each boss, not to mention that the norms are fluid and ever changing. So the *answers* are found by knowing the *questions* to ask—and by having the intent to figure out the political norms. This is why we jokingly announce in our workshops that there are three answers to every question that any participant might have: (1) "We'll get to that after the break," (2) "What does the group think?" and (3) "It depends!" Seriously, each savvy high-integrity political tactic should be stamped with the words IT DEPENDS and AS APPROPRIATE. We know you'll keep these qualifiers in mind as you now master the rest of the book's individual- and leadership-level savvy tactics.

Chapter 8

Know the Corporate Buzz

What's Your Jacket?

Dusty Baker, manager of professional baseball's 2002 National League Champion San Francisco Giants and the 2003 pennant-winning Chicago Cubs, has said that each player's reputation is his "jacket." Every time a new player joins his ball club, Dusty sits down and asks that major league star what he thinks his jacket is and how to improve it. For you to be truly successful, you need a similar examination of your corporate buzz, the jacket you wear. People form perceptions of you, your strengths, and your drawbacks. These perceptions can become frozen icebergs that block or enhance your influence and power. Your corporate reputation, or rap, follows you and impacts personal and team credibility. Are you seen as smart and technically good, but functionally narrow? Are you viewed as an executor, but ineffective at managing people? If you're seen as a leader, is it in a narrow slot or across a broad spectrum to add strategic business value?

Perception *Isn't* Reality, but It Might as Well Be!

You've heard the phrase "Perception is reality." We prefer saying, "Perception isn't reality, but people sure make decisions based on it." Compared to the Power of Person style, Power of Ideas people don't think as much about how they're perceived. They don't focus on image, so they don't make time to examine or shape perceptions about themselves or their teams. If you don't shape your image, who will? If you don't know your buzz, *that's* part of your buzz! Let's examine how to discover your reputation and which traits (positive or negative) matter in your organization, so that you can better manage your corporate buzz rather than let *it* manage you.

Three Categories of Corporate Buzz

It's fundamental to understand what buzz will propel or hinder you, and the following three categories are helpful.

- *Positive Buzz.* What characteristics do you want associated with your name? Obviously, positive traits include being a team player, knowing the industry, being proactive or multitasking, having a strong work ethic, and going the extra mile.
- *Negative Buzz.* Jeopardizing labels that convey a gap, discount you, or threaten your career include low intensity, disloyal, lack of urgency, and failure to fit the company mold.
- *Positive but Limiting.* Other characteristics and qualities sound positive, but marginalize you with boundaries on your expertise or career. The label may either be deserved or unfairly generated by sabotage.
  - *"Juan's a technical expert."* Now Juan runs the risk of not being seen as having a cross-functional perspective.
  - *"Denise is a terrific project manager."* Uh-oh. Is she capable of running an entire function? Does she have the power base or influence for a leadership role?
  - *"Hassim always makes his numbers. We can count on his sales projections."* A supersalesman is branded as indispensable in the field and blocked from management or a higher-visibility business-development function.

— *"Tamara is a perfectionist."* Is she a peripheral nitpicker who bogs down others?
— *"Oscar is a loyal follower, a real behind-the-scenes contributor."* Hmmm . . . he's certainly not a leader, is he?

Different Strokes for Different Folks

How do you know what traits really matter, what corporate buzz will help or hurt you? Here comes the "when in Rome" part of organizational savvy. Knowing what your company or culture considers favorable or unfavorable press helps you to decide which perceptions to reshape by "managing the airwaves," which you'll learn later.

Are you seen as "nice"? In some companies it's crucial to be nice, as in parts of the Midwest, where there's a premium on people skills. Poor listening skills or inflexibility lands you in coaching to learn to play better in the sandbox. Other companies ostracize you or send you to remedial counseling for being "nice." We once visited a client who had relocated from an East Coast insurance company's friendly climate to a competitive major California software company. She was told to aggressively challenge others' ideas in meetings since the environment applauded demonstrating research rigor more than a cooperative spirit. She confided that she couldn't hack it in such a tough-minded culture and it was a bad fit for her. In some companies, if you're not ruthless enough in cutting heads or being demanding with your team, you're branded with career-limiting buzz as "too nice." Different strokes for different folks. Different companies, different cultures.

The Roots of Corporate Buzz

Astute leaders identify which traits to emulate or evict, the characteristics that they seek or shun. They know that desirable traits differ from one organization to another. Here are some of the signposts to notice. Tracking these roots of corporate buzz won't tell you what labels are actually attached to *you*—just what is considered to be good, bad, and limiting buzz in your particular organization.

Corporate Priorities. A clump of corporate buzz clues is lodged in the formal organizational priorities and officially favorable characteristics.

- *Vision, Objectives, and Taglines*. Priorities are suggested in goals, strategies, annual reports, missions, manuals, standards, and slogans. It doesn't take a brain surgeon to see how FedEx's "On time every time" former tagline summoned the savvy leader to be on time to meetings. The Peace Corps' mission isn't congruent with voracious greed about compensation. Official priorities are clues to desired and cursed traits.
- *Published Core Values*. Published guiding principles or core values such as integrity, customer focus, and respect constitute positive corporate buzz targets. Orientation materials and training clue you into desired norms. Imagining the opposite of these standards gives a bird's-eye view of the negative buzz qualities to avoid.
- *Leadership Competencies*. These written standards are appraised and often measured in survey feedback. They are reinforced on wall posters and in training programs, executive-coaching initiatives, and employee handbooks.

Corporate Culture. Instead of in official written clues, this cluster of signals is found between the lines, through intuition, and in conversation.

- *Informal Norms and Unwritten Rules*. People can and will tell you the less overt norms for success and favorable buzz. It's not that these rules are purposely kept covert. They may even be expressed in orientation sessions or training. They are simply the less unofficial traits people say are needed to fit the company mold. We've already said that they flow from top management behaviors, what's actually rewarded, and the influence of country, culture, economy, and other business norms.

- *Who's Promoted or Ditched*. Analyze the descriptors surrounding corporate heroes, role models, people who are promoted, future stars, and company legends. Learn by contrast from those who are ousted, demoted, dressed down, transferred out, or simply seem to be "untouchables."
- *Informal Artifacts and Rituals*. Notice cherished artifacts like trophies highlighting a prized quality, lobby artwork hinting at a key value, and old equipment that purposely maintains a link with the past, founders, or tradition. Hertz's headquarters has a Model T Ford in the lobby, Wells Fargo Bank has its stagecoach, and Pepsi Bottling Group displays traditional bottles as a bridge to its past. A ritual can reveal a core value, as Apple Computer's past "beer blasts" announced informality and fun as norms.
- *Historical Lore*. Other organizations have a history rich with legendary anecdotes. This traditional lore is instructive and discloses values for getting ahead. Genentech, the parent of the biotech industry, shares its lore at every employee and vendor orientation. Venture capitalist Bob Swanson called Stanford University's Dr. Herb Boyer to request a brief meeting in his lab. This ten-minute meeting ended up as a three-hour meeting at a bar on San Francisco's Clement Street, where the two sketched plans for the fledgling company on a napkin. Embodying values of informality, science, and entrepreneurship, the moment is commemorated in a bronze statue of the pioneers.
- *Idiosyncratic Practices*. Companies have popcorn machines and Ping-Pong tables in hallways. Others have offbeat job titles—chief evangelist, officer of fun and inspiration—signposts that a sense of irreverence is embraced. Best Buy's fun-loving and hip culture was hinted by our wonderfully spirited client's first e-mail signature, "Warrior Princess of Training." One company's managers collectively decided each other's salaries, posting them openly on a flip chart for discussion. Norms of open

collaboration about normally sensitive issues trickle through the organization.

Seniors' Biases. Official corporate priorities and informal cultural norms don't negate powerful people's off-the-record personal preferences as additional markers.

- *Seniors' Agendas*. An executive may adopt a new focus or value after working with a consultant or corporate coach, or after reading about a new leadership principle. These endeavors can alter what makes for positive or negative buzz traits.
- *Strategic Change Initiatives*. Monitor the CEO's expressed philosophy and observed whims, but any manager may install a strategic initiative that influences what's in vogue.
- *Your Own Boss's Biases*. Savvy leaders don't watch the sky for high-level management clues while tripping over what's on the ground right down the hallway. They test the shifting winds at the top while staying in touch with their own manager's preferences.

Crisis or "Crunch Time" Switches. Wanted and unwanted qualities can quickly change because of external factors. A crisis like public fury about an environmental stance, negative media coverage about corporate governance, or a traumatic safety mishap can create a taboo or behavioral norm. Don't be caught off-guard when a standard operating procedure is now frowned upon. We know a CEO who became extrasensitive about "loyalty" when people were bailing out of the company due to scrutiny about a scandal. Suddenly, mere figures of speech like "the good old days before the merger" or comments about how "the old company" operated became kiss-of-death blunders that branded one officer as "disloyal" and cost her a promotion.

Before the dot-com crash, one Fortune 500 software CEO revealed his status-conscious nature in an interview, saying that he had no respect for anyone who did not own a Montblanc pen! He put in black and white his culture's Power of Person preference for a prestige-oriented image. In a later seminar, the group brainstormed carrying such power-related accessories as fitting its company's power-image culture. A perceptive Power of Savvy vice president reminded the group about crisis-time switches: "Wait a minute. Don't buy into that stereotype based on our usual culture. Lately, we're in a cost-cutting mode, so a Montblanc pen might brand you as frivolous. My boss tells me to steal the Motel 6 pens!" Touché! The winds can change good or bad buzz.

The Scorecard for Your Next Job. Former chairman of the Joint Chiefs of Staff and U.S. Secretary of State Colin Powell has always scoped out the positive and negative traits for success in his current job, but also for the next job he sought. This approach is exemplified by a company comptroller asking the treasurer or CFO what different skill sets and qualities are essential for the next step—for instance, possessing a more strategic financial-modeling capacity.

If One Person Tells Me I'm a Horse . . .

Now you know the target kind of buzz you'd like. Unless you have a job working for the Psychic Hotline as a mind reader, you're probably wondering, "But how do I know what the rap *is* on me?" You can blow off feedback and the following clues to your buzz as wrong, insignificant, or coincidental. But remember the adage "If one person tells me I'm a horse, who cares? If two people tell me I'm a horse, I might give it some thought. If three people tell me I'm a horse, it might be the source of considerable concern. If four people tell me I'm a horse, I'm going to buy myself a bit and saddle." So explore as many of these avenues as possible in your self-research project.

Ask Others. Your network can tell you what others are saying about you, your unit, or that new project you're pushing.

- *Colleagues.* Peers know your public image. Ask people you trust to give you the straight scoop without pulling their punches. Make sure they're wired in enough themselves to know, and that they don't have an ulterior motive for feeding you false information. (Just because you're paranoid doesn't mean people aren't out to get you!)

- *Direct Reports*. Your team may have access to more data than your peers, since others may be less cautious about leveling with them. They may be eager to help out, but make sure they don't tell you what they *think* you want to hear. Remember CEO disease? Reassure them that they won't become messengers who are killed for bearing bad news.
- *Cross-Organizational Contacts.* Tap into people outside of your area. Enlist "murmur mentors" from your contacts at trainings, cross-functional meetings, or corporate functions.
- *Managers.* Use your boss as a confidante, depending upon your relationship and whether she is open and honest. A fellow Power of Savvy style friend can be asked at lunch in a casual manner. Make sure the boss knows you can handle straight feedback. If your manager is more formal, use sanctioned times such as appraisals. Sometimes, your boss's boss has a broader perspective, but solicit this input only if it's safe, appropriate, and (usually) after you've interviewed your own manager.
- *Clients and Customers*. Seek feedback through conversation or surveys about your strengths and growth areas. This feeds you buzz about your potential traits. Asking customers will also send a message that you want to improve your service to them, which is a great side benefit.
- *Past Associates*. Since people at a former company now have nothing to lose, they might be forthcoming with you about your past buzz. You probably wrapped up your behavior patterns and any related buzz in a package and brought them with you to your new job.
- *Contractors, Suppliers, Vendors, and Consultants*. We sometimes get complacent with our behavior toward those who consider us their clients, so they can serve as a valuable truth serum about our best and worst traits.

- *Mentors.* Since they are usually not in your current chain of command, they can also be candid, especially since that's part of their role.
- *Friends and Family.* This group knows you at your best and worst. They can provide insights into qualities that may transfer to work situations as your corporate buzz.

Listen. Keep your own ear to the ground for what people are saying. Don't hire a gumshoe to wiretap phones or bug associates' cars! But do pick up on perceptions through casual conversation, friendly but revealing jokes, or thinly veiled annoyance. If you take the floor at the end of a meeting at 5:05 p.m. and someone jokes to a neighbor, "Better call in for pizza," it's a safe bet he sees you as a blowhard who will ramble late into the night. If a team member timidly asks if you really want him to follow protocol to the T, you may be seen as too stuck to red tape, an extreme left-side flaw. If a peer hems and haws before answering your question, you may have a reputation for being aggressive. If a subordinate sighs with exasperation and asks, "Can we please just stick to the core issue and not miss the forest through the trees?" you may suffer from paralysis of analysis. You also probably have low credibility, or why would she ever dare to criticize you?

Self-Awareness. Savvy leaders are courageous professionals willing to study their assets and shadows through these resources:

- *Self-Assessment Tools or Checklists.* Magazines and books give glimpses into your buzz through self-awareness instruments. We offer one such self-assessment tool, the Organizational Savvy Skills Assessment, to rate your own level of political savvy. It is available through the Web site address in the back of this book.
- *360-Degree Survey Feedback*. Your company might provide instruments and profile feedback as part of ongoing leadership development, so take the data seriously. You can also receive feedback from others about your own organizational savvy prowess by

obtaining the assessment instrumentation available in the back of *Survival of the Savvy*.

- *Mentors and Coaches.* Here's a luxury many executives don't afford themselves, even when the company offers the opportunity.
- *Workshops.* Even if a workshop doesn't include a formal feedback instrument, skill practices usually include feedback from the instructor or fellow participants.
- *Assignments.* Notice what tasks, competencies, or subject matter areas are tougher for you to master and those you cruise through and easily assimilate.
- *Reading.* Executive briefs, newspapers, or professional publications may be easy to understand in some content areas but hard in others. Notice the kinds of articles you flip to or avoid, since these may reveal the same gaps people see in you.

Observe Treatment You Receive. You can guess if your buzz is good or bad from treatment and events. But this doesn't tell you *what* is being said about you. So don't merely conclude that your stock has gone down if you receive an inadequate bonus, budget, headcount, meeting time allotment, or recognition. Go further and analyze *how* you're treated when you're informed of inequities and what exact buzz traits this treatment might indicate.

Interpret the *kind* of assignments you get—functionally restricted ones or the cross-organizational visible ones? What messages are you sent by the kind of information that is disseminated to you? Are you buffered from meetings with certain kinds of customers, due to a perceived lack of experience in that industry? Do people give you carefully timed schedules and scripted talking points because you're known for being a loose cannon or a blabbermouth? Do people come to your meetings on time? Don't read *too* much into these events, but don't ignore a consistent pattern. Start figuring out the qualities and labels it might point to as you analyze your buzz.

Stereotypes. Make educated guesses about labels that might circulate about you based upon *nothing* you personally do or say, but generalizations stemming from your functional area, gender, country of origin, ethnicity, geographical region, marital status, religion, or industry. We often ask what negative labels, fair or unfair, are attached to various functional areas:

- *Systems or Information Technology:* "nerds . . . techies . . . geeks . . . jargon junkies . . ."
- *Finance:* "bean counters . . . number crunchers . . . bottlenecks . . . budget-slashers . . ."
- *Sales:* "used-car salesmen . . . money-grubbers . . . overcommitting liars . . . exaggerators . . ."
- *Human Resources:* "touchy-feely . . . soft . . . out of touch . . . charm schoolers . . ."
- *Legal:* "nitpickers . . . bottlenecks . . . loophole lizards . . . manipulators . . . liars . . ."

Of course, we're not trying to siphon away your professional pride or reinforce stereotypical boxes that imprison people in unfair or inaccurate perceptions. Negative names do volley across functions, so we'd be naïve to ignore them as a source of corporate buzz. We remember a playful sales manager introducing a colleague from Credit as the "sales prevention manager."

A Launching Pad for Increased Impact and Influence

You now know how to figure out what corporate buzz you do or don't want surrounding you or your team, and you know how to discover how you stack up against these traits. You know if you have a troublesome informal dossier following you. This courageous attempt at self-knowledge forms a launching pad to increase your organizational impact, because now you're ready to move into the street-smart actions of the remaining chapters. By placing your ego in your back pocket to discover your corporate buzz, you are positioned to change and reshape it if necessary. But the first step is to look in the mirror without distortion. This is the core of savvy leadership—caring about truth over ego. Such knowledge and humility (left-side) can eventually bring power and influence (right-side) to individuals and teams.

Chapter 9

Weave a Safety Network

Jim Brenner (not his real name), a sales training consultant we know, received a frantic call from a client at a retail giant telling him to check his fax machine. It was an urgent memo from his client's manager's boss reading:

> **Urgent Memorandum**
>
> *TO:* All Vice Presidents and Regional Managers of Sales and Marketing
>
> *FROM:* Sam Savage, Executive Vice President of Sales and Marketing
>
> *RE:* The Brenner Strategic Selling Skills Program
>
> It's come to the attention of the Executive Team that Jim Brenner's Strategic Selling Program has permeated the company. Some of you have spent exorbitant amounts on this training. Therefore, Brenner is being scrutinized, so by Friday, December 7, I require full disclosure of how many salespeople you've sent to his seminar, along with your business rationale, the exact amount you spent, and what *if any* results in increased revenues or newly acquired accounts have accrued. There will be a full investigative report published within two weeks.

After Jim cleaned up the puddle under his chair (!), he asked his client to explain the story behind the ferocious fax. His client confidante revealed that Savage Sam was an Overly Political (OP) egomaniac who had spent $2 million installing a sales revenue tracking system. Its software included a particular model of account management that was a bit different from the approach taught in Jim's course. The main purpose of the sales management technology wasn't sales training, and Jim would have adapted his model to be compatible, but the EVP was threatened by Jim's sterling results and reputation. Jim was becoming part of the sales culture, so to protect *himself* from playing second fiddle and to guard his own pet internal consulting project, Sam was trashing Jim's program.

Fortunately, Jim's program evaluations were glowing and resulting revenue increases were well documented, both for new and seasoned people. Many regional managers wanted the program so their districts would gain similar increased sales and prospects. But what really saved the day was that Jim's network of allies was strong with top executives, not only within the sales division but throughout the multinational conglomerate. He had close formal ties from the training sessions, and informal bonds from people stopping him in hallways, calling for advice, or inviting him to submit selling tips for the company intranet. He liked his clients and invited them to pro football games. Many considered him a friend and all endorsed his work. One VP even lobbied on Jim's behalf to Savage's boss and cc-ed Savage on these positive e-mails. The "investigative report" was never published.

A Decent Boldness

Some Power of Ideas managers equate networking to "kissing up," or an imposition on people's time. As politics-avoidant people avoid corporate events, their overly ambitious counterparts are tying together the shoelaces of colleagues to beat them to a table of powerful people. The proper balance is again a middle-ground approach. Savvy leaders view networking as a "decent boldness." This ethical politics strategy is the bare minimum if you're serious about greater organizational influence and impact. Jim Brenner's network gave him a heads-up about the sabotage effort, stood up for him, became a forum for lobbying and promoting, and protected his reputation.

So avoid Self-Talk that frames networking as being pushy for an appointment, elbowing into conversations, or shamelessly working a room. Recast networking from a shotgun-style collection of every business card you can get into meaningful contact with people. Balanced, tactful networking never crosses the ethical line. Yes, *boldness* is required, since building connections means leaving your safe foxhole. Networking requires risk-taking when you ask for meetings with seniors or people who know them. But it's a *decent* boldness that conveys respect for others and an interest in getting to know them.

Schmooze or Lose

Transform negative associations of "schmoozing" into merely "interacting," just as you'd mingle with your guests at your own wedding rather than sit alone. This strategy is about visibility, not vanity. It's about giving, not just receiving. Here are the payoffs for knowing powerful seniors, unofficial influencers, and emerging leaders beyond your own organization.

- *Insurance for Bad Times.* Companies operate on a "What have you done for me lately?" basis, which makes it dangerous when you have a bad year. Anyone, no matter how successful, can have a slump. If you lack a strong network, a performance dip can hurt you in spite of a strong track record. Your network helps to protect you.
- *Makes You a Known Quantity*. You have a better chance for job advancement if you're a known quantity: "Oh, yeah! I know her. She briefed me on a project she spearheaded." Imagine a senior instead saying, "I don't know her." In a vacuum of information, most decision-makers go with the known quantity.

- *Access.* Often, especially when you're new to an organization, you can't beg, borrow, or steal a meeting with higher-level managers until you network, gradually gaining exposure and receptivity. Networking gains you access to people, information, resources, favors, and support.
- *Feeds You the Real Buzz.* You may play a wonderful game of "Mirror, mirror, on the wall, who's the fairest of them all?" but if your mirror is a carnival fun-house distorted mirror, you don't have an accurate image of people's perceptions. Your network can level with you about your reputation, more accurately reflecting your corporate buzz.
- *Protection.* Whether mudslinging is a malicious ambush or a lame potshot, your network gives you a heads-up warning and sticks up for you. Jim Brenner's network saved his programs from being struck by lightning. When sabotage hits you, that's *not* the time to build a network. It already needs to be in place.
- *Endorsement.* When lobbying for approval, you can first advocate for an idea with your network of closest stakeholders. Now they're in your corner as you approach more distant, resistant decision-makers. We can't overstate the importance of having a wide array of people endorsing your thinking, philosophy, and results.
- *Manages the Airwaves.* Your network is a vehicle for reshaping your buzz. To alter perceptions, you need your support network to contradict negative buzz and broadcast positive buzz. Your grapevine can sprout favorable impressions about you instead of making corporate life thorny.
- *Business Knowledge.* If you don't network across the company, you have functional tunnel vision. Cross-organizational networking broadens your scope and strategic view.
- *Job Satisfaction.* A manager said, "Those hallways are mighty long," to express his corporate loneliness. Instead of being a stranger in a strange land, you'll enjoy work as you widen your network. Expanded visibility is energizing, fulfilling, and fun.

Networking Reminders

The savvy, ethical executive networks with grace and decent boldness especially after making a transition from one company and culture to another. She knows who her allies are and patiently spends time developing working relationships with them. She has a keen sense of proper timing for what it takes to create change, as well as when to network for rapport versus idea support. She leads her new company to do the right things (Power of Ideas) by using a tapestry of power allies and key stakeholders (Power of Person). She epitomizes Power of Savvy relationship building, using these networking guidelines:

Think NOW. There's no time like the present. Don't wait to build your network until you urgently need one to support an important idea or protect you from an underhanded rival. It doesn't work to scurry about creating a network in the midst of a brush fire. Your firefighting unit must already be in place—up, down, and throughout the organization.

Think HIGH. Build relationships in high places. This is where the *bold* in "decent boldness" comes into play. You need powerful allies, not just strength in numbers. Arranging meetings and conversations with seniors involves understanding their current goals. If you know their shifting priorities, you might send a related magazine article. Even if they've seen it, they'll be impressed that you are on their wavelength and bold. "Here's a smart, creative person offering value and knowledge." Network upward by interviewing officers to learn from them. Executives like to talk about their accomplishments, and you'll develop a cross-organizational perspective while showing that you value learning. Others see you with a senior who may later drop *your* name!

Think WIRED-IN. If you can't network directly to a senior, meet with common associates who *do* have a connection. They get a sense of you, your experience, your knowledge, and your potential. Become visible to many people without dropping your regular responsibilities or being seen as a manipulator. People might *not* be impressed, but it can't hurt unless you say, "I want to build up my career image and have you talk me up to the boss."

Think WIDE. Don't only network within your group. This builds an insular support system that becomes inbred and perpetuates silos. Besides, your team and department already know and respect you. So cure your cross-organizational agoraphobia. Especially if you're in a staff function such as human resources, legal, information technology, or finance, your credibility and power base strengthen exponentially when you plant one foot firmly in the line business.

Think OUTSIDE. Go beyond company boundaries, joining more professional affiliations or volunteering to serve on the board of a nonprofit organization. You never know whom you'll meet who knows a high-level officer in your company. View golf memberships, conventions, and civic events as also having networking benefits.

Think WHY. If you don't have a "good reason" to meet, remember that getting acquainted is a valid objective in itself. Of course, you have to respect proper channels and seniors' time, but don't let your fears or assumptions about them become cop-outs. They may *want* to know you. Use travel as a good excuse. People are more likely to meet if you "just happen to be in town." Since you're away from family anyway, why not nudge yourself to have dinner or coffee with someone new to expand your network? Find bridges of reasons to meet by finding out their agenda. You might call to say, "I served on a committee that explored the wireless technology possibilities and I know you're working on this in your division. Care to swap war stories?"

Think BIG FUNCTIONS. Entire books exist about making connections at large events, because many people are in the same boat of feeling awkwardness or aversion around these settings. Many powerful people are just as uncomfortable as others at such functions, so they appreciate when someone approaches them and guides the conversation. At a celebrity benefit gala someone we know was confided in for two hours by a Hollywood box-office megastar. He confessed his relief to have her to "buffer" him from the crowds, who assumed that he was a natural at mingling. He wasn't. So you never know. If you bump into a senior at a function, talk about industry trends and use open-ended questions to learn about his interests rather than monopolizing airtime. Other times, humor, small talk, or just being you is all you need.

You can network with many people efficiently at mixers, company events, nonprofit benefits, trade shows, and conferences. Take plenty of business cards, ask for the other person's card first (which will lead to reciprocation), be a great listener rather than trapping someone with your monologue, and keep conversations short so you can follow up later. Graciously excuse yourself when you are ready to move on, simply saying that you've promised some clients or colleagues that you would catch up with them, that you've enjoyed meeting the person you're leaving, and that you hope to stay in touch.

Think PAST. Contact former colleagues, friends, associates, customers, clients, and suppliers now and then just to maintain contact. You never know who might be connected.

Think MENTOR. As long as you're networking, find a politically savvy mentor, regardless of her current power status. You'll learn and benefit greatly from an organizationally astute mentor. This particular networking effort is less about building your power alliances and visibility, and more about more ways to expand your savvy.

A Safety Network

A broad network forms a safety net for anyone in any kind of political arena. Both Ronald Reagan and Bill Clinton were brilliantly art-ful with networks—even more so than most politicians. Reagan was called the Great Communicator, and Clinton could convey empathy to people from any walk of life while weaving his web of power brokers across the nation. So think about how you can construct a network of powerful allies and connected associates. Decide whom to include, whom you've ignored, who is an untapped resource already in your sphere, and how you'll forge more conscious networks. Remember that none of this requires compromising your integrity or ethics.

Chapter 10

Manage the Airwaves

Melting Icebergs

You can't change that people form and circulate buzz, but you *can* change your response. You can become the pilot of your corporate buzz, guiding how word about you travels through the company. Instead of being a victim of a negative reputation permeating the informal airwaves, broadcast your *own* buzz. Melt frozen, caked-up corporate buzz icebergs—those obsolete perceptions that linger. Reinvent and reshape your "rap." Plant seeds with people to create new impressions, capitalizing on your strong network. Paradoxically, you can obliterate negative gossip about you by "blowing your cover," which involves admitting when some of the negative traits surrounding your name are valid. Finally, if you know that a saboteur will try to pollute the airwaves with negative talk about you, especially directly to your boss, try to get to your boss first to buffer any behind-the-scenes attack. Let's double-click on these proven tactics to manage the airwaves as a political pro.

Broadcast Your Own Buzz

The first way to speed the evaporation of negative icebergs of frozen corporate buzz is to never surrender the "reputation radio" to others. Many extreme Power of Ideas victims of disparaging gossip throw up their hands and give up. Grab back the reins by staying connected and active in broadcasting what *you* want said about your work and function. Examine how you cast *yourself* in your organization. What you say about yourself flows from your Self-Talk about your role and identity, because your thoughts influence what comes out of your mouth. Notice and change any discounting labels that you attach to yourself when in public. Do you need a new campaign manager?

We remember George, an extreme Power of Ideas research scientist in a major pharmaceutical company. He had earned himself the off-putting reputation of being overly nitpicky about analytic data. No wonder. In our workshop, he introduced himself by saying, "I'm the resident techno-geek!" Here was a well-meaning Borderline Under Political professional who regularly put a great big bull's-eye on his back *begging* others to see him as overly technical and detailed. Don't be like George by announcing your own negative buzz!

Reinvent and Reshape Your Rap

Besides what you *say* about yourself, modify how you *act* to avoid reinforcing any negative corporate buzz. Our "techno-geek" friend George often butted heads with a dominating Power of Person woman. Lucy frequently treated him as weak and lacking power by talking dismissively to him at meetings. One day, George called one of us to brag, "You would have been proud of me. I built up my power image"—a tactic we'll discuss later—"with Lucy. No more Mr. Nice Guy! She quoted some clinical results and I showed her up in front of everyone. I corrected her . . . to the *third* decimal point! I showed her, didn't I?" George was gently coached, "You showed her all right, and everyone else, too . . . that the buzz on you is correct—you're a techno-geek!" George immediately grasped how his power strategy may have countered his weak image, but perpetuated another perception—as being overly technical.

Beyond broadcasting your own buzz and purging self-defeating self-labels, politically sharp people are dogged about *behaving* in ways to support healthier buzz. Some years back, Dan Rather concerned network executives as seeming too hard and unapproachable. So image makeover specialists dressed him in a sweater to soften his persona. If you have a reputation like George's as "overly detailed and technical," how might you reinvent yourself? Ideas from workshop alumni include:

- Avoid jargon, academic titles, or esoteric references unless you're sure they bring credibility.
- Provide bulleted cover pages and summary pages for longer reports.
- Occasionally, carry around the *Wall Street Journal* or *Harvard Business Review* to show general business acumen. Of course, read these publications so that you can refer to their content intelligently and become fluent in business lingo.
- Link your technical details to other parts of the company. What do they mean for supply chain, operations, sales, marketing, quality, and other staff or line functions? This shows you're aware of the whole company, not locked in your own world.
- Mention top management catchphrases or agendas, short-term corporate objectives, and long-term strategy. Demonstrate that you *do* see the forest through the trees.

Perhaps you come off as "lacking a sense of urgency." If your organization deifies quality instead of quantity or speed to deadline, it might not matter. But if your company works at "net speed," you can make some savvy behavior changes:

- Be punctual at meetings and let people know they can call you at home if needed.
- Give progress updates and tell people ahead of time if you're not going to meet a deadline, providing new milestone targets.

- Cite your priorities to top managers and show them succinct written goals and dates.
- Speak up more so you're seen as action-oriented.
- Change your vocabulary to insert more words related to "action," "now," and "urgency."
- Adjust your speaking pace to be more clipped and to the point, not slow and rambling.
- Anticipate people's objections and be prepared to respond with concrete steps.

Plant Seeds with Embedded Impressions

Without communicating false information about yourself, you can ethically plant the seeds of new perceptions as you interact with people—in hallways, at lunches, during chats before a meeting—in the hopes they will spread updated buzz about you. Imagine that people see you as "a pushover and too accommodating" of performers who don't pull their weight. A friend tells you that your team wishes you'd stick up for them more and that peers disrespect you for not disciplining problem performers.

Based on this chapter's suggestions, you can broadcast your own buzz by describing yourself as "demanding" and gradually reinvent your image by acting tougher in meetings, challenging others' ideas, and reducing personal small talk before getting down to business. You can also plant seeds that generate a different impression. At lunch with an associate, drop hints about your way of working, anecdotes, or other tidbits that relate to this perception of being "too nice." This is a more subtle than direct strategy, leaving it up to your lunch partner to interpret what you've said and broadcast it in the airwaves as new buzz. You start new positive gossip about yourself without saying something stupid like "By the way, would you mind spreading around that I'm really *not* a wimp?" Here's how to plant these impression seeds:

- *Anecdotes and Topics of Conversation.* At lunch, we're *not* suggesting that you insist that your colleague pay, nor should you snap at the waiter if he's late with your order! That would be gauche. Instead, adroitly steer the conversation toward topics that show you in a new light. You apologize for being late, due to a tough performance appraisal in which you held someone's feet to the fire for not performing up to par. You compliment your boss for finally shutting down a boisterous task force member, a long overdue reprimand. By inserting conversational vignettes that contradict your negative buzz, you plant seeds for budding new perceptions. By contrasting example, a different person's negative buzz was that she was "intense and in people's faces," always seeming "right." She decided to listen more, but also to casually mention to others how she'd changed her mind on an issue after talking with a common colleague. She planted the seed that she wasn't so rigid about her stance and was becoming less "intense."

- *Turns of Phrase and Expressions*. Speak in ways that mold a different impression of your value system from what the scorned trait implies. For the midmanager shaping new buzz of *not* being a "pushover," he can consciously use expressions like: "Hey, sometimes you have to lay it on the line for people," "It's not my job to be the most popular guy in the company," or "As long as I'm the head honcho, I know sometimes I'll be seen as the heavy, but it comes with the territory."

Blow Your Cover!

A paradoxically potent way to reshape corporate buzz is to blow your cover. Do the counterintuitive. Admit that you're working on some aspect of your negative buzz. Whatever the problem trait is, openly ask for and welcome feedback on it. This nondefensive strategy won't make you vulnerable, except with the most unreasonable people. This tactic uses mind over matter—if you don't mind, it doesn't matter! This reverse tactic earns political reputation points with several kinds of people.

- *Well-Meaning Worriers*. These colleagues are in your corner but stay silent when someone bad-mouths you, for fear of guilt by association. When they see you nondefensively acknowledge your buzz by asking for help with the alleged trait, they are relieved to see you courageously own up to your foibles. Their previous efforts to protect their own image might make a 180-degree turn since they've wanted to support you all along, but have been awkwardly silent due to the hush-hush air around this issue. These worriers may now become warriors who protect you: "Hey, he's aware of the issue and is working on it. I heard him ask his team for help. It's no big deal anymore."

- *Bad-Mouthing Buzz-ards.* Typical rumor-mill junkies pass along buzz they hear about you. They don't particularly mean you harm, but are just keeping the corporate "Uh-Oh Squad" intact. So blow your cover to surprise them and enlist their goodwill. Now they realize you're no dummy and that maybe you deserve a fair shake. If people aren't really trying to hurt you, a preemptive strike against yourself makes it unnecessary for them to play the game. They may decide that talk is cheap.
- *Samurai Saboteurs.* If someone uses your negative buzz against you in a group, don't act defensive about the label you're sick of hearing. People mutter to one another, "See how defensive he is about this? The truth must hurt." Don't show that the buzz is valid by emotionally denying it, explaining it away, or taking offense. Each rebuke highlights how serious the bad rap must be, or you wouldn't have such energy about it. Instead, do the unexpected and face the music, talking openly about a trait you are working to change. This tactic takes the sail out of the saboteur's wind. Yes, we *mean* to say it that way rather than "takes the wind out of his sails."

Get There First!

Sometimes you do your best in private to defuse a volatile conversation, but it's clear that an adversary plans to trash your name in the corporate airwaves. The aggressor might flat out threaten to tell your boss how unprofessional you are or "make sure others know you're not a team player." Or, you get wind of the stink your assailant is flushing into the system when an ally tips you off. Once you know a saboteur is going after you, it's pointless to confront him since this may only accelerate his panicked plan to sully your image.

Should you stoop to his level and institute your own trash-talk campaign? We recommend taking the moral high road unless you're absolutely forced to play hardball and go on the offensive (which we'll address later). Striking back can get *you* fingered as the one with poor ethics. In sports, when there's a personal-foul penalty, it isn't always called on the first person who shoves or hits another player. Often, the one who counterpunches winds up being flagged for the penalty. But you don't have to passively say, *"Que será será."* Let's say you know Jerry is leaving a conflict you two just had and plans to go tomorrow to your boss, Bev, to badmouth you. You don't have to wait and wonder how badly he'll dump on you. Instead, get there first. You can go to Bev and say:

> I wanted to catch you before your nine o'clock to tell you that you may have one more item on your plate today. You and I know that sometimes Jerry and I don't see eye to eye on every issue. We got into it yesterday about the conversion process and it got a little heated. Neither of us was at our best and we each said some things that were below the belt. I'm not here to take your time lobbying for my side. We can discuss the conversion issue whenever you want, but I recommend that we three do that together, to be fair. I just didn't want you to be caught off guard if Jerry stops in today, because I know you're on a tight deadline.

What have you accomplished? You've demonstrated respect for Bev's time with the heads-up and by not trying to work the content issue now. You've taken the moral high ground by *not* trashing Jerry, allowing for conflict between professionals, and admitting that you both lost your cool yesterday. Now, when Jerry barges in on Bev ranting and raving about how unreasonable you were during your skirmish, you'll come off smelling like a rose. Even if he is verbally disciplined and low-keys his behind-the-scenes assault, you've still given your boss advance notice compared to relinquishing the airwaves entirely. Now rewind the videotape of the scenario and pretend that Jerry got to Bev first. She calls you into her office wanting an explanation of what went on since you were described as flying off the handle. No matter *what* you say or *how* you respond, you'll sound defensive, apologetic, or blameful. So if you expect a saboteur will slander you by going behind your back to someone in power or who has access to the corporate airwaves, get there first. You can still hold on to your professionalism while blunting and diffusing the attack.

Now You Can Be the Boss of Your Buzz

It's impossible to prescribe exact steps for reshaping every potential negative trait. Instead, we've given you the right questions to ask so you can pinpoint your own problematic buzz, along with five tactics for tailoring a personalized plan to address any particular reputation: (1) broadcast your own buzz, (2) reinvent and reshape your rap, (3) plant seeds with embedded impressions, (4) blow your cover, and (5) get there first. None of these tactics alone form a panacea to halt negative perceptions of you or your team, but taken together they represent a powerful elixir for curing any corporate buzz ailment. They result in your proactively managing the corporate airwaves that impact your reputation, influence, and success.

Chapter 11

Promote Yourself with Integrity

If you want to sell a car, you can't keep it in the garage.

—SHARON GRUNDFAST, SENIOR MANAGER
AVON PRODUCTS LEARNING AND DEVELOPMENT

Witness the countless books on selling yourself and the many classified ads for jobs that list self-confidence as a qualification. It pays to build your visibility and credibility by standing out from the crowd. Management self-help guru Tom Peters's eleventh book is *Re-imagine!* The business champion says to "brand you," since the most important product you'll ever make or market is yourself. Think of the clutter in people's minds. One way to have seniors and others know your expertise and contribution to the company is to promote yourself with integrity.

Selling Yourself Isn't Selling Out

Letting people know about ideas you initiate or results you achieve is neither conceited nor crass. You're not show*boating*—you're show*casing*. You're *not* stealing credit, exaggerating your contributions, or plagiarizing. You first need to tweak any flawed Self-Talk—blocking messages about pride, modesty, or bragging that you may have received when you were a tadpole. You'd think that this savvy strategy would be comfortable for left-siders since it *is* about substance, sharing how your work and ideas make a positive difference. Sadly, many Borderline Under Politicals (BUPs) or Under Politicals (UPs) are mired in doubts about self-promotion and worry that they will turn off people.

Many women are still taught to avoid self-promotion and may therefore become more modest, leading to inaccurate buzz that they're weaker. Researchers document how this stereotypical tendency is a double whammy because data also show that men are promoted based upon future potential while women are more likely to climb based on past accomplishments. Some women, especially less political ones, are uncomfortable with promoting their accomplishments, yet it's ironically the very skill set that some organizations require for career success.

There's always a judgment call about how loudly to blow your own horn, but unless you blast it in people's ears, it won't sound like noisy racket. People may even *want* to celebrate your accomplishments. Just be sensitive to company culture and read what could be too much hype so that if you're a Borderline Overly Political (BOP) or Overly Political (OP), you can monitor yourself to lean more into humility. But if you're a left-sider, you can probably advertise your work more. Isn't it your responsibility as manager? This doesn't mean you'll use people or deceive others about your contribution. You deserve to promote yourself with integrity, merging *class* with a little *sass*.

Put Your Handprint on Your Work

Get involved to be more public about your work, so that your contributions and know-how aren't kept secret. Some people keep their work under a rock as if it were a snake, almost viewing deserved credit not as a *handprint* to put on their work, but as *fingerprints* put on a police blotter. Enthusiasm and positive pride are contagious. You don't have to promote yourself in a pompous, hype-oriented manner. You can let people see your accomplishments in a spirit of sharing your excitement about being able to help the organization. This is comparable to a musical performer being complimented and, instead of patting himself on the back, more graciously commenting about how much fun he has performing, how blessed he feels, or how much pleasure it brings him to see others enjoy his work. So don't feel guilty or shy about your hard work, results, or capabilities. You can tastefully (blended with humility) promote yourself and your work. You're again networking up, down, and across your company, but now it's to obtain exposure for your talent and achievements.

- Document your work contributions—save testimonials, congratulatory notes, job objectives and achievements, favorable appraisals, and records of accomplishments. Keep a diary of your projects. Consider developing an internal résumé that captures your profile of results, talents, and skill sets, especially as they grow each year.
- If you have a trusted friend in your organization, you may be able to help one another. If somebody else blows your horn, the sound travels twice as far! Connect with a sponsor, someone senior who promotes your achievements for you.
- Get involved in decision-making, serving on committees and cross-organizational task forces to demonstrate your interdisciplinary grasp of the business.
- Deliver an executive briefing. Conduct a seminar or brown-bag lunch for the general population. Sponsor an external conference on an area of expertise at your organization.
- Write an article for an internal newsletter or professional publication. Make reprints of the article to e-mail or send to strategically pinpointed people in your network.
- Create an award or contest with conduct-related events or ceremonies. Your name will now be associated with a standard of excellence for safety or quality. Find catchy brand names for these

awards, like one electronics firm's "Customer Now" initiative that distributed awards for innovative customer-focus ideas. The contest didn't even originate in the customer service department.
- Get involved in charitable campaigns or sports competitions within your organization.

Put Achievements under the Umbrella of "Organizational Learning"

Organizational learning is a huge buzz phrase in today's corporations. The emphasis on learning is illustrated by how many companies have a chief learning officer. Top leaders buy into the notion of organizational learning, so you will sound less like a brash braggart if you leverage this concept. When you ask a senior for a meeting and your agenda is to promote yourself, don't necessarily describe the topic as your "achievements" or "results." Instead, place the ideas or accomplishments you're sharing under the umbrella of "organizational learning."

Maddie, project leader of a task force that benchmarked ways to save money on shared services technology within her division, called the president of a different division and said

> Hi, Molly. I enjoyed meeting you at last month's town hall forum and I happen to be passing through Chicago next week. I'm hoping to schedule a short layover so that I can cab downtown for a cup of coffee with you. I'd like to tell you the results of the Technology Options Task Force, because I believe that what we learned for our division could be of tremendous relevance and benefit to your business. I'd only have a half hour, but it'd be nice to get better acquainted.

Maddie was smart and savvy to give her accomplishments "legs" by offering to explain what she had "learned" (not "achieved" or "accomplished"). You won't sound self-serving or arrogant, since you're not saying, "Hi, I want to tell you how great my department is." As long as you don't tell people how to run their business, they're not likely to resist such a meeting. Besides, you can't lose what you don't already have! Seniors will respect your decent boldness: "Here's a competent person with a novel approach, company interest at heart, and some guts, too." This tactic also forces you to take needed time to harvest the learning from a project instead of simply moving on to the next task. This is a valuable habit to practice.

Share Credit while Getting Your Share

One way to promote yourself is to thank others, which should appeal to left-siders' goodwill and team spirit of humility. If you're a Power of Ideas person not prone to taking much credit yourself, you'll like this practice of sending out thank-you e-mails to team members for projects, task forces, or special initiatives that you spearhead. Be detailed, with specific recognition for each team member's unique contribution rather than using general, global praise. This shows you're a great manager, building a motivating work environment. Positive recognition is one of the top motivators, according to workplace motivation researchers. PeopleMedia found that 80 percent of the ten thousand people they surveyed said that more than money they wanted their manager's recognition. So the buzz on you will be that you're a morale-boosting leader.

Here's one last important reminder about these effusive but genuine appreciation e-mails: be sure to cc key individuals—your boss, possibly his boss, and the managers of people on the cross-departmental team you led. You're putting your handprint on the project even as you share credit and recognition. It's clear you're the leader because you're the one sending out the kudos. This strategy promotes your leadership role and expands your visibility while helping others.

You can call this manipulative, but there is nothing wrong with broadcasting your involvement in important initiatives in creative ways. Incidentally, there may be further corporate karma benefits.

People love to talk about their boss—the good and the bad—so they'll promote *you* in glowing ways if you give them reasons to do so. Here, the receivers may tell other people you recognized them publicly, further spreading their own accomplishments as they praise your magnanimous nature. They might even like talking up important people (you) to their friends since it elevates their status.

Use Elevator Speeches to Avoid the Elevator Shaft!

What Is It? The Elevator Speech is a common term in sales training, marketing, and branding workshops, but underutilized in the organizational politics arena. This self-promotion tool is a quick pitch about your overall job or current project. It gets its name from the hypothetical scenario of a top executive stepping onto an elevator and asking what you do. Or, he knows your general position but asks what you're working on these days. This opportunity can arise in a hallway, at a cocktail party, or by running into someone at an outside function. You squander the moment if you wing it or just answer with your title. A savvy manager knows that job title alone throws him in the hopper with a cast of many like him or requires translation for someone to understand his value. The key is, *when asked,* to have various ways to set apart your job or the initiative you're promoting.

A balanced Elevator Speech avoids low-profile Under Political mistakes such as changing the subject to "those Mets," winging it on the spot, or reciting the same pre-scripted speech without adapting it to the receiver's rank, style, situation, or priorities. You'll also steer clear of typical OP blunders such as giving your pitch without being asked, speed-rapping without pauses, or overhyping your role without sharing credit with your team. Savvy leaders know there's no formula for success and no one right way to sell your role for every situation. In many organizations, the top leaders don't *want* to be sold if they are more analytic, in a sales-aversive culture, or far left on the Organizational Savvy Continuum. You might even scrap self-promotion altogether and simply build rapport in other ways. But where going unnoticed is a career flaw, the Elevator Speech provides a valuable visibility advantage.

Guidelines for Elevator Speeches. The Elevator Speech is actually shorter than a "speech" (thirty seconds, a minute, or two minutes), and not really a "pitch" since that would usually be "over-the-top selling." Below are some criteria to consider in crafting what to say about yourself.

- *Concise.* Is the speech short with some punch to it?
- *Contribution.* Does your Elevator Speech highlight your tangible bottom-line, tangible benefits to the company?
- *Corporate Value.* Do you link your contribution to strategic goals, values, or objectives?
- *Credibility.* Do you mention your track record, qualifications, or results as appropriate?
- *Commitment.* Does your excitement and enthusiasm for the company show?
- *Confidence.* Do you replace wishy-washy wording and speak with conviction?
- *Culture-Sensitive about Self-Promotion.* Is your amount of hype appropriate to your company culture, topic, and receiver? Do you show that you're savvy enough to share the right amount of credit based on company norms and your style?
- *Creative.* Are you clever and innovative, or dry and unwilling to take a risk?
- *Conversational Tone.* Are you natural and down-to-earth, or slick and presumptuous?

Interactive Pitches. Unless you're slam-dunking a thirty-second pitch or introducing yourself in a group with many others, you can take the suggested conversational tone a step further by making your Elevator Speech interactive. You "chunk" your pitch to deliver it a sentence or two at a time, pausing periodically to check if the other person wants more. You "leak out" each piece gradually and see if your listener wants you to elaborate. This interactive delivery requires a strong enough opening sentence to accomplish one of two goals:

- *Stand Alone*. In case your audience won't want more or might step out of the elevator a floor earlier than expected, you need the one sentence she's heard to be clear, pithy, and memorable ("I coach our National Accounts salespeople to cure their corporate stage fright so that they win more customers at large-scale presentations").
- *Tease*. If you're confident the person has enough time for further interaction, you can be purposely vague while tempting elaboration. You make each sentence provocative and creative enough to pique curiosity ("I make sure our company is never again seen as the Rodney Dangerfield of the marketplace like we were at the last shareholder meeting").

Besides "giving your fish more and more line" by unpeeling your Elevator Speech in bite-size, engaging one-sentence chunks, you can also be interactive through closed-ended or open-ended questions. One director of sales training for a wholesaler used these approaches to pitch his seminars to his internal client business managers:

- "You know the classic problem of our sales forces complaining instead of selling?" Pause for response . . . "Well, I move our salespeople from whining to winning."
- "Does your sales force waste time and productivity on whining?"
- Reacting to a question: "What do I do? Well, to explain, let me ask you, what do your salespeople gripe and whine about?" . . . (presuming that they *are* like most salespeople).

Dare to Be Different. Leave a lasting impression as a creative contributor. After all, the only fish that always go with the current are the dead fish! There's a risk to being controversial, but in many cultures it's respected. We know a corporate entertainer who answered the "What do you do?" question on airplanes by quipping, "I'm a corporate motivational lounge lizard." This quirky image invited fellow business-class travelers to laugh and ask for clarification. He could then explain his Vegas-style musical comedy act that lampooned any company's challenges in order to help people to laugh at their problems and improve motivation. The point is that besides feeding the listener a sentence or two at a time, stressing benefits, and avoiding the usual job titles ("I'm a motivational speaker"), the consultant dared to be different and memorable.

Sentence Stem Templates for Elevator Speeches. Experiment with a version of the sentence stem "You know the problem we have with [highlight a company business challenge]? Well, in my role as [provide your job title or role], my team and I solve that problem by [describe related activities and contributions]." You may prefer the framework of "goal" and "meet that goal," or "challenge" and "address the challenge." You can draw out the problem through questions about it or just position the issue yourself before explaining how you help. Whether you use declarative statements or questions depends on the time you have (are you on floor five and he's getting out at seven, or have you pulled the alarm button to stop the elevator?), your style, and reactions you get. Besides a problem, goal, or challenge focus for your Elevator Speech template, here are other packaging structures to use for self-promotion with punch.

- *Loss Focus:* "Our company loses [amount] each year because of [root cause of loss]. As [title], I head a group that prevents/cuts down this bottom-line drain by [explain the team's activities and outputs]."
- *Opportunity Focus:* "I'm excited about the company's chance to [cite the opportunity in bottom-line terms]. My task force is helping us to capitalize on this opportunity by [describe the actions and how they relate]."

- *Benefit Statement Focus:* "As [title], I deliver [name the output, service, feature, or activity], which brings/creates/ensures [state the resulting general company or customer advantage], and satisfies our need for/to [link the advantage to a company need]."
- *Empathy Focus:* "If my understanding is correct, you've been concerned about [name a problem, issue, concern]. My [name the group] team helps by [describe the team's activities, outputs, and impact on the concern]. My role is [give your title or function]."
- *Excitement Focus:* For more "sober selling" in a non-promotion-oriented culture, share your accomplishments as a self-disclosure of excitement or pride in your team: "I'm very excited about the [cite achievement] my team worked so hard to accomplish, because they made sure that our company [state the strategic benefit gained or liability avoided]."

A Pop Quiz. Use the Elevator Speech criteria list on preceding pages to critique the following examples. They aren't perfect and on paper they lack a conversational tone. They may have too much hype for your culture or lack enough humility, but they do demonstrate most of the guidelines. The first example uses a question-oriented interactive mode and tees up a problem. The second is more declarative in style, positioning a corporate challenge that is addressed.

- "You know that problem we've noticed with losing top management to the competition?" Pause for response . . . "I think Jerry quoted a cost of three hundred thousand per position in replacement dollars, not to mention the morale and productivity drain. Well, my team reduces that loss by installing incentive programs to reward seniority and motivation skills training for level V and W managers. As VP of human capital retention, I help us to build our managerial bench strength and stop the bleeding of attrition."

- "I'm our director of targeted marketing, working with a super crew. As you know, since we're just breaking into the high-tech vertical niche, we need to look like a bigger player to create a positive industry image and land contracts. My team uses high-tech electronic marketing campaigns aimed at Route 128 high-tech firms to drive business to our sales force and meet the new strategic revenue goals."

A Self-Promotion Pro

A workshop alumna, Susan, demonstrated the protective shield of self-promotion when she called to report her experience of leaving her pharmaceutical research job to join some senior researchers who were launching a start-up venture. She was excited and relieved to escape her previous job, because a coworker, Jeanette, had become inexplicably malicious. Jeanette had avoided her, didn't respond to phone calls, and dropped the ball on deliverables while blaming Susan. Susan passively resigned herself to being patient until she could leave this ugly atmosphere and the mystery would end.

Susan took a new job at the start-up and did great work, rejuvenated by the change of venue and dynamics. At first, not wanting to make waves, she characteristically let her results speak for themselves (a Borderline Under Political on the Organizational Savvy Continuum); but then she heard that Jeanette was joining the firm. Uh-oh, what to do now? Susan leafed through our seminar workbook and decided to adopt a slightly more political style position. First, she wisely decided it would be inappropriate to tell the senior researchers about Jeanette's previous sabotage, because that would sound as if *she* were a saboteur. Instead, she checked out her corporate buzz with associates and learned that she was seen as a bit aloof.

Susan decided to make sure the management team had a clear picture of her contributions and hard work but also knew her as a person *before* Jeanette arrived on the scene to sabotage her success. She started to cc management on e-mails about her work and invite people to lunch to discuss important findings. She accepted holiday party invitations that she used to consider a waste of time, and she actively chatted up her excitement about her team's progress. Formerly, she'd viewed this as a nuisance. Now she realized she had little choice in order to protect her credibility and to be sure that she—not Jeanette—purposefully created her organization's picture of her. Susan even wrote up a few quick Elevator Speeches and taught them to her team so that they learned to "strut their stuff, too," as she put it. She gradually showed herself as a competent, loyal, fun research manager who knew the ropes and was well connected.

Jeanette arrived and picked up right where she'd left off, trying to bad-mouth Susan. Susan heard through the grapevine that Jeanette's husband was out of work and her son was applying to an expensive private school. Susan found out that at their previous company, another researcher had leaked word about Susan's coming to the start-up. Now Susan figured that Jeanette resented being excluded and wanted the same opportunity. Since Susan finally had a network to tap for knowledge, she was privy to information she had no way of knowing before. Susan didn't approach Jeanette at their new company since that had failed before, and she had studied the company culture enough to know that management would view gossip or trash-talk as off base.

After six months, Susan got a promotion and Jeanette earned corporate buzz as politicking too much and being divisive. Susan told us she'd had some ambivalence about self-promoting since it went counter to her ingrained Self-Talk that "this is bragging, and bragging is unattractive. My results should be enough and I don't want to have to schmooze." But she had consciously reprogrammed her thoughts to view selling herself as a channel for gaining the recognition she deserved, elevating her image, and shielding herself from sabotage without getting her hands dirty.

Graduation with Honors

We listened carefully to Susan's postmortem and congratulated her for all of the workshop's savvy tactics that she had implemented for high-integrity politics. Jeanette did try to trash-talk her way in front of Susan for a promotion, but Susan had constructed a safety net against this sabotage. She deactivated her political buttons with reprogrammed Self-Talk about self-promotion so that it was no longer distasteful to her. She discovered the corporate buzz about herself and her team by exploring her reputation. Then she reshaped these perceptions to manage the airwaves. She networked with decent boldness to gain visibility and access to key power holders. She became a student of power dynamics, politics, and unwritten rules. She realized that the research firm's noncombative culture would frown upon her even hinting at Jeanette's previous sabotage. In this case, advance warning would have seemed uptight. She promoted herself and her team's work, so that her network was aware of her contributions and would stick up for her in case of potshots from Jeanette. Graduation with honors!

Don't Be Invisible

Promote yourself and your team ethically to prevent you from disappearing into a corporate black hole. Amy, the invisible woman who you met in our introduction, had far too low a profile and was a carefully kept secret before she approached the executive vice president with her unique idea. She virtually had a bull's-eye on her back for her superior to steal her ideas. She didn't share her idea with others or let people see her handprint on the innovation. She didn't document her accomplishments or sell herself to Sam as indispensably connected to the successful rollout of her value strategy. Had she incorporated this chapter's tips for increasing her presence within the organization, her odds for recognition and her political stock might have risen, perhaps even dramatically.

Chapter 12

Pump Up Your Power Image

To Be Feared or Loved, That Is the Question

In 1515, Niccolò Machiavelli wrote that princes are better off being feared than loved. It's still believed true by certain political styles. Recently, a highly political ladder climber was sent to one of the authors for remedial coaching. On the first day, he looked his coach sternly in the eye and barked in his staccato-clipped voice, "I'm here. I'm a prisoner. But you would be sitting in this room alone for two days if you weren't as tight with my boss as you are." By the end of two days, the gruff power tripper acknowledged that he had learned something, but we would never have had a fighting chance if it weren't for his perception of our power base.

Left-side Power of Ideas people who believe power resides in their substance alone assume that others will support ideas that make good business sense. Meanwhile, right-side Power of Person people wonder, "Who in power supports this idea?" Overly Political (OP) players may even obsess about this question. So savvy leaders increase the perception that they are powerful, or at least well wired into position power. Without simply changing the title on your business card or crossing the integrity line, you can (1) build your power base, (2) enhance your personal impact, and (3) avoid muffling your meeting impact. Ethically pumping up your power image and aura raises your lobbying potency and success while diminishing the sabotage aimed at you.

Build Your Power Base

In a sense, this is a goal of the entire book, since the best way to be wired into power is to actually gain it through high-integrity politics. You'll increase your influence with right-siders if they perceive you as having a power network, as being aligned with key people, and as spending time with seniors who recognize your ideas. Of course, there's no replacement for having an enduring reputation as competent, ethical, and loyal to the company . . . but a power base can't hurt you with more political colleagues.

Your Real Power Base. Weave a vast, wide web of high-level people who know you, your expertise, your track record, your integrity, and your political astuteness. Hopefully, these seniors will mention they just had lunch with you, visited your team for a briefing, or respect your work. Learn what's important to seniors and talk their language. Show that you're up to speed on their agenda and you're a broad-based business partner who can help and interest them. This doesn't mean you're a robot, clone, or yes-person. Don't just use their pet phrases and nicknames to manufacture connections; read up on issues of concern to them. Broaden yourself with periodicals and books that you know executives are reading. If you don't have time, you can be conversant enough by subscribing to Soundview's *Executive Book Summaries,* eight-page reviews of the current business books. You also need tributaries to people without official power but who are cohorts, confidantes, and assistants to seniors.

Perceived Power Base. Besides having actual power and a power network, you can increase the *perception* that you have power, which obviously bumps up against each person's value system. It's about creating the impression, without lying, that you are connected and possess official or informal influence power. These moves can obviously cross your own ethical or company culture lines, but what can you do that fits your values and company? Depending on your organization, it may be inane to maneuver for a corner office, have an assistant record the outgoing message on your voice mail, join a prestigious country club, eat at the "in" place, or have an assistant call you "Doctor" just to convey position. But these are tactics workshop participants have brainstormed. Many power aficionados do prescribe *looking the part*—as if you are successful and control resources—such as by throwing a party or picking up the tab at an expensive dinner with seniors. One manager joked, "I have it! I'll marry the boss's daughter!"

You need to look in the mirror and across your company to know what constitutes crossing the line or looking presumptuous. Maybe it's enough for you to introduce a senior at a luncheon, thus implying a bond, or to become a mentor to cast a longer credibility shadow while also helping someone. Consider working on key, high-visibility projects, especially with line versus staff responsibility. Needless to say, don't do this unless you are confident that you have the skills to carry it through successfully. Perhaps you will delegate more tactical jobs to others, since doing them is not only inefficient, but conveys a lower position. We assume you'll be respectful of your company norms and other people rather than adopting an inappropriate power posture.

Enhance Your Personal Impact

We once coached an information-technology vice president sent by the chief technology officer at a huge insurance firm's securities arm. We pressed to understand why the CTO didn't consider Jeff to be executive material. The CTO finally blurted, "It's his shirts! He buys them with the collars too small. His neck seems short and stocky and he looks like a penguin!" Other factors may also have doomed him, but his appearance was the final knockout factor for a top executive position. Professionalism, power, and image are intertwined, so enhance your personal impact. This includes how you dress, accessorize, present yourself, talk, and behave so that you convey an aura of power and importance without being arrogant.

Remember that these days it isn't all about pomp and throwing around your weight abusively. Egocentric charisma no longer defines top leadership. More and more great companies' great leaders carry an air of personal humility, taking Teddy Roosevelt's famous advice to "speak softly and carry a big stick." Still, looking confident does suggest power. There are countless books, workshops, tapes, videos, and coaches to enhance executive presence. We merely remind you to create a "power zone" in your interactions—an air of possessing potency and credibility. You'll say "Oh, yeah" to the ideas below, but don't let familiarity lead to complacency about image. Especially if you *do* have position power, all eyes are scrutinizing you on such variables.

- *Fitness.* Watch your physical condition, stay in shape, and optimize your energy and vigor. A healthy and fit appearance conveys potency instead of weakness.
- *Clothes Call.* Dress for success, and *consider* a power wardrobe to communicate position and prestige. You can do this without being flamboyant. Don't go into debt or be transparent, and forget it if designer suits are wrong for your culture. Some people may interpret "power dress" as status-driven, fake, or brash. Dressing well doesn't take a lot of money, just noticing what's in and what's out. One caveat: if you are a midlevel manager and you notice that the very top executives wear blue shirts and white collars, and Armani slacks with tassled loafers, *do not* emulate them. You will simply look foolish for overreaching. Some people dress more *casually* than others, as if to say that they can get away with it. But you may risk censure, subtly or directly. Overdress slightly when in doubt. You can always scale down.
- *Accessorize!* It's shallow in many companies, but looking the appropriate part is important. This can include your briefcase (a tattered knapsack or classy splurge?), your pen (a cheap ballpoint

with a chewed cap?), and your jewelry (a plastic-band sports watch or a status symbol?).

- *Groom or Doom.* Historians report that the fastidious British prisoners in World War II German camps on average did better at surviving the wrath of the Gestapo than POWs whose grooming fell by the wayside, along with their attitudes about the future. Don't be lazy about grooming (gnawed fingernails or fine manicure, mop-head or well-styled hair, shaggy or well-trimmed beard? For many companies, women are advised to keep hair fairly short and away from the face). Be sensitive to the company culture regarding beards and mustaches. Most corporations today are relaxed about this, but in direct customer-relation jobs, such as banks and front-counter positions in a financial services branch office, they may be frowned upon.
- *Order In.* Watch your eating habits at power lunches (heavy sauces to splotch your tie and career, or a light salad that lets you speak without spewing?). And needless to say, don't chew with your mouth open, don't talk with food in your mouth, and don't hesitate to blot your mouth periodically with a corner of your napkin if you do sport facial hair.
- *Your Hangouts.* Check your car (dirty and cluttered with toys or clean and presentable?) and your office (disheveled and unkempt or Spartan with business awards prominently displayed?).
- *Act the Part.* Much of your power image is conveyed through your eye contact. Do you sheepishly avoid eye contact, blink excessively, or just as bad, drill through people's brains with laser vision? Posture is critical, so stand and walk without a slump or slouch. When you are stationary, experts suggest occasionally putting your hands on your hips, standing with feet shoulder-length apart. Move purposefully to convey an impression of being busy without being harried. Carry something work-related with you to let people know you're responsible for getting things done. A person's gait speaks volumes.
- *Say What?* Speak with vocal volume, tone, and rate that suggest urgency and clout, which does *not* mean loud volume and

speed-rapping. Hesitating for emphasis is fine. But err on the side of speed and slightly revved-up volume. Purge your vocabulary of tentative language (more on this in a later chapter). Add power phrases with punch, such as "I'm confident," "It's now or never," "Nobody can do this as well as we can." Also, watch your articulation and annoying verbal mannerisms, "ya know?" Hone your presentation skills to ensure crisp, clear formats and a compelling delivery style. We have a strong culture of stand and deliver, so this is a critical skill-set.

- *Take Charge.* Be organized and manage your time well. If you can't be in charge of yourself, how can you be in charge of others? Complete your tasks promptly and decisively. Be willing to make the tough decisions so that you're recognized as a take-charge person. This includes delivering hard messages and holding people accountable. Your goal isn't to be Darth Vader or a hatchet man, or to be indifferent to an employee with a serious problem at home, but to have a power image that is benevolently potent.
- *Get Rid of the Monkey on Your Shoulder.* Consider that top leaders don't get bogged down in details. Do people bring you issues or problems only to have you solve them prematurely, or do you get in the practice of training others to exhaust their own ideas before burdening you?

Don't Muffle Meeting Impact

By pumping up your power image, you maximize influence, visibility, and respect for your ideas and expertise. You have few chances to make an impression on seniors, so meetings are critical. Don't squander the moment. Make sure that people know you were at the meeting!

- *Preparation for Natural Conviction.* Prepare thoroughly for meetings that include bosses. Try to glean their formal and informal priorities about the meeting's agenda items, so that you can arrive with a strong, carefully thought-out point of view. This allows you to convey natural conviction, to demonstrate leadership by speaking early with commitment, and to stand your ground if people push back.

- *Pay Attention to Where You Sit*. Get to the meeting early to avoid seating that distances you from the action. This *doesn't* mean sitting next to the senior; just avoid being where it's hard to inform the conversation. Some people suggest sitting adjacent to the senior, but you risk not establishing enough eye contact to gain entry into the discussion.
- *Prevent Being Marginalized*. Being marginalized means being shut out or shoved into a low-impact box. Give thought to what you'll do if others knowingly or unwittingly marginalize you by interrupting you, talking over you, or diverting the focus. Protect your right to have a say and get your ideas discussed through tactful phrases to regain the floor, such as:
  — "Janie, I'm interested in your take, but when you're finished, I'd like to finish what I was saying."
  — "OK, Will, go ahead and finish your point. Then I'd like to get back to what I was saying."
  — "Dan, before we go in another direction that I'm sure will be constructive, I'd like to get feedback from the group on my idea."

Positive Power, Not Abuse or Fake Role-Playing

Clearly, your goal in pumping up your power image is not to rule through intimidation or to play some charade as a top-floor Goliath. You don't want to come off like a power-drunk megalomaniac or mob boss, just someone who exudes confidence that comes from within and that conveys conviction and constructive power. The tactics in this chapter must be adapted to your corporate culture and can backfire if you overdo them. But revving up your power image without flooding the engine is easy if you remember to use ethical means and savvy political skill.

Chapter 13

Address Hidden Agendas

Use Your Sniffer

Listen to your gut instincts. If something an associate does starts to smell fishy, it may *be* fishy! He says one thing to you and something else to others. Someone pushes unreasonably for an illogical idea or suddenly changes his body language. You deduce that he's afraid of losing something. You suspect a pact between several people who stand to gain by impeding a project. Maybe someone is an overly methodical thinker, or he *could* actually be stalling until an ally shows up at a meeting. A peer trashes or freezes out your idea, quashing any open forum. Your issue disappears from the agenda, is pushed to the bottom, or is tabled. Is the schedule just jammed or is the meeting being railroaded?

It is no secret that corporations sometimes harbor manipulators who orchestrate events for their own versus company benefits. Their hidden agenda can be about getting into someone's hip pocket, avoiding blame, plotting to leave the company, staging a coup against a rival, or steering clear of a politically undesirable assignment. The devious associate may have ulterior motives that are patently selfish—a bonus, a promotion, a pet project, visibility, covering his tail, or winning a boss's favor.

Notice that above we said "*listen* to your gut instincts," and not "*trust* your gut instincts." We don't want you to become paranoid or suspect a conspiracy at every turn. We'd worry if you automatically acted on your every instinct, since people can misread others as a result of past deceits or their own insecurities. Even if someone is generally a manipulator, it doesn't mean she has a selfish agenda in any particular instance. In other words, protect yourself from mistakenly assuming ulterior motives through these "gut checks":

- *Check Your Track Record*. We've said, "Don't be a chump," but ask yourself if you have misjudged people in the past, distrusting innocent colleagues or wrongly making villains out of people. What's your general aptitude for reading motivations?
- *Check for Factual Clues*. Listen to your hunches about hidden motives, but validate these suspicions with data. Facts are more reliable than feelings alone, especially if your track record includes some speed bumps—times you thought you saw something in the dark when nothing was there. Confirm your assumptions with others you trust, observe actual behavior, and listen for other evidence.
- *Check for Logical Leaps*. Take into account a person's political style and past self-serving actions, but reality-test your gut sense for *this* situation by grilling yourself on:
  - — What public gains or losses will occur if his idea is implemented or another is blocked? Can you connect the dots to any potential payoffs (such as power, money, approval, status, exposure, or loyalty to friends)?
  - — What private gains or losses might compel him to push his agenda or block someone else's?
- *Check for Body-Language Tip-Offs*. Sharpen your ability to detect body-language signals. The real experts are FBI agents, customs agents, auditors, poker players, negotiators, and law enforcement officers. These people's livelihoods and often their lives require a keen X-ray vision to see through lies or misrepresentations. They know what to look for as tip-offs—an eyebrow twitch, a clenched

jaw, dilated pupils, the snicker, poor eye contact, or a change of subject. Do you sense when people have secretly been working an issue behind closed doors, maneuvering with people in private or making special deals before the decision-making meeting? Admittedly, it's hard to detect schmoozing in the shadows due to its covert nature. But you *can* develop informal political polygraphs. A backroom operator gives herself away with throwaway comments: "There are rules, and then there are *rules,*" or even, "Rules are made to be broken."

Listen to your gut but don't be too quick to suspect power-oriented or greed-driven motives. Remember that the person may still be behaving ethically within the Power of Savvy style, but just pushing hard for some business direction he believes will help the company. Also, haven't *you* ever had self-interest *and* there was concomitant company benefit? You might be misjudging intentions based on your own resistance to any level of self-interest or politics whatsoever.

Your Friends May Come and Go, but Your Enemies Accumulate

Politically naïve people may be correct in detecting hidden and selfish ends, but falter in how they address these private objectives. Lack of verbal discipline is a stumbling block when encountering hidden agendas. Virtues like uncompromising honesty, resistance to kissing up, and a tendency to wear integrity on one's shirtsleeves can become liabilities. We coached one director who was usually politically shrewd but, when he detected hidden agendas, allowed his ego to let him insert his foot in his mouth and catch athlete's tongue. Don't let your integrity seduce you into blurting out every hunch about a hidden agenda. Especially with seniors and power-obsessive or easily threatened colleagues, use discretion. You can accomplish your business goals *and* live to talk about it if you practice verbal discipline.

Wounding the King

In our introduction you met Larry, a regional vice president (RVP) for a large retail corporation, who ended up in hot water because he confronted two seniors about their secret bonus-motivated agenda to open as many stores as possible, caring little about profit margins. This earned Larry the corporate buzz that he was rigid and not a team player. Larry was devastated about his new "dead man walking" status, but realized he'd shot himself in the foot.

When we playfully asked Larry to tell us his title again, he looked confused and replied, "RVP." We asked the titles of his two visitors. A knowing grin crept across his face as he sheepishly murmured, "Senior vice president." Then we asked, "We don't know that much about corporate structures, but can you get those guys fired?" Larry rolled his eyes: "No." He nodded as we said, "Larry, you just wounded the kings. You accused these guys of either being stupid or lacking integrity. The problem is . . . *the kings are still alive!* They know you're onto them, they have power and the ear of seniors at headquarters, and they want to take you down."

Larry could have argued against the store opening by just tackling the profit issue and demographics, ignoring the hidden agenda, and by blending agenda—offering *two* store openings a mile or two down the street. He "got it," but it still ticked Larry off as he threw his hands up in exasperation. "But I'm *right* about their true agenda! They *don't* care about the company as much as their own wallets!" Gradually, Larry was able to see that in this instance being "right" got him the booby prize. Being in charge of his reactions would have been more savvy than letting his emotional outrage or sense of nobility lure him into ambushing himself.

A Street-Smart Recipe for Hidden Agenda

We're not saying to never confront hidden agenda or to always play it safe. But choose your battles carefully and know whom you're wounding. Larry was impatient, impetuous, and lacked verbal discipline. Other than that, he handled the situation perfectly! Seriously, he meant well and acted on behalf of the company, but his inflated sense of integrity tarnished his image. He could have followed this recipe for handling hidden agendas: see them, stow them, survey them, and strategize them.

See Agenda. There's an entire carnival sideshow of freakish techniques people use to push a pet issue. But the clues to hidden agendas are sometimes in what *doesn't* happen. Sherlock Holmes once solved a murder by what *didn't* happen. Neighbors said dogs that usually barked to ward off visitors had been silent the night of the murder, so the sleuth deduced that the culprit was a family member. It might *not* be a coincidence when someone "forgets" to put your item on the meeting schedule or to mention your contributions at a meeting.

Stow Agenda. You've detected the hidden agenda. We beg you to "put a sock in it," as a beloved great-grandmother admonished her cantankerous but lovable husband whenever he went off on a rant. Just store away the hidden agenda in the back of your mind. Instead of losing control and divulging your instinct, stay in control—of yourself. We're advising you to *check*—check your mouth, and check the facts! What if you're wrong? What if the situation is not as underhanded as you suspect? Self-interest isn't always mutually exclusive to company welfare. So be prudent unless someone's hidden agendas start to smell like company compost.

Survey Agenda. Later, keep tabs on patterns you observe in the person, watching the kind of issues he supports or blocks. Ask your network of trusted people to verify your hypothesis about a hidden agenda. *You* might not be able to confirm it, but someone else can. Find an insider to clue you in on the person's motives and hot buttons. Then, when you *do* validate the agenda, *still* keep a sock in it!

Strategize about Agendas. There are many ways to skin a cat, or in this case, skin a snake. If you *do* decide to tackle the hidden agenda with the OP party, you'll benefit from the savvy influence vocabulary in the next chapter, which will help you navigate this dangerous territory without tripping ego land mines. Also, ask yourself the following strategic questions:

- *Will You Work the Hidden Agenda or the Business Issue?* Just because you know the hidden selfish motive doesn't mean you should name it. You can more safely address the presenting business issue. Larry should only have argued his profit concern based purely on the numbers, logic, and merits of his business case. He could have discouraged the store opening by pointing out the competition in the area, showing the density of nearby restaurants, and proposing alternative locations that would generate more revenue, all without naming the hidden agenda about bonuses. Steer clear of covert territory that's hard to prove in order to protect yourself in case you're wrong about a hidden agenda. Besides, even if you're correct, your adversary is probably cunning enough to cover his tracks so that you'll end up looking callous to accuse him of ulterior motives. What's your true business need? Is it to show him up as a sleaze or to help the company and avoid blocks to your own goals? Just stick with the facts.
- *Will You Win the Battle Only to Lose the War?* You may avoid the issue altogether if you'd win the battle but at too great a cost. Take into account the person's position power, political style, and your respective power networks. Unless you or the company will get into hot water if you *don't* work an issue, you may let some issues go. This might earn you the freedom to argue other issues without being seen as a constant nitpicker.
- *When and Where*? Plan when you'll surface the issue. In spite of our caution, if you must confront an actual hidden agenda, there are pros and cons to doing it in public. If you meet in private, the accused may appreciate the face-saving effort and respect for his

ego, or he could figure that you can't prove anything without witnesses. In a group, the risk is much greater of creating a public uproar, but you might want to do so for protection. Just know that either choice means you risk "wounding the king," especially if you do so in open battle.

Trust the Godfather's Savvy Verbal Discipline

Mario Puzo's book *The Godfather* became a stunning Francis Ford Coppola film in which Marlon Brando plays Vito Corleone, the Godfather, and James Caan portrays his oldest son, Sonny. In one fiery foreshadowing scene that leads to Vito later being shot, the Sollozzo family visits the Corleones to sell them on the idea of sharing the heroin trade for the city. They reason that the Sollozzos have the drugs and the Corleones have the police and judges in the palms of their hands. Vito says that he must say no because drugs are a "dirty" and "dangerous" business. The Sollozzo negotiator, attempting to win the Godfather's approval, offers to guarantee the Corleone's entire investment if they agree to this mobster partnership.

Sonny becomes excited about this enticement, leans forward in his seat, and expresses his renewed interest. Seeing his naïve son tip his cards, the Godfather calmly interrupts, tells his son to sit down, and apologizes for not teaching his children to avoid speaking out of turn: "I have a sentimental weakness for my children and I spoil them as you can see; they talk when they should listen." He then respectfully declines the Sollozzos' offer and graciously wishes them well in their venture. After the Sollozzo representative leaves, the Godfather says to Sonny, "Whattsa the matter with you? I think your brain is going soft. . . . *Never* tell anyone outside the family what you're thinking again!" Sonny's revealing his innermost thoughts later gets Vito ambushed since Sollozzo hopes with Vito out of the way, the heroin regime would be formed, because Sonny is "hot for the deal."

The saying goes "Keep your friends close and your enemies closer," which Corleone demonstrates with tact. It's always vital to practice verbal discipline in deciding how much of your *own* agenda to share, but especially when confronting *others'* hidden agendas. Don't be so outspoken about hidden agendas in peers or bosses that you go on their list for retaliation. Whether tempted by your Power of Ideas integrity or Power of Person ego, tread lightly around secret motives. Your friends may come and go, but your enemies accumulate.

Chapter 14

Respect Ego and Turf with Savvy Influence Vocabulary

"Pioneers Are the Ones with the Arrows Sticking Out"

We say this tongue in cheek to clients so they don't swallow whole every appeal for "honest, straight talk" without first chewing on who's dishing out this management morsel. Is the request for honesty coming from a leader like former New York City mayor Ed Koch, whose famous "How am I doing?" slogan was a symbol of openness, or from a leader more like Attila the Hun?

It's your job to *present ideas,* but sometimes these opportunities for shining become realities of fizzling. Other times, when seniors advance their ideas, you're not doing your job unless you *challenge ideas*—reality-testing a stance or bringing up factors that haven't been considered. Now you're really on thin ice, but treading lightly doesn't mean you can just pretend the boss hasn't proposed a bonehead approach.

Whether these situations are career catapults or career catastrophes hinges partly on the language tools you'll now refine. These savvy influence vocabulary tools determine whether as a carpenter you build yourself a bridge to others or construct a box (a wooden box). Sometimes, the person you need to approach is so vengeful and hotheaded that you need to weigh the pros and cons of whether even to speak the truth, since you could end up as a pioneer with arrows sticking out. For self-protection, we'll wind up this chapter by reminding you to respect ego and turf.

Words Have Impact

For decades, we've raised companies' "emotional intelligence" by teaching listening and speaking skills, but interpersonal performance improvement falls outside the scope of this book. While *Survival of the Savvy* mainly examines organizational influence at a strategic level, this chapter treats it from a tactical vantage point. Nevertheless, our communication focus stems from a political rationale more than from a human relations perspective. Later, when we focus on ethical lobbying, we'll strategize the *content* of your influence efforts. For now, let's hone your political *vocabulary,* because the words you use have tremendous impact:

- *Words Create a Power Image*. Words convey power or impotence, confidence or insecurity. Your ideas must make a strong business case (remember the "Where's the beef?" TV commercial), but the actual vocabulary you use to sell your content also creates either a favorable or unfavorable aura.
- *Words Avoid "Wounding the King."* Accessing a full range of savvy influence vocabulary prevents you from insulting an ego-sensitive senior, colleague, or customer. In a heartbeat your word choice can trigger a stakeholder to dismiss your *idea,* or dismiss *you*.
- *Words Prevent You from Giving Ammunition*. If you say something the wrong way to the wrong person, some people will go after you. Don't provide them with the bullets they need to bring you down. The wrong language in a public meeting or e-mail becomes evidence to justify their attempts to sabotage you. Cap-

italized words in writing can have the same effect as yelling in oral communication. Watch out for poorly selected phrases in e-mails: "You're OFF BASE on this system integration scheme." "There's NO WAY the boss will even consider this fantasyland budget until R&D is slashed!" The capitalized words are made even more inflammatory by adding provocative descriptors such as *scheme* and *fantasyland.* You've just handed a crafty, competitive colleague a smoking gun to forward to cronies while saying, "See how unprofessional and judgmental Joe is? He's not even giving you or me a chance."

We've seen how your *internal* Self-Talk word choice has remarkable *self*-influence, so now we're reminding you how much your *external* word choice influences *others*. Since words can empower you or *dis*empower you, let's troubleshoot your influence repertoire by exploring weak and harsh influence vocabulary as different from balanced and firm language.

The Pussycat Factor: Weak Vocabulary

In some cultures being apologetic is desirable, such as Japan or even in parts of the U.S. Midwest. According to Deborah Tannen's research in *Talking from 9 to 5,* women more than men use qualifying language and soften needed criticism with praise, by being less direct, or by nurturing a receiver's feelings. Politically less powerful people, regardless of gender, can screen out self-diminishing phrasing that detracts from their ideas:

- *Tentative:* kind of; sort of; I think maybe; if it's OK with you.
- *Apologetic:* I hate to bother you, but; I'm sorry I haven't really thought this through; my team didn't have time to rehearse this presentation.
- *Self-Discounting:* this is outside my expertise, but; I'm not the best person at financials, but; here goes nothing; you probably won't agree with me, but.

- *Ambivalent:* I might be wrong since I keep second guessing myself; would it be crazy for me to suggest; I keep flip-flopping on the best approach to take.
- *Vague:* Using general, global statements without specific recommendations avoids risking a clear stand. This comes off as all fluff, and smart people see it for what it is—a stalling tactic based on lack of expertise or confidence.

Sometimes you'll purposely use weak vocabulary approaches to achieve an objective. You may want to be self-deprecating to convey humility if you have a reputation for being abrupt. You might purposely lower expectations by qualifying the parameters of your preparation, so that listeners admire the risk you've taken in presenting a work in progress. You may intentionally keep an early stance vague so that no one opposes you.

However, weak language usually lowers respect from others, especially more powerful and politically oriented associates. Don't open the door for them to be dismissive or view you as lacking credence and impact. If an Overly Political (OP) senior is teeter-tottering in his perception of your power image, soft vocabulary may tip the scales just enough to put you on his "diss-miss" list. Stronger vocabulary helps you manage impressions and strengthen your power image.

The Piss-Off Factor: Harsh Vocabulary

There's a fine line between being confident and becoming curt or gruff. Harsh vocabulary is occasionally the right choice, but usually it erodes rapport, shuts down negotiations, alienates or silences teams, and endangers careers. Top managers want your ideas, but they don't want them shoved down their throats. Tough, callous language with a Less Political superior may merely lead to his rejecting your recommendation. But if you cross the line with the wrong senior, you can end up on his hit list. We've seen people cost themselves a huge promotion with a couple of ill-conceived phrases.

Remember, egomaniacal people who also have position power receive a steady diet of accommodating language, so they may not be used to forthright language and points of view. They may project more aggressiveness onto your vocabulary than you intend. You're walking on thin ice if passion for your idea or your own ego leads you to any of the following phrasing:

- *Autocratic or Threatening:* this is how it's going to go down; I've decided and I expect cooperation; if you won't do what I'm asking, I'll find someone who wants the job; I'm not asking you, I'm telling you; as head honcho around here, I'm mandating that we; don't cross me on this or you'll be sorry; if you have a problem with my proposal, talk to Danielson, because he's behind this; this is policy and we're not going to break rank; your insubordination is being duly noted.
- *Opinionated:* obviously, the right strategy is; I know what I'm talking about; I went to Wharton, and the school of thought there was always; I've been around here for eleven years so I think I know a little something about the company culture; the facts plainly show; trust me on this, I ought to know.
- *Critical or Abusive:* you're being so shortsighted; this is a waste of my time; you're being penny-pinching by being unwilling to invest in the future; that idea is silly; how reckless; did you stay up all night to dream up that harebrained idea?; oh, I can't wait to hear what you have up your sleeve now, Swami.
- *Blaming:* come on, suck it up and take a risk instead of always wimping out; you didn't do your homework; I wouldn't have to authorize overtime if it wasn't for your faulty capacity plan; you blew it on the projections, so now we have to.
- *Exaggerated:* this is the *only* way to go; *anyone* can see we should just; here's what we *have* to do; if we meet with the consumer group, it'll be a *total* disaster; what I'm proposing is *the* answer to our problems; we should *never* acknowledge any truth in the union leaders' concerns, since that *always* leads to Pandora's box being opened.

Common Sense Isn't Always Common Practice

You might feel insulted by the above reminders, since everyone knows to avoid being abusive, disrespectful, or blaming. Here's the problem—common sense isn't always common practice. In a high-stakes discussion, you may not be at your best. Years ago, author Michael Morgenstern made headlines when he was fined $10,000 for punching his girlfriend in the face. This made national news because of its irony in that Morgenstern had written the bestseller *How to Make Love to a Woman*. We sometimes *know* much better than we *do!*

This language issue is subtler than it looks. Even Power of Ideas leaders who shun being blatantly abusive can accidentally cross the line into different kinds of harsh vocabulary. Their sense of rightness about their ideas (their focus on "substance power") may lure them into sounding too opinionated, matter-of-fact, or absolutist:

- "This one's a no-brainer . . ." You've insulted a senior with less technological know-how.
- "Anyone can see the liability issues . . ." The other person feels slighted since she's less aware of current employment law than the human resources left-sider.
- "We *have* to use a damage-control strategy that's less reliant on new technology . . ." A touchy CEO reads this harmless language convention as presumptuous and barks, "No, we don't *have* to do anything, and by the way, do you know who you're talking to?"

Vocab Rehab: Presenting Ideas with Firm Language

Avoiding either weak or harsh vocabulary, the balanced Power of Savvy leader aims for firmness in his word choice. Let's put a magnifying glass on firm vocabulary to further calibrate it. Within the firm range, you can choose either "invitation" or "conviction" language. Again be strategic, based upon your audience. Even balanced wording can detonate the "fight" response in an ego-sensitive, power-oriented, and turf-protective extreme Power of Person individual. So it's key to use judgment even with how firm to be, modulating judiciously between "invitation" and "conviction" word choices.

• *Invitation.* Correlated more with the left side of the Organizational Savvy Continuum (but appropriately so, not weak), this word choice is more provisional and safer with a defensive Borderline Overly Political or clearly Overly Political person. Since you might threaten her even though you're being firm, *not* harsh, play it safe by using phrases like these: *what if; would it be possible; one alternative we might explore; I'd appreciate your ideas on a direction; we're leaning toward this vendor but need your input and guidance.*

These invitation-style lead-ins within the firm language range still present your recommendations but in a more *ask*-oriented manner. You're not apologizing—just showing respect by inviting the other's consideration. You stop short of venturing into the weak or wimpy range. It's the discreet option when your recipient is power-focused, you sense tension in the room, or you're unsure and cautious about the reaction. It's wise to state your view more deferentially and then to gradually ramp up your fervor. Why jeopardize your position right off the bat with too strong a stance? It's hard to backpedal when you've overstepped your bounds.

• *Conviction.* Now we edge toward the right side of the Organizational Savvy Continuum yet remain within the firm vocabulary range. Conviction language avoids being harsh (OP), but still conveys strength and self-assurance to generate a power impression. You're stating your case in a bolder, *tell*-oriented fashion: *I recommend; we strongly suggest; my advice is that we; based on my experience; our point of view is.* Many Power of Person seniors respond well when you're authoritative without being presumptuous. If you don't cross the line into harsh wording, this more declarative method of packaging your ideas raises seniors' estimation of you as you earn task-level trust.

The conviction flavor of vocabulary is advisable when you know your audience respects self-assurance and admires people who take a stand. If a senior *asks* for your input, he's saying that he considers you the consultant and wants your expertise. So there's no need to soften your stance through invitation language. Lean into a conviction tenor if you're worried that a Power of Person senior doesn't hold you with high regard power-wise and you want to put your best foot forward with a slightly more forceful posture.

Now Tell Your Face

Kindergartener Johnny raises his hand and shyly asks his tenured teacher of twenty-nine years, "Ms. Grissom, do you like your job teaching?" A bit taken aback, the burned-out veteran answers, "Why, of course I do, Jonathan." An awkward silence follows and Johnny murmurs, "Then why don't you tell your face?" Johnny only believes his teacher's words if her body language is congruent with her answer.

You can sabotage your firm influence vocabulary if you forget to accent your words with confident body language and a committed-sounding vocal rate, tone, and volume. Research shows that emotional impact experienced from a message depends up to 90 percent upon nonverbal and vocal elements over actual content. If you carefully select *invitation* language to counteract corporate buzz that you're "intimidating," but speak with a clenched fist and abrupt clip to your voice, people will still sense a gruff demeanor. You can also betray purposefully selected *conviction* language with insecure stammering or tentative eye contact.

Challenge Ideas with the Balanced Response Technique

Someone suggests a direction you know is flawed or incomplete. You must get her to see factors that she's ignoring, explore other options, or drop the strategy altogether. How do you reality-test the idea without becoming the heavy? With a boss, you don't want to commit a career-limiting move. With a peer or subordinate, you don't want to alienate the person or create bad press in the corporate airwaves that you are argumentative or judgmental.

A hasty person on either side of the Organizational Savvy Continuum reacts like a bull in a china shop when challenging ideas. The Power of Ideas style snaps back with a substance knockout factor, stopping his boss dead in her tracks: "But you're not anticipating the lawyers' reactions" or "We tried that a few years ago and it didn't work." The Power of Person style gets jittery about the top-floor power elite's response and tries to slow his manager's momentum by name-dropping: "Look, I don't think Louise will ever stand for this" or "What makes you think Katie would ever let Mark implement a new system without an RFP?"

Unskilled rebuttals trigger the ego radar of more defensive people to go into red alert mode. We need a way to sneak input past the Overly Political (OP) or Borderline Overly Political (BOP) individual who is trawling for insults that aren't even there. The stealthy Power of Savvy person knows how to constructively criticize the ideas of *any* senior, regardless of political style, and of *any* BOP or OP, regardless of rank. Even when endorsing an idea but giving suggestions for enrichments, package your reactions with the protective bubble wrap of a technique we call the "Balanced Response."

This skill simply holds up the pros and cons of an idea, giving each side a fair shake even as you challenge or enrich it. This calls to mind the scales of justice, giving an idea its day in court. You still use firm vocabulary, but embed it in a special Balanced Response structure. You will fly under the radar of ego and have a greater chance of being heard without negative repercussions. The steps are to (1) listen empathically to the idea, (2) sincerely focus on the merits of the idea, (3) firmly surface your concerns, and (4) avoid the words *but* and *problem.*

Listen Empathically to the Idea. Nonjudgmentally paraphrase the person's thoughts and feelings so that he feels fully heard and knows that you really understand his viewpoint before responding to it. Let's say your manager wants to redesign the monthly financial consolidation reporting process so that every department submits its numbers in its own format to minimize hassle. Use active listening skills to "reflect back" the essence of his idea, showing empathy for his emotions and rationale until he signals you've tracked him (*not* necessarily agreed):

> Joe, you seem confident that we'll build stronger networking relationships with each business unit if we shift from our common, universal monthly financial reporting template to a format that's more customized to each function's needs.

You restate the boss's thoughts and feelings until he gives some signal that you've understood his perspective. You now pause, showing that you're letting his proposal sink in and that you weren't just going through the motions of listening. "The skill of reflective listening is one of those 'soft skills' that have recently gained credence as driving business results," according to Jim Bolton, CEO of Ridge Associates, one of many excellent consulting firms that deliver rigorous training on this deceptively challenging corporate competency.

Sincerely Focus on the Merits of the Idea. Genuinely voice whatever you see as positive elements in the idea. Emphasize the merits with specifics and sincerity versus providing token lip service. Prove that you've fully absorbed the concept and honestly see the benefits of the suggestion. You're showing a Power of Person individual due respect for image, turf, and ego. You're showing a Power of Ideas colleague substantive respect. Through this good-faith display of how you're on board with certain aspects of the idea, you better prepare the other person to also hear your concerns or disagreement. To continue with the financial reporting template idea:

> Joe, I'm with you on the value of each business head seeing us adapt to their world. They always complain finance is locked in our ivory tower, out of touch. So I like the approach from a political perspective. We'd be forced to really understand each area's business from the inside out as we decipher their figures. I can also see some risk-management advantages of letting each department speak its own language to us, since they'll have their guard down.

This focus-on-the-merits step goes way beyond transparent gimmickry or global statements—empty phrases like "Great idea," "I can see you've put a lot of thought into this," or "Your idea has real merit." These platitudes are meaningless unless you go past them, expressing the idea's specific merits (even if you'll later show them as overshadowed by the downsides). This step helps you think in less black-and-white terms, so that you see the ambiguity that is corporate life.

The Balanced Response mentality can become a liberating way to find something positive in any idea. If you agree with the goal, say so. If you understand the rationale behind the idea, cite it. If you see the obvious passion or level of preparation that went into an argument, appreciate this. If you disagree with the purpose or end but admire the advanced thinking behind the tactics, reinforce it. If the actual formatting or packaging of the idea is impressive, show approval. If the person simply had the chutzpah to dream up an approach so off-the-wall, award some *cojónes* points! ("Don, I have to hand it to you. You don't back off of controversial moves. That's what makes us a market leader in innovation.")

Firmly Surface Your Concerns. You've now earned the right to respond with any downside points. You're taking this risk so the boss sees what he hasn't factored in, what he might face in moving ahead. You're raising issues tactfully, after first listening and identifying what you like about his idea, so he's not tuned out:

> Joe, you've probably already factored this in, but just to be sure, have we considered the extra time it'll take our department to compile, process, and distribute the monthly report if we're comparing apples and oranges? I'm worried the goodwill we build by working more closely with groups could be counteracted by delays in completing consolidation reports. Of course, a way around this challenge would be overtime for staff or devising a system that transposes the diverse data into the new integrated methodology. Could we explore some of these possibilities?

Notice that we show good faith by suggesting possible ways to address any concern we surface. We also use the "invitation" end of the firm-vocabulary range, stating our issues in the form of a provisionally stated concern and question. However, we can also use the "conviction" approach to firmly state concerns, still without totally dismissing a proposal. So while using the Balanced Response, we still continue to modulate our vocabulary and we consider the receiver's political style and position power.

Moving away from the financial reporting example, you can use *invitation*-oriented sentence stems to surface concerns. They might include phrases such as "Considering the reactions we might get from the union, *do you think we should consider* checking in with the representatives first?" "*Are you as worried as I am about* the resistance we typically get from QA about compliance issues?" "*How concerned are you about* the overtime costs we'll face if we shoot for this 24-7 standard for maintenance of the equipment?"

On the other hand, sample *conviction*-slanted lead-in phrases are "Steve, we agree about the upside of conducting a public forum given the furor. *I'm concerned about* how local media could seize on the forum to push their editorial views." "Martha, *a challenge we'll face* in training the service reps in listening skills is that call handle time will initially increase while they feel awkward with new skills." "Louise, *if you're serious* about delaying the layoff announcement, *an issue we may face* is rumors circulating and the potential resentment when we finally break the news."

Avoid the Words But *and* Problem. In linking step 2's *merits* and step 3's *concerns,* choose a word other than *but* or any of its cousins, such as *however* or *nevertheless. But* discounts everything you say before it: "Tom, I like your great-looking tie, *but* those shoes . . ." What's Tom focusing on, his tie or shoes? The word *but* is a huge eraser, undoing the empathy of step 1's "listen empathically" and step 2's "focus on merits." Also notice that we avoid the word *problem.* It might be a sheer matter of semantics, but some seniors bristle at this word as if it were profane. You can argue this word is not a "problem" if the tone of voice is all right. We prefer playing it safe by reframing *problem* into *challenge, concern, issue, difficulty, obstacle,* or *factor to consider.*

Balancing, Not Copping Out. You are not shying away from strongly stating your reservations when you use the Balanced Response format. You can reject the idea outright, just in a more palatable, less dangerous manner. You might even speak to your boss after a meeting where you used this tactful technique to disagree further: "Joe, I didn't want to say this in the group, but I actually feel more strongly than I let on during the meeting. I have three serious reservations about the customized finance report . . ." At first glance this approach looks dangerous, but what might you accomplish? You prove that you respect your manager's image—you didn't want to show him up—and that you have the courage to tell it like it is. Most managers appreciate the deference while valuing your strength of will in taking this risk.

Your goal is to lower the odds of adding insult to injury, as well as *injury* to *insult*. We're purposely switching the wording order of this cliché. You want to prevent the *injury* of retaliation you could suffer when you disagree with a senior, withhold 100 percent agreement, or show that he hasn't fully analyzed a situation. The *insult* is the nonexistent, imaginary one that your receiver may read into the situation. The Balanced Response avoids adding injury to insult.

Treat Hyperactive Ego Glands

I have never been hurt by anything I didn't say.

—CALVIN COOLIDGE

Chuck, a Borderline Under Political (BUP) engineer, works under Carla, an Overly Political (OP) information systems director who was the architect of a major technology infrastructure she installed three years ago. Chuck approaches Carla with needed upgrades to the system. She resists the changes, gets defensive, and sees Chuck's ideas as criticism of her intellect. Chuck means well, coming from a "substance power" perspective, but winds up in hot water as his boss thinks, "How will this make me look? Why didn't I think of this idea? How will I look for not thinking of this?" Meanwhile, the technology atrophies, the company suffers, and word gets out to "just lie low."

Carla might even perceive Chuck's idea as threatening her power base and either sabotage him overtly or undermine him. She may blindside Chuck by claiming his ideas as her own or embellishing her role in formulating them. Since Carla filters any proposal through her intense need to look good, Chuck needs to suggest the upgrades with great care and interpersonal dexterity. You already know how to incorporate savvy influence vocabulary to firmly present and use the Balanced Response technique to challenge ideas; but sometimes an OP ego is so fragile, it is like a frayed wire ready to short-circuit. Chuck may need to use extra tactics:

- *Reinforce Her Contribution*. "The system was great when you devised it. We would have been in trouble without it. But something you said to me yesterday got me thinking."
- *Plant the Seeds for Her to Think of the Idea*. "Have you had any time to think about the current configuration of the system installation given the new factors that exist?"
- *Stroke Her Ego*. "I was wondering if you had time to help me

think through some potential enrichments to the system since you're the resident technology guru."

- *Face-Saving Lead-ins.* Get used to injecting phrases like *as you know* or *you've probably already been thinking this, but . . .*
- *Remove Any Inkling of Blame.* "There's no way anyone could have predicted the growth we've had since the system conversion, not to mention changes in peripheral technology. But since these variables have entered the picture, I'm wondering . . ."
- *Link Your Idea to Image.* "I'm excited about the visibility and kudos these upgrades will get our function" (aka, "Hey, boss, do you realize how great I can make you look?").
- *Use* We *Language.* Partnering with the senior lowers her feelings of blame or criticism and helps you gain some visibility and credit if she likes your idea.

A major Under Political style risk is to so revere integrity that verbal discipline goes out the window. The peril is then in unwittingly triggering a hypersensitive ego. Carefully plan your approach to reduce the danger of political fallout. Keep the Overly Political (OP) boss informed and *never* let him think you're going around him. If you bring in a consultant, ask if the OP wants to select one to show that you respect his turf. This face-saving dance and tiptoeing around turf will be less annoying if you can reframe image-sensitive people—these self-protective thorns in your side—poor souls who happen to have hyperactive, oversecreting ego glands. It's not their fault. They need your help!

Your challenge is reminiscent of the Rogers and Hammerstein musical *The King and I,* in which Anna helps the king of Siam to save face due to his massive ego. She learns that he has earned the reputation (buzz) as a "barbarian" who is out of touch with the rest of the world. England is considering making Siam a protectorate. To save the king from himself, she wants to suggest that he invite the ambassador from England and his entourage to a fancy state dinner featuring a dance to *Uncle Tom's Cabin* to prove that he is cultured. Anna knows the pompous king will never agree if the idea comes from her, so she implies that since he is wise and all-knowing he must already have a plan for what to do about his quandary. The king says, "You guess." So Anna bows to his helpless appeal for assistance by pretending to play a guessing game as she feeds him the answers to his dilemma. The king, with arms folded in grand repose, listens to Anna "guess" that "you will not fight with your visitors" from England but will instead "give a banquet in their honor. You will entertain them in a grand manner. In this way, you will make them all witnesses in your favor. They will return and report to the queen that you are most certainly *not* a barbarian." The king (with secret relief) retorts, "This is what I shall have intended to do!" Anna plays the king like a violin.

Reframing "Manipulation"

We can almost hear your thoughts screaming, "What a pain in the butt! This is a nuisance to have to play this game instead of just telling this blowhard he's full of crap. Are you kidding me? If I have to help him save face anymore, I won't be able to look at my *own* face in the mirror." Change your Self-Talk or you'll drive yourself crazy maneuvering around ego-trippers' defensive reactions. Judgmental attitudes about respecting ego and turf might also include worrying that you are "manipulating," but don't we also manipulate objects to make them function more effectively? Keep in mind that the word *manipulate* has many definitions, including these from a Webster's dictionary:

ma-nip-u-late

1. to work, operate, or treat with or as with the hand or hands; handle or use, especially with skill
2. to manage or control artfully or by shrewd use of influence, often in an unfair or fraudulent way
3. to falsify for one's own purpose or profit

Only the second and third definitions connote unethical means or ends. Even the first part of definition 2 above can be noble. It's the "unfair," "fraudulent," and "falsify" that fall outside the realm of integrity. Remember that "unfair" doesn't simply represent not telling the person what you are doing. It must also involve ill will and deceit against the other's best interests. With power-hungry political tyrants, you're influencing a positive course of action for the organization. You're assisting an ego-challenged despot to avoid his own self-defeating overreactions and paranoid self-protective shields. You're treating his hyperactive ego gland.

"Do I Speak the Truth or Defer to Ego?"

The Power of Savvy political style involves deciding daily when to kiss up or get kissed off, whether to dummy up or *be* a dummy by not appeasing an ego-tripper. Surviving *and* thriving at times means swallowing your own ego, but this is the price of the dream. You can win the game without shame if you remember at times to heed Abraham Lincoln's advice: "It is better to say nothing and be thought a fool, than to say something and remove all doubt." We can't tell you when to be silent. Remember the answer to every single question you may have about when and how to implement the strategies in this book: *it depends*. You will decide whether to speak truth to power or defer to ego, but when you *do* take the risk, the savvy influence tactics we've reviewed can help you save your idea as well as your skin.

Chapter 15

Ethical Lobbying

The Price of the Dream

The Power of Savvy leader embraces politics as a necessary, invigorating arena of corporate influence in which to sell ideas, get deserved credit, receive optimal consideration for career advancement, and win resources or budget for his team. Under Political (UP) leaders need to shift their blocking attitudes to gain increased influence and impact, realizing that ideas themselves may *not* be compelling enough on their own. Sometimes, for ideas to bear fruit and results to flourish, recommendations need to be prepositioned and pre-sold through ethical lobbying. Conversely, power-tripping leaders can increase their integrity, realizing that it's not always fair or wise to approach key stakeholders beforehand.

Group decision-making meetings are sometimes where the action is, and sometimes are not. Underpersuasive individuals lose endorsements for the ideas they champion by waiting until the formal meeting as others are meeting *before* the meeting. Meanwhile, overzealous counterparts turn off others by jumping the gun or going too far in their attempts to secure prior approval. This chapter elevates influence skills beyond last chapter's language techniques by mapping out a step-by-step strategy to impact stakeholders through ethical lobbying.

You're Not on Capitol Hill!

Don't worry. You haven't just switched careers to join a Washington, D.C., lobbying group or Congress, where every idea is lobbied and *then* groups lobby for the lobbying groups. If lobbying conjures up images of unethical manipulators supporting agendas they philosophically oppose just to win votes, please let this association float down the river. Nothing we suggest means compromising your value system. Our definition of organizational politics includes using formal *and* informal avenues for getting things done in organizations. But this is not to be confused with "playing politics"—a catchphrase used to describe untrustworthy people who lack substance or scruples. Lobbying is ethical if you don't hide that you're seeking approval and if you don't exchange favors by betraying your value system. You can play aboveboard and retain your integrity, supporting causes that are good for the organization.

Organizational savvy includes reading what's politically correct in your company. If an issue really *will* be first discussed at a decision-making meeting, it's savvier to wait until that sanctioned forum. You'd be silly to break the unwritten rules. But if people are getting the inside track on you by persuading others in advance as you lose your edge, you'll be behind the eight ball by not joining the crowd. What are the ingredients of ethical lobbying?

Manage Your Political-Favors Bank Account

Stephen Covey's self-help landmark, *The Seven Habits of Highly Effective People,* describes the "emotional bank accounts" we have with everyone we know. Covey says we constantly make positive relationship deposits through character and caring, or negative withdrawals through disrespect and mistreatment. We add a political spin to this bank account metaphor by including the informal chit system that exists in organizations. The familiar phrase "I cashed in a lot of favors on that one" confirms that we operate in a support system partly dependent upon the balance in our political-favors bank account. Organizational influence partly involves collaboration, alliances, and favors. But it doesn't have to wind up in smoke-filled back rooms characterized by the adage "Scratch my back and I'll scratch yours." It's just human nature and an organizational reality that giving support is appreciated and raises the odds that a powerful colleague might become an ally. To reap the best return on your political bank account investment, practice these accounting principles.

Remember—You're Still a Good Person! Just because you understand favors doesn't make you opportunistic. You won't only interact with people who can help you or only support someone with strings attached with ulterior motives. If the idea of exchanging chits or favors connotes ruthless ledger-keeping, reframe it as helping others. We all want to do the right thing and help others, and there's a lot to be said for corporate karma. If positive payback kicks in and you derive future benefit, so be it. Maybe you deserve it.

Back to Networking. Build your network with an eye toward gathering a surplus in your political-favors bank account and paving the way for ethical lobbying. The wider the "net" in your network, the more potential "fish" you catch to support your ideas. Support comes from surprising places, like an executive administrative assistant who is critical to your political stock regardless of position power. Mind how you treat *everyone*. Word travels fast and the grapevine can become awfully thorny. We know a consultant who was blackballed from high-level construction assignments at an engineering company because he was curt with someone who he didn't realize was a top manager. Yet, we know that you won't network callously—using some people, dropping others you don't need, or only helping those who are linked to power. You're not like the faker at the cocktail party feigning interest while scanning the room for a more important person.

The Profit of Favors. Gaining favor through favors doesn't make you a Machiavellian if your heart's in the right place. Be available to people and invite them to call you after hours. They won't actually call at 3 a.m., but it makes an impression when you're willing to go the extra mile. Lend support to others' ideas and projects. If you can't devote time to a project, you can still visibly endorse work and ideas in meetings and conversation. Look for ways to help people save face and get out of jams. Pitch in at the eleventh hour if colleagues are in trouble. You're also helping your company by doing these favors. But organizational savvy entails hawk-eyed awareness of your impact. Be careful about whom you support and whom you cross when lending a favor or supporting an ally. Weigh the potential political consequences before voicing approval if someone's good idea is being challenged. You might be building up your influence credit rating with one person while simultaneously creating a deficit with another. Don't blindly grant favors without knowing whose list you could end up on for vengeance.

Appreciation Is an Account Asset. Don't underestimate the value of expressing strong appreciation when people do *you* favors. While you don't want to show grudges, you do want to show gratitude. If you don't show sufficient appreciation, you may be committing a major faux pas. Send thank-you notes with copies to key people, so your benefactor knows you took extra steps to broadcast his help and team-player status. Even if the person doesn't consciously expect acknowledgment and even appears to shun it, don't mistake modesty ("It was nothing, just part of the job") for lack of appreciation for *your* appreciation.

Sabotage Destroys Your Political Bank Account. Be careful to avoid accidental sabotage. You may unwittingly harm a person important to your success. We've said a favor for one person can ignite resentment in another who feels slighted or dislikes the person you help. Sometimes you'll blow it—misspeak, unknowingly blemish someone's strategy, divulge information you forget is confidential. If you hurt someone's interests or feelings, immediately own up to the mistake or it may be seen as conscious sabotage. Apologize and assist in salvaging the situation. Sometimes we add insult to injury because we're so embarrassed that we procrastinate having an uncomfortable conversation. Then the misdeed snowballs in our minds, and we further hide from it. Now we've really painted ourselves into a corner.

Associates may regard you as lowering your political bank account balance with them if you're too busy to lobby for their venture or you have already committed to supporting a competitor's stance. Don't burn bridges if you can't support colleagues or must turn down their request. When rejecting a request for help, show that you've carefully considered the appeal and demonstrate your goodwill while graciously declining support at this time. A "no" right now doesn't need to close the door for future collaboration.

Bridges can also be burned when others inadvertently sabotage *you,* even though you forgive them. They clumsily smudge an idea you express in a meeting, receive funding that decreases resources for your team, or decline your appeal for support. Even if you may totally understand, some people become paranoid on you and spiral the situation into a much bigger deal. They feel so guilty that they avoid you, accuse you of being angry, or think you'll sabotage them, so they act in self-defense. To help them to save face, reassure them, and acknowledge that reasonable people can end up on opposite sides of issues. Let them know you believe that life is for *giving* and *forgiving*.

Devise Your Game Plan: Analyze the Political Landscape

Once you have a surplus of work favors with your network, don't just wing it or explain your idea the same way for every conversation (just as you wouldn't do for Elevator Speeches). Effective lobbying requires surveying the political horizon, mapping out the power and influence relationships involved, anticipating levels of support or objection, and strategizing the best approach for persuading each stakeholder. You act less like a skeet shooter with a quick trigger finger and more like a head coach for a football team. You scout and watch film on the other team to understand how they play the game, then you script a tailored game plan that matches up best for that unique team. Salespeople among our readers may be thinking, "Oh, yeah. In other words, *sell*!" That's accurate reframing, but add political savvy to your usual selling efforts so that you draw up a lobbying game plan for each issue, decision-maker, and influencer.

Political Climate and Timing. When should you tackle this issue? How will the overall climate in the organization be affected by your idea? Is the company so turbulent or distracted that it's a bad time to make your recommendation? What forces support you in presenting your agenda now and what factors dictate patience? For example, is it wise to push for labor-intensive process improvements while people are working pedal-to-the-metal to finish a new-product release? Should you lobby to send all employees through a new corporate identity orientation when workforce reduction announcements are looming? You might come across as rearranging the deck chairs on the *Titanic*!

Influence and Power. On a scale of one to ten, what is each stakeholder's formal position power or informal influence? Judge how much her official or unofficial rank or status matters for ultimate project go-ahead. Take into account approval chains, connections, and subject matter expertise for the given issue. Decide who matters most for achieving your critical mass of support. In a time crunch, save less influential people for later or don't even worry about securing their advance support, especially if you determine that the person is dead set against your initiative.

Political Style. What is the decision-maker's placement on the Organizational Savvy Continuum? If she has a Power of Ideas style, adjust the positioning of your idea to provide more substantive rationale. If she has a Power of Person style, factor in more power and image considerations. Be especially careful to strategize for the extreme spots on the Continuum. Be careful to avoid setting off the Borderline Overly Political (BOP) or Overly Political (OP) styles' turf and ego alarm, and be wary of the Borderline Under Political (BUP) and Under Political (UP) styles' potential content-level turnoffs. Political style also influences your influence-vocabulary selection, how much attention you give to presentation packaging, and whether you first need endorsement by powerful others before lobbying a certain individual.

Your Own Influence, Power, and Political Style. How does the stakeholder view your formal or informal status and your placement on the Organizational Savvy Continuum? Is your power and influence greater, less than, or equal to the person's you're lobbying? For this issue, does it matter? Remember your own potential blind spots when you ponder this question.

Your Political Favors Bank Account. Do you have enough of a surplus to approach this person? Have you ever sabotaged this stakeholder? Does she view you as neutral, an enemy, or an ally? Do you possess enough power to earn her attention even if the networking relationship is absent or negative? If she has formal or informal influence and your account is overdrawn, you may need to pave the way by first regaining goodwill. You may even need to develop a "taste for crow" as you approach this player.

Agreement Level. What's the stakeholder's anticipated level of agreement or disagreement with your idea? Are you privy to any insider information from your trusted network? Has the person supported ideas similar to yours? Are there any hints in presentations on related issues that can help you project how she may react? Consider contacting those people you know will lend support, because if they hear you've met with other key stakeholders and not them, they could feel slighted, taken for granted, or out of the loop. Besides, your strongest allies may help you coplan how to secure further support.

Changeability. Regardless of her current attitude, what's the stakeholder's likely flexibility on the issue you're lobbying? This is a subjective judgment informed by her political style, your knowledge of past patterns, and the current status of your political balance sheet with her. How often have you seen her vacillate? Is she open-minded or does she refuse to budge once she's made up her mind? You might decide to cut your losses after unsuccessful initial lobbying, or not even invest time in approaching her at all.

Power Networks and Connections. What are the connections between this person and others critical to project approval? You may or may not mention who else is in favor of your lobbying idea. If you strategically reference a knowledgeable person who has promised support, LP people might respect your ally's expertise. An MP individual might be more inclined to throw you his support if the name you drop is someone with power. On the other hand, he might not like your supporter or might have political reasons for not buying into an issue regardless of other endorsements. Is this stakeholder someone who can help you influence another stakeholder? Based upon your analysis, decide the ideal sequence for approaching your pool of decision-makers.

Blend Agendas. People do things for their reasons, not ours. The word benefit means "good fit," so package your ideas in ways that meet others' business needs and priorities. Blend your idea with the agendas you've analyzed as relevant to your stakeholder. Properly "tee up" your idea like a golfer preparing his ball for a drive. Master salespeople ethically reposition their product slightly differently to highlight how it supports various buyers' unique needs.

Presumably, by now you know your stakeholders' business hot buttons because you have networked and learned their goals long before any lobbying situation.

Now, size up which of their goals, charters, objectives, performance issues, and business strategies link well to your lobbying idea. Many of your stakeholder's biases may be irrelevant to your idea or won't fit logically, but others may tie in easily. Get into the habit of explicitly linking your idea, initiative, or program with your decision-maker's efforts. Use some sort of boilerplate sentence such as "*An idea that fits well with your goal of* [quickly integrating the two cultures of our newly merged company populations] *is my idea for* [introducing ongoing team-building workshops], *which addresses your needs by* [establishing monthly cross-functional communication sessions, which will get people from both organizations talking, reduce negative judgments, and help us all see we aren't so different]."

In ethical lobbying, you want to blend agendas the way a consultative salesperson does. High-integrity salespeople seek to understand customer needs before positioning a product or program. For instance, we know a savvy internal corporate-training manager who teaches listening skills. He has ethically linked his listening skills workshops to a variety of company business needs:

- To *retention concerns,* since poor communication with one's manager causes attrition.
- To *sales growth,* since listening increases rapport, explores customer needs, defuses objections, and makes sales presentations more relationship-oriented.
- To *teamwork and morale* improvement, since listening improves rapport and trust.
- To *profit,* since listening reduces bottom-line-draining errors.
- To *negotiating skills,* since listening surfaces others' underlying positions.

- To *quality* programs, since facilitators need listening as a group process skill.
- To *service,* since understanding customer expectations is essential to world-class service.
- To *diversity,* since empathy creates tolerance and acceptance of individual differences.

The comedian George Carlin understands how it all works: "The environmentalists finally got it right. They figured out that no one wanted to give any money to swamps and jungles. So now they call it 'wetlands' and 'rain forests.'" But you're not just a spin doctor playing a word game. Go past verbal cosmetics to make true substantive links, showing exactly how your plans align with the other's goals. You're not some "Slick Willie" camouflaging an idea with words to slip it past someone who wouldn't otherwise approve it. That tactic will bite you next time around.

A helpful filter for discovering a stakeholder agenda that might relate to your idea is to adopt the mind-set of a change-management consultant. Every new idea that is implemented represents an organizational change—an ending to the status quo. Therefore, analyze what public endings would result for this stakeholder if your idea moves forward and what private endings she might fear. With more private or deceptive political individuals, you'll have a harder time cracking the code on covert losses, since these might include selfish concerns that she keeps more private. But try to figure out how your idea impacts her world positively and ways to minimize any anticipated concerns. Of course, ethical lobbying means you'll admit when your idea doesn't support, or even contradicts, the other's objectives or philosophy. This way, the buzz on you will be that you're trustworthy, and the decision-maker will believe you the next time.

Compromise Your Idea. Being savvy involves compromising, as in our analogy of the musician paying his dues by playing commercial tunes so he is noticed. Super sports agent Leigh Steinberg, the inspiration for the hit movie *Jerry Maguire,* tells how future NFL Hall of Fame quarterback Warren Moon was cut in 1997 by the Minnesota Vikings. Moon had made $5 million a year with the Vikings but was offered $750,000 to play second string for the Seattle Seahawks. Warren set aside his ego and took the job, after which the starter was hurt and Warren led the league in passing and received a lucrative contract the next year. Just as Moon took a step backward to move two ahead, you may need to alter your idea to gain acceptance.

A high-tech corporation invested millions in a huge quality initiative that was even made a major condition for a merger. However, the eventual leadership team later abandoned the program, so the quality directors felt like unwanted stepchildren. A resourceful quality training director saw the handwriting on the wall and compromised by repackaging his quality curriculum under the umbrella of "business effectiveness." He made substantive changes beyond cosmetic repositioning of content, eliminating some courses and adding others.

You can't always get your idea implemented totally intact, so compromise and get *some* of what you want. Once your partial idea is in swing, gradually guide it more fully toward your initial vision. Just because you give a little to gain a lot doesn't mean you're selling out. Giving a large fish plenty of line allows you to reel it in. Taming a wild stallion demands mounting and allowing a horse to take you where it wants before you gradually guide it into your control.

Give Up Credit. Decide whether this stakeholder will want some credit for your idea in exchange for his support. If you need a senior's approval, getting 25 percent credit for a program and giving up 75 percent as if he had initiated it is better than keeping 100 percent credit for an idea that goes nowhere. You'll still receive more exposure than if the idea dies. Besides, you are helping the company and you can always let insiders know how instrumental you were with an idea. But you need to strategize to make sure you don't lose too much credit. Make yourself indispensable to a power-oriented ally, as Amy from our introduction could have done. Position yourself as a subject matter expert to ensure data-oriented credibility while showing appreciation for the ally's cross-departmental selling skills, connections, and charisma. Paint a picture of the two of you rolling out the idea so that "*we* have greater success and our department receives resources for the next project." You'll feel good by knowing you make a difference in your organization by being less attached to receiving all of the recognition. Remember that "off the record" the Power of Person senior knows the truth and depends on you. Also, people often figure out the truth about who conceived an idea or did the lion's share of work.

Planned Spontaneity. Mark Twain advised, "It usually takes me more than three weeks to prepare a good impromptu speech." You might call a stakeholder to chat informally or casually raise your idea off-the-cuff. These "spontaneous" methods are often as carefully planned as formal meetings. If you or your assistant requests an appointment, consider that different people view scheduled meetings as either respectful or an imposition. The invitation, timing, and location of lobbying all send messages about respect, power, openness, and other dynamics that impact the reaction. Meeting on others' turf may either give them more control *or* make them relax and be less protective. Consider tactical seating. Sitting directly across from someone can be either confrontational or ensure good eye contact; right angles can seem supportive, and side-by-side is more collaborative. Will you be alone or with other people, and will this affect your plan? Run all of these logistics through your political savvy scanner.

Taking It to the Streets

John Wooden, Hall of Fame basketball player and coach said, "I believe that failure to prepare is preparing to fail." You've certainly prepared through all of the political-landscape plotting you've completed. You've planned the work, so now work the plan. Your idea and strategic plan for lobbying others represent the engine of a boat carrying your idea forward, but *you* provide the steering to ensure that the idea successfully reaches each stakeholder. You bring your systematic lobbying blueprint to the table, plus so much more—such as your business wisdom, personality, intelligence, industry knowledge, technical expertise, and street smarts. You'll also want to be resolute in your use of the following interpersonal skills.

Listening versus Arguing. What do you do when someone proposes an idea, you point out an obstacle, but she doesn't listen to you? Do you shut down, feeling pushed or unheard? If so, isn't it just as likely that others will respond to your lack of listening in the same way? Make sure you constantly hone your nondefensive listening, paraphrasing, and empathizing skills. They are lifesavers when others are resistant to your ideas. After all, ethical lobbying isn't a monologue or a "duel-logue"—it's a dialogue.

Savvy Influence Vocabulary. Use vocabulary in the firm range, adjusting for political style and the issue's volatility. If sensitivity or ego is involved, you may choose the permission-requesting *invitation* mode of firm language. If the person views you as lacking intensity, use *conviction* wording for a more authoritative pose. If dissent surfaces, use the Balanced Response as an interpersonal crutch to prop you up and keep you from stumbling into losing your cool.

Honesty. You lose the moment you bull-sling, especially with Power of Person seniors, who spot it in a heartbeat. Never make up an answer, since eventually BS catches up with you, and instead of looking all-knowing, you'll look immature. Savvy seniors don't expect you to know everything, just where to find the answer. If a senior sees a flaw in your plan, don't deny it. Acknowledge the concern with empathic listening and respond with benefits that outweigh the flaw. Think of a way to adapt your idea to address his objection (back to constructive compromise), since one objective of lobbying before a meeting is to discover in advance how others might disagree during the group discussion. Savvy leaders purposely shop their ideas around to allies who will play devil's advocate before their toughest critics in a future meeting can skewer their concepts. With critics, they leverage any real objections by asking, "If I can resolve this understandable concern, is there anything else blocking your support?"

A Cultural Option to Ethical Lobbying: Sober Selling

It's usually appropriate to champion an idea you believe is good for your company, but in some companies where it's considered too self-focused to promote *yourself* with integrity, it might even be crass to promote an *idea*. If your culture, the players, your role, and the specific issue make lobbying inappropriate, "sober selling" is an alternative posture. Some top managers don't want to be "sold" and instead want you to share the pros and cons of each side of an issue that you've researched and benchmarked. Adopt this sober selling style of informing more than persuading or influencing, leaving top managers to their own conclusions (unless, of course, they ask for your bottom-line recommendation). Your role may be to foster informed leadership decisions, so objectively present the business-case analysis for each side of an issue. Sadly, some slick operators with hidden agendas misrepresent, distort, or filter data even when appearing unbiased. We've all heard the maxim "There are lies, damn lies, and statistics." In this chapter, we've assumed that you *do* have integrity and that you are *not* in a lobbying-averse situation.

Ethical Lobbying Requires Perspective

Life is too short to strategize every issue. If an idea is advantageous to most people, you might not need to bother with detailed planning, especially if you anticipate little resistance or your idea already has momentum. Still, illogical resistance to good ideas can crop up like weeds when you least expect it, a dynamic we uncovered when we discussed addressing hidden agendas. So exercise your ethical lobbying muscle until it becomes strong yet easily flexed.

Political savvy is partly about not pushing the river. Naïve political players let their passion for their ideas and sense of values turn into brash, provocative stances. The politically adept use flexibility to avoid painting themselves into corners with nonnegotiable, rigid stances. If you're astute, you know that organizational change takes time. Winning approval for most ideas is less like a speedboat that cuts a sharp turn; it's like a cruise ship whose turn is a wider arc. So, remember the Serenity Prayer that is widely used in the Alcoholics Anonymous organization:

Lord, grant me the serenity to accept the things I cannot change,
The courage to change the things I can,
And the wisdom to know the difference.

Chapter 16

Conversational Aikido to Defuse Sabotage

> I want to be able to open up all the windows and let the wind blow in without blowing me over.
>
> —ANONYMOUS

When *They* Get the Benefit and *You* Get the Doubt

We believe in giving the benefit of the doubt. But when the *other* person gets all the benefit and *you* get all the doubt, you're eligible for lifetime membership in the Naïve Club. Astute people don't let trust in human nature blind them to the darker side of organizational life. It's great to trust people, but if you trust someone who abuses power, burns you, or siphons recognition into his own gas tank, chances are you *won't* survive many risks with him.

The positive political tactics we've discussed help you *prevent* becoming the target of a corporate-politics rogue, but our strategies are not bulletproof—you may still have to face saboteurs' weapons: sarcasm, insults, questions about your competence, insinuations about your motives, blame, withheld resources, marginalization of your function, and freeze-out ploys. Politically savvy leaders need the poise and peaceful power gained from the art of "conversational aikido."

George Leonard's *The Ultimate Athlete* popularized the discipline of aikido as a helpful metaphor. Unlike a Western boxer's use of force against force, the Eastern martial arts such as judo and aikido use the athlete's balance and the energy of the attacker for self-defense. Sometimes, playing tough with push-back tactics analogous to boxing is unavoidable, so we'll also visit the need to get tough with others and even occasionally use constructive sabotage yourself. "Playing hardball" in these last-resort ways is presumably for the right reasons: to survive an attack from a person who is dangerous to you and to protect the organization from danger.

Jack Be Nimble, Jack Be Quick

Don't let your faith in people become *blind* faith, since blind faith becomes vulnerability. Since shifty political players are tough to pin down or catch in the act, adopt these safeguards.

Be Careful about Favors. Here's where last chapter's concept of the political-favors bank account gets tricky. Be wary of favors or trusting what might be feigned confidence or praise from untrustworthy colleagues. Sometimes, an "inside scoop" is the manipulative ploy of a game-player. You may be getting duped into saying something that earns ostracism while the instigator denies any knowledge. Make sure you're not being used as a mouthpiece, doing someone else's dirty work while he avoids taking responsibility. We know an unsuspecting, good-hearted accounting executive vice president who made the mistake of participating in a gossip grapevine that was first planted by someone else. The naïve UP who tells us his Monday-morning-quarterback story has now been labeled a toxic rumormonger while the real saboteur has come out smelling like a rose.

We recently coached Ramon, who was trying to get out of the corner into which he'd painted himself. Ramon had naïvely believed Sasha, who had sold him on a controversial advertising idea that ridiculed the competition (with clever but extremely aggressive half-truths). Fearing that her provocative publicity scheme would be frowned upon by the highly ethical EVP of sales, Sasha manipulated Ramon into presenting this questionable business practice as an "innovative way to take bold risks" against the company's pesky rival. Sure enough, when top management's eyebrows were raised and Ramon looked to Sasha for support, she left her colleague hanging out to dry.

Stall for Time. If you doubt someone, you may need to be cagey or evasive to be safe. What if you're uncomfortable being associated with an individual's project, but refusing to support him would place you in the bull's-eye of this sabotaging sniper with connections? You can avoid committing to his idea without lying or misrepresenting your position. Stay neutral and stall for time with phrases like:

- "That idea merits some thought. It'll be interesting to see how it all shakes out."
- "I'll certainly weigh all the pros and cons. I appreciate your wanting my support."
- "That's an intriguing direction you've proposed. It bears study and consideration."
- "To be frank, the jury's still out on whether I'll have time to actively help you. I want to make the right call so that if you get my support, it's my wholehearted endorsement. Thanks for keeping me in the loop."

Once the in-your-face demand for support is sidestepped, you can consult others about the best path to take and investigate further signals yourself. This way, you're like a poker player holding your cards close to your chest until you can see how the game unfolds with the other player's cards—his real agenda and next steps.

Get out of the Middle. If you're caught in the middle of two warring adversaries and both are power trippers demanding your alliance, try to gracefully extricate yourself. Tactfully support each of them, which is admittedly tough if one says, "If you're not with me, you're against me." As you respond to such appeals, try making the analogy to a divorcing couple who can both be your friends if everyone agrees that *no* one is totally right or totally wrong. Ask the person to consider your situation in the same light as this common personal dilemma he's probably encountered.

Practice Conversational Aikido

A saboteur tries to push your button in a group with a biting or dismissive remark to tarnish your credibility. You're trapped in a "damned if you do, damned if you don't" situation that Gestalt therapy founder Fritz Perls called the "top dog–underdog" game. If you sheepishly wimp out or apologize, you reinforce your weaker-underdog image. If you fight back with top-dog anger or sarcasm, you feed the saboteur's resolve and create buzz that you're immature or belligerent. Here's where the skills of *conversational aikido* will earn you more points than staying stuck in the meek underdog role or in clumsy attempts to regain the overpowering, winning top-dog position.

Check Your Self-Talk. Don't jump to conclusions, thinking every caustic comment is a calculated power play in an antagonist's master plan. Don't become like the two psychiatrists who say "Hello" passing on the street and both wonder, "I wonder what he meant by that." Don't read sabotage into every edgy comment that comes your way. People do have bad days. Others are just interpersonally unskilled. Don't scurry to analyze the political terrain or frantically strategize a response. Even if a person *is* trying to discount you, unless he's powerful, who cares? Maybe your attacker is flexing his muscles as others laugh at his immaturity or lose respect for him for his ruthlessness. If you can see the selfish ladder-climber is trying to step over you, everyone else can, too! Is this encounter worth escalating? Don't let your own ego or political buttons hook you. Bleed your ego out of the situation. Instead, listen to your Self-Talk and keep yourself in check.

"Put-Aside" Responses for Put-Downs. Often, a saboteur wants to go one *up* on you with a put-down that downgrades your power image. You're late to a meeting and a control freak snidely comments, "Hi, Terrance. Nice of you to make time to join us." Some of us automatically respond to this put-down tactic with a *put-down* response of our own (abrasively retorting, "Excuse me, your highness!"), proving that we're hooked and just as much under the saboteur's control as if we had slinked out of the room. Or, we may offer a *put-up-with* response (sheepishly mumbling, "I'm so sorry . . . uh, I guess I sort of blew it again, absentminded me. I'll try to do better") or some other meek apology that reinforces our underdog status. We recommend a third option, a *put-aside* response that smoothly sidesteps falling into top-dog or underdog traps and instead maintains an adult, professional, and neutral position. The put-aside alternative demonstrates that you're above ego or power skirmishes. You protect your image without chickening out or getting hooked.

Alissa attacks her peer Matt by blindsiding him in a project status meeting: "Thanks for nothing, Matt. You're not pulling your weight around here, maybe because you're hanging out in the fitness center pulling weights there." What are Matt's options?

- A *put-down* response: "Look who's talking! I don't see you staying here till eight o'clock like I do. Maybe if you were staying late, you'd know that there are fewer interruptions and more real production taking place then. Besides, who appointed you CEO?"
- A *put-up-with* response if delivered in self-deprecating manner: "I'm really sorry. I guess I just thought I'd fill in and catch up later. I thought I was making up the time well enough by staying later, but I guess I should watch my clock better. I'm sorry, everybody."

- A *put-aside* response if handled in a matter-of-fact, even voice tone: "Alissa, you're obviously upset with how I arrange my flex hours and might even be questioning my commitment to the team. I'd be fine discussing my contributions now with the group, but I suggest that you and I meet later off-line to work this through so that the team can focus on the revenue strategies we're here to map out."

The pros and cons of each response depend on the power dynamics, but the last one is more neutral and actually stronger while being less challenging. You attempt to "put aside" the personal issue so that the group can return to the business issues at hand. The savvy message is that you're not intimidated and are confident enough to acknowledge the heat. You don't back down or get sucked into fighting. You treat the insult casually as if it's not emotionally charged, refusing to take the bait. This defusing posture is like a matador sidestepping the bull.

If you instead use a put-down response, the attacker controls you as if you were what we call a reverse puppet. Any knee-jerk response to deny and angrily state the reverse of your saboteur makes you like an angry teenager who out of rebellion automatically rejects what his parents say. He instantly does the reverse of what's wanted by his folks, thinking he's now taken back power. He feels in charge, but if he's defiantly doing the opposite of whatever his dad or mom wishes, he's still given up self-control. He's no more the master of his destiny than if he were to snap to attention whenever his mom or dad speaks. The adolescent's behavior is still being determined by his parent—not by free will.

Appropriate Humor. Sometimes a well-placed humorous retort can halt a saboteur without retaliation or intimidation, functioning as a put-aside response. If we return to the sarcastic put-down about arriving "on time for a change," a put-aside posture could be achieved through a humorous retort like "Yep, it's a whole new world that's opening up for me. I even had time to try this new custom they call breakfast!" Perhaps you smile and pat the person on the shoulder as you say, "Well, I finally opened that new alarm clock you sent me in appreciation for all my contributions to the team!" The point is to be creative, balanced, and prepared. Convey that you aren't hooked or attacking the other, just rising above the game—putting aside the put-down. Of course, some types of humor, like flippancy or sarcasm, come off as a put-down loss of control instead of being smooth and graceful.

Winston Churchill had a long-standing feud with Nancy Astor, the first woman elected to the British Parliament. At a party where the proper English lady found the statesman to be offensively inebriated, she confronted him: "You, sir, are drunk!" Churchill's put-down comeback was "Madam, in the morning I shall be sober, but you shall still be ugly." This response might top a put-down artist's list, but in many organizations his insulting reply would merely lose respect. The put-down style also perpetuates the battle. Sure enough, on another famous occasion, during a Churchill speech, Lady Astor heckled him saying, "Winston, if you were my husband, I would flavor your coffee with poison!" Churchill snarled back, "Madam, if I were your husband, I should drink it!" And the beat (or beating up) goes on.

On the other hand, a put-down return can be so clever and nonoffensive that it suavely serves as a tactful put-aside response. This kind of creative and appropriate put-down was delivered by Oliver Wendell Holmes, who was quite short in stature. During one of his weekly scholarly smoking-room gatherings, a pompous colleague patronizingly remarked, "Dr. Holmes, I should think you feel rather small in the midst of all of us bigger fellows." Holmes didn't miss a beat as he quipped, "Yes, I feel rather like a dime amongst pennies."

If humor is part of your verbal equipment, what style does it convey? Is it self-deprecating (a put-up-with style) or more aggressive (a put-down style)? Can you create a window of opportunity to make a positive impression through well-placed, balanced humor that skillfully puts aside any attack or criticism you receive (a put-aside style)?

Listen Nondefensively. We've already used active listening to convey respect and empathy during ethical lobbying and when challenging ideas with the Balanced Response, but it also has the power to defuse sabotage. In a noncontroversial, matter-of-fact fashion, simply put into your own words the sentiments your antagonist is expressing and invite elaboration. By repackaging the attack into less loaded language, you show courage without provoking, de-escalate the conflict, and buy time before your next response. Often, if you mirror back a saboteur's remarks in a nonaccusatory manner, he'll back off since you've put a spotlight on his ploy for all to observe. Matt could reflect Alissa's cut about being late, "Wow, you're really ticked about the delay I had on the way here. What's up, Alissa?" Now, watch Alissa backpedal her way out of her put-down statement.

Ask for Specifics. A nonretaliatory way to disarm a saboteur's inferential mudslinging and keep labels from sticking (such as "incompetent," "dragging your feet," or "undermining this team") is to actively listen in a way that rewords the attack into less derogatory language and then ask for specifics. Force your aggressor to flesh out his subjective, self-serving accusation with behavioral examples to back up any negative claim about you or your team. Even if the person has position power, he often backs down or admits the accusation "came out wrong."

- *Accused of Being Incompetent.* "Maurice, you have some real issues with whether I'm qualified to head the team given that I wasn't promoted from within the company. Since I can't change that fact, what kind of background information would be helpful to increase your confidence level?"
- *Accused of Dragging Your Feet.* "Naomi, you're bothered by what you see as a lack of urgency in my deliverables. I'd be both-

ered, too, if someone held up the team's progress at a critical time. But I'm surprised by this, so please help me to understand what milestone date I missed or which specific project parameter I dropped the ball on."

- *Accused of Undermining The Team.* "Wow, Kevin, your message is pretty clear that you don't think I'm into this project as much as everyone else. I gotta assume that somehow I just let you down in some way. Since I'm baffled by your resentment, how have I not pulled my weight or fulfilled my end of the bargain?"

Respond with Firm Vocabulary and Balanced Responses. After neutrally reflecting back the attacker's concerns, if you *do* need to respond with a countering position, lower the political risks with a noncombative tone and savvy influence vocabulary that's firm rather than harsh or weak. Firm wording assumes the same posture of maturely putting aside the negative put-down rather than getting sucked into a bickering battle, so that you're perceived as cool and collected.

Unless your aggressor is a vindictive senior holding all the marbles, consider challenging the person's accusation through the Balanced Response technique. The tactic is trickier now since you're not just challenging *ideas* being discussed. Here, the issue is the smearing of your reputation. Rigorously control your Self-Talk, use empathic listening to de-escalate the emotions, and recognize any merits in the saboteur's content (OK, so you *were* late to the meeting) but *not* his unfair labels, inflammatory conclusions, or emotional venom (you're *not* validating his conclusions about your attitude). Pause and censor the word *but* coming out of your mouth. Finally, firmly and fairly surface your concerns about any untrue implications or accusations:

- *Listen Empathically.* "Wow, Alissa, you're really annoyed that I'm late to the meeting."
- *Acknowledge Merits.* "I know my absence bogs down the group's productivity, especially when there's going to be a vote,

because we agreed everyone should be present before any consensus decision-making."

- *Surface Concerns without Saying "But."* "Alissa, what's hard to ignore is your linking my lateness to my commitment level. My contribution, hours, and work product speak for themselves. I was late today because of a safety issue Eric had me managing, so I suggest we move on. Later, you and I can clear the air to get back on the same page. Or, if you want, we can work the issue right now, but only if the group agrees."

Please don't get caught up in the actual content or style of the above example. The point is to track the Balanced Response steps and notice the lack of weak or harsh language. After you listen empathically and acknowledge merits, you surface your concerns. You retain a strong, even stance and avoid resorting to counterpunching. You show flexibility for alternative next steps. Doesn't this sound nice and tidy on paper? We know tremendous self-control and skill are required. We obviously suggest great care in using the approach with powerful superiors. Sometimes, it's wiser to just absorb the blow or to simply listen empathically and express apologies without overdoing the weak language.

Recently, when good-natured nine-year-old Carrie tried to ask her school deskmate, Meg, to please not talk as much while the teacher was explaining, the chatterbox Meg was angry at the little Virgo. Later, when the children were each announcing how their year was going, Meg embarrassed Carrie by saying, "Well, Carrie is really irritating the way she always hushes me." Instead of getting angry, Carrie found Meg later and said, "I'm sorry you're so mad about my shushing you. I can understand how that bothers you. I do want to hear Ms. Lang, so please tell me if there's a better way to say it. I really hope we can be better friends in the future." If only adults were as skilled.

Rely on the Group. Professional group facilitators are taught to avoid locking horns in a power struggle by turning the issue over to the team, especially if a resistant participant doesn't hold rank.

Conversational aikido uses this nonprovocative, safe move. If Sam hears that politically maneuvering Jacob has been spreading buzz that Sam's been taking credit for the team's progress, a savvy strategy is for Sam to let the group decide how to handle the issue. In a nonchallenging way, he expresses surprise at the strong view that Jacob's expressed and consults the group to reality-test Jacob's stance. Sam self-discloses to the group that he believes he's played an equal role and is open to taking group time to discuss the issue if they agree with Jacob. A few red flags with this approach are crucial: First, try other put-aside methods to defuse the sabotage put-down ploy, such as humor, nondefensive listening, asking for specifics, the Balanced Response, or firm vocabulary. The group may resent your appeal to them if there's a time bind, so be sensitive. *Never* use this tactic with someone who has high position power and can banish you.

Sometimes You *Have* to Play Hardball

You don't have to fight saboteurs blow by blow if you practice conversational aikido. Using others' energy against them lets you keep your balance and dignity. They don't lynch you and you don't flee the battlefield. We've offered a palette of options, but you're the painter who mixes and matches colors for each scenario. Unfortunately, at times you must act more forcefully against someone, because if he gains power, he'll hurt the company or unfairly burn you—get rid of you, marginalize you, or blame you. You've tried noncombative methods to no avail. The person won't back down and rejects your efforts at win-win, cooperative conflict resolution. You cannot work it out and it comes down to being *you* or the other person. These are the sleep-disrupting times when you may have to play hardball.

First Soul-Search. While overly political players invented this art of corporate warfare, it's less comfortable for newcomers to the political arena, and the politically avoidant dread it. When this last-resort measure is warranted, don't wait too long or back down from taking steps to prevent a foe from grabbing power. On the other hand, you also don't want to abuse this last-ditch survival strategy, so let's call it what it is—sabotage. Only use it with the most cutthroat of enemies who will otherwise wreak havoc. It might mean using negative buzz or threatening to go with information to a boss, customer, or person your opponent would fear. Perhaps you tell someone that you have ways of making life more difficult or are willing to take an issue public that you know she'd rather keep in the shadows.

Don't use this tactic every time you run into an SOB, since it's too easy to rationalize your *own* unfair behavior by thinking, "He's a snake, and if it's him or me, I'm the better option for the company. The ends justify the means." Well, they *don't* when the SOB ends up being *you.* Test yourself by triple-checking all your signals that the other is *intentionally* out to hurt you or the company.

Make sure the battle is worth fighting, because it will affect your image and your political standing. In real hardball, a pitcher sometimes purposely feels he must pitch "high and tight" to brush the batter off the plate or even hit a batter to intimidate him. This may work, but it can also make the batter so mad that he hits a homer on the next pitch or his teammates rush the mound for a brawl. Be sure that you don't get all charged up with righteousness and rough somebody up before doing some soul-searching, checking the facts, and wondering about the consequences. You may not have judged the situation correctly and you could get into deep trouble, even lose your job.

"Pick Battles Big Enough to Matter, Small Enough to Win." This quote from Jonathan Kozol counsels carefully weighing the decision whether to play hardball. But you can fight appropriately, as shown in the next vignette, an actual dilemma that unfolded on the top floor of a megacompany where we consulted. When two corporate giants merged, our Power of Ideas coaching client in the

older company agonized over a "kill or be killed" situation. He knew that the newer legacy company was trying to put its people in all the top positions in the resulting merged executive team, for which the CEO was rapidly making membership decisions. So far, only officers from the younger, skyrocketing giant company had been selected, due to their aggressive manipulation and put-down style of lobbying.

Curtis, a Less Political (LP) sales and marketing veteran in the older organization, knew that if his Overly Political (OP) counterpart in the newer partner company, Tim, got the nod, it would mean curtains for his own job stability. Tim was known for discriminatory behavior toward minorities, to the extent that some of his own cronies had nicknamed him the Beast from the East. Curtis once heard Tim say in a meeting, "I'm worth a hell of a lot of money, so I don't want any of you attractive ladies hitting on me. Unless, of course, you offer something in return." Besides this humor that offended many, Tim had recently alienated a major customer by answering yes when asked at a high-visibility meeting whether the sales organization had an overseas customer support system "on soil and in country." Tim falsely claimed such capability for sterling customer service when he knew that his company was in fact only outsourcing this function to loosely managed affiliates. Ultimately, developing the proper full-time infrastructure to service the new global account proved tougher than anticipated, with many glitches that surprised and angered the customer, eroding trust between the businesses.

At a regional sales meeting, Tim told Curtis he considered him an "obsolete dinosaur" and wasn't afraid to tell the CEO. Considering Tim's lack of judgment under the spotlight, his unethical customer relations, and the dangers of further corporate imbalance on the executive team, Curtis truly believed Tim's appointment would be horrible for the company. He agonized for days but finally decided to actively take on Tim and maneuver against him behind the scenes, a tactic he'd normally never consider. He told his coach, "I have to do it. My friend Leanne is close to the CEO. I'll ask her to tell the CEO about the sexual harassment comment in the meeting and the customer service misrepresentation. Planting these seeds of doubt about Tim's ethics is a service to the company." This decision to play hardball worked since Curtis won the seat and six months later Tim took a job elsewhere after his primary powerful supporter left the company. To further legitimize Curtis's tough decision, it soon surfaced that Tim was guilty of some highly questionable financial deals with prospective customers and suppliers, involving favors and kickbacks.

When you play hardball, you're going beyond conversational aikido, but in the right circumstances we still consider aggressive ploys to be part of high-integrity political tactics. Curtis gave his legacy organization executive team representation, helped the overall company steer clear of years of potential injury from Tim, and protected himself from being sabotaged. Curtis had wrestled with himself to be sure this last-resort strategy was appropriate given the situation and alternatives. Nothing he did was dishonest since everything Leanne told the CEO about the managerial marauder who was simultaneously mudslinging Curtis was true.

Do Your Hardball Homework. Savvy, high-integrity leaders who assertively jump into a political skirmish or turf battle with another executive balance courage and values with a realistic assessment of their chances of success. Their decision is based on political astuteness and political homework. Before going to battle, they make sure that they have done the following:

- *Detected Power Dynamics.* They have studied the power positions, the power connections, and the political styles of key players, as well as the competing agendas.
- *Done Ethical Lobbying Analysis.* While the idea being lobbied isn't substantive, but personal, they are still lobbying to get something done (to keep an unethical person from gaining access to a top job, counter an attack with a counterattack, pre-

vent someone from infiltrating the company with an idea that would poison morale and so on), so they complete the same process they did when lobbying for any idea. They consider the right timing, the right setting, and all the other factors we examined last chapter.

- *Installed Their Safety Network*. They have used their network to first get feedback about their plan before launching such a high-risk strategy, created allies in their corner, and identified an internal advocate as Curtis did with Leanne.

At times we have seen savvy people fight for an issue despite personal risks and only a small chance of success. In these situations, they felt that the cost of not acting—to their integrity or to the company—was too great. Even then, they did all of the things above to improve their chances and to make an informed choice about the risks involved.

A Dirty Word in Politics . . . *Forgiveness*

High-integrity political strategies won't always prevent sabotage, and this chapter's savvy conversational tactics or outfoxing your enemies won't always make things right. If you do lose out in the end, sometimes your only saving grace is to move on with eventual forgiveness. If you hold on to residual anger so long that it eats you up with ulcers, then the saboteur has beaten you twice—once in the political arena and once in your mind and heart. One Nazi concentration camp survivor inspired his son by letting go of bitterness, proclaiming that the Nazis took five years of his life and that he refused to give them one second more.

Forgiveness doesn't mean condoning, forgetting, or being an easy mark for the next person. But it's an attitude shift to release yourself from a prison you're imposing on yourself. Dr. Jerry Jampolsky is the founder of the first Center for Attitudinal Healing in 1975 and along with his wife, Dr. Diane Cirincione, has inspired dozens of such centers all over the world. The organization is a wonderful nondenominational organization providing emotional support to people with catastrophic illness. Bishop Desmond Tutu, John Denver, and other dignitaries and celebrities have been on the advisory board. Dr. Jampolsky has written a life-altering little book simply entitled *Forgiveness: The Greatest Healer of All,* maintaining that living without forgiveness and holding on to anger is like taking poison but expecting someone else to die. Do you want to be happy or do you want to be right?

Forgiveness puts us one thought away from totally overcoming sabotage. A forgiving attitude requires us to reframe saboteurs as people in pain and to interpret their attacks as cries for help. San Francisco comedian Michael Pritchard visits elementary schools across America to curb bullying and invite young victims to feel compassion for bullies. He tells kids, "Hurt people hurt people." If the kids don't derive peace of mind by trying to help the attacker, they can at least calm themselves by wondering how unhappy the bully's life must be. Does he live in a desert of no love? Is this the only way he can feel worthy? Why is he seething inside? "Hurt people hurt people."

We'll never forget being asked to coach an overly political, vindictive executive with a reputation for being so brutal and conniving that we didn't even want to be in the same room with him. We took the job as a favor to our HR client, who needed help with somehow taming this tiger. Only when we worked with the tyrant did we learn that this wounded warrior had been abused as a child and as a young adult had lived in his car for seven months, two of those months with a child. His eyes glistened as he said that he wasn't proud of how he had been greedy and cutthroat to obtain and protect his power position, but that he'd made a vow to himself to never again let his young son suffer deprivation. Eventually, this hurt person who had hurt others softened his abuse of others but he always maintained a protective posture, and for understandable reasons. We couldn't help remembering a wonderful, simple quote: "Be kind to other people. Everyone walks a rough road." This compassionate, noncombative spirit even toward our opponents seems a fitting close to this chapter and is embodied in a quote from Sun Tzu's manual *The Art of War.*

> *Build your adversaries*
> *a golden bridge*
> *from which they can retreat.*

PART III

LEADERSHIP SAVVY TACTICS TO DETECT DECEPTION

Chapter 17
A Leadership Wake-Up Call

Work "Between the Ears" and Merge into the Savvy Zone

You may worry that our many ethical-politics tactics will take too much time or make you seem too political overnight. Bear in mind that many strategies take no extra time because they involve qualitative changes in how you carry out existing activities: monitoring your influence vocabulary, gracefully responding to an attacker, factoring political style preferences into a big proposal meeting, respecting turf issues while working with a power-conscious peer. Also, much political savvy happens "between your ears," where no one can see you use new insights: reading power dynamics, scanning people's actions for hidden agendas, picking up on unwritten rules when taking a new job.

Granted, many of our recommendations involve observable behaviors, so adding them all to your repertoire would be seen as overkill, especially in a less political culture. You'd be crazy to suddenly employ ethical lobbying, triple your networking activity, use new techniques to spread word of your accomplishments, and grill dozens of people for the inside scoop about your corporate buzz. Relax! Take your time and just imagine that you're gradually merging onto the road toward increased savvy. You wouldn't jump into the ring with the world champion after first learning to box. Likewise, if you instead need to *decrease* your political activity—scaling back your overly political temperament—you can also calibrate this transition to a more values-grounded treatment of others. Otherwise, people will suspect you've been medicated or have had a lobotomy.

A Steward for Your Organization

So far, we've sounded an individual wake-up call about politics, using a zoom lens to focus on your own organizational impact while maintaining your integrity. It's now time to sound a leadership wake-up call—switching from an individual close-up zoom lens to a wide-angle lens to survey the political culture of your whole team, department, division, or company, whatever your sphere of power may be. The past few years have shown rampant increases in competitiveness, deception, and self-interest over company welfare. What's needed is nothing less than a revolution in leadership development—a transformation that rests largely in the hands of business schools, corporate universities, and corporate learning officers. But the responsibility also falls upon your shoulders as a leader. After all, regardless of your level, you are a steward of your organization's political health. Therefore, parts 3 and 4 of our book explore why there is such deception in business, how you can detect it, the skills needed to rescue your organization from negative political activity, and how to build a more constructive political atmosphere. Perfecting your political savvy at the leadership level can have a rehabilitative, nourishing impact on your organization's overall results and success.

Preventing Leadership Blind Spots

In shifting from individual to organizationwide power dynamics, our goal is determination, not despair. Awareness is a launching pad for hope and practical answers. Make no mistake—*all* organizations are political. Just because your company may be *less* political doesn't mean your culture is *non*political. Some companies attack destructive politics but overestimate their progress. You don't turn the corner just by announcing new values or leadership competencies like "integrity." As one client proudly alluded to such ideals, an insider confided, "If they *really* knew . . ." Touting apolitical leadership values may sound like a groundbreaking position, but doing so won't automatically build a healthy political shelter that will stand. In fact, such "nonpolitical cultures" often stumble in the following predictable ways:

- *Inoculation*. Wishing away the problem with ethics training or corporate communications about apple-pie leadership values like "integrity" can even slow down deeper culture change. People can point and say, "See, we've inoculated everyone," but the result may simply be that people can claim they've been cured and are even freer to continue maneuvering. It's like insisting that people exercise regularly, but then letting them devour junk food and smoke.
- *Opening Pandora's Box*. Employees who already have integrity wonder why an explicit program should even be necessary and may resent it, while overly political people are quick to justify their behavior, claim integrity, and cover their transgressions.
- *Token Efforts*. Some new leadership values are little more than public relations gestures. Without concrete skills for attitude change, the intervention is like a dry heave—lots of energy but no real substance! Leaders need to do more than raise the integrity banner.
- *Underground Politics*. When leadership efforts *are* genuine, politics may become even more dangerous. The culture transformation can drive overly political, slicker operators underground, where they work subversively with greater care to cover their tracks. Their maneuvering is now subtler and harder to detect, making it more devious. There *is* such a thing as a wolf in

sheep's clothing. One CEO in a more openly political organization said, "At least around here, when someone is in the penalty box, you know it."

Organizational Politics: A Front-Burner Issue

A number of economic, societal, cultural, and global trends form a combustive chemical reaction making corporate politics a survival-level issue for leaders. Complacency is more dangerous than ever.

Economic Fears. The sagging economy, dot-com crash, rampant downsizing, global competition, and soaring unemployment rates combine to create a mind-set of scarcity, fear, and crisis. In conditions of economic and financial threat, even in altruistic nonprofit agencies, people can become politically predatory.

Pressure to Deceive. Fear is increased by the constant demand on corporations by Wall Street analysts to appear attractive to shareholders. Analysts exert pressure to report ever-rising quarterly numbers, sparking frantic CEO efforts to pump up earning statements, hype the stock, cut worker pay to inflate stock values, and bury any mistakes in divestitures and restructuring. All of these ploys are part of a destructive gambit that many CEOs feel they must master to avoid embarrassing analyst meetings. The danger is that they become hostage to their own deception.

Corporate Greed. Ambition and the promise of mind-boggling financial rewards that await corporate ladder-climbers seduce people to become self-serving and overly political. *Barron's* "Executive Excess 2003" study found that the highest-paid CEOs had the most mediocre performance and greatest pay inequity. Among fifty companies with the most layoffs and underfunded pensions, CEOs earned paychecks that surged 44 percent the next year, compared with a median 6 percent pay increase in other organizations. Jim Hightower's *Thieves in High Places* reports that the twenty-five companies with the highest-paid CEOs, COOs, and CFOs in the years from 1999 to 2003 (with salaries totaling $23 billion) saw their stock plummet 75 percent, prompting *Fortune* magazine to call the list "the twenty-five companies with the greediest executives." No wonder Hightower offers new names for such greedy executives: kleptocrats, grabbateers, vulture capitalists, profiteers, sleaze whiz, corporados, terrortunists, and pillage idiots. Corporate cronyism isn't the only culprit. The *Harvard Business Review* article "Why It's Hard to Do What's Right" reports that, incredible as it seems, compensation experts warn boards of directors to inflate CEO pay to reassure Wall Street that they have top-notch leadership talent.

The greedy and the overly ambitious dance along the foul lines, test the limits, flirt with censure, and rationalize breaking the rules. You may incredulously ask, "Why do these people think it's OK to break the rules?" The answer is—*because they can!* Some people cynically believe that breaking rules is resourceful, enterprising, and creative. David Geffen, now worth almost $4 billion through his DreamWorks brainchild, falsely told William Morris Agency he'd graduated UCLA after discovering that a college degree was required for advancement. He then intercepted and destroyed a letter sent by UCLA to set the record straight. Why do we marvel at the extent of ethics fallout when people constantly look the other way and shady behavior becomes a rewarded norm? Movies, TV, literature, and pop culture tend to sanction borderline conduct, antisocial behavior, and illegal activity by glorifying antiheroes like Tony Soprano, Bonnie and Clyde, Thelma and Louise, and corrupt cops. However much we may enjoy this genre of entertainment, perhaps our cheering mavericks and villains in fiction is a hop, skip, and a jump away from tacit endorsement of real-life self-entitlement, rule-breaking, and corporate crime.

The Scourge of Scandal. Some corporations are now notorious clichés as business school case studies for crossing ethical lines and even for criminal behavior. High-visibility debacles have ushered in a new era of corporate liability, legislation, massive penalties, FTC and FBI investigations, CEO salary disclosures, shareholder outrage, and public relations fiascoes. Scandals can gut profits, morale, performance, and investor confidence. Through the mayhem, companies spend millions scrambling to police themselves, provide ethics education, and mend their reputation.

Corporate atrophy and avarice scream out from bookstore shelves with titles like Hightower's *Thieves in High Places,* David Callahan's *The Cheating Culture: Why More Americans Are Doing Wrong to Get Ahead,* and Arianna Huffington's *Pigs at the Trough: How Corporate Greed and Political Corruption Are Undermining America*. Corporate scandal is so woven into the fabric of life that late-night talk shows, jokes, and pop culture make business ethics a commonplace topic. Who could have dreamed that a CEO's infamy would make him a pop icon captured in song parody?

Pirate of the Year

You won't see shaggy beards or earrings or a patch over one eye,
Today's discerning pirate prefers Armani and a tie.
Bluebeard never went to school but he'd have no chance today,
He'd need a Bachelor's in Accounting and a Harvard MBA.

There's Presidential propaganda about making all this stop.
What's keeping us from taking back the mansions and the yacht?
There's no end to this crime wave, the news is never dull;
Even Martha Stewart's flag has cross-bones and a skull.

Without the old direct attack, I'm having trouble keeping track,
Of where the treasure is and who the Captains are.
But one man stands out from all the rest for inspiring investor fear,
Hip, hip hooray for Kenneth Lay, Pirate of the Year!

—DAVE HICKMAN, FROM THE ALBUM *NOTHING LIKE A TRAIN*

The Cost of Negative Politics. Leaders ignored the bottom-line drain of organizational politics when businesses were flush, but now they pay attention to this buried line item on the balance sheet. Millions are lost when competent employees avoid voicing ideas for fear of ego-driven superiors who might disagree or feel threatened. We've seen many good, valuable people run out of organizations. Many companies with cutthroat political reputations suffer diminished market share and difficulty in recruiting talent. Who wants to work for or do business with an organization infested with ladder-climbers and "empty suits" who run amok? Now, factor in attrition due to the political revolving door, power plays, scandal, or disgust about politics, and the costs are astronomical. A politically derailed executive's job costs $300K–$500K to replace. This doesn't include the intangible costs of customer loss, diminished morale, or interruption to business flow. The Conference Board declares that rehiring costs 241 percent of a mid-manager's annual salary, 176 percent of an IT professional's salary, and 150 percent of an exempt professional's salary.

Ethical Politics as a Leadership Competency. Corporate executives are asked to feed their companies' future leadership pipeline, corporate universities abound, and the status of chief learning officers skyrockets. As companies clamor to build leadership bench strength, organizational savvy is called front and center as a development need. Political skills are now emphasized in competency models, appraisals, coaching, human resources planning, and training needs assessments. Less political technical functions like engineering, R&D, and information technology must partner with line colleagues, calling for increased organizational savvy. Staff functions are redefining their roles by becoming business partners with line counterparts, demanding a reinvigorated power image. Politics is targeted for discussion in companies' women's networks such as Deutsche Bank's diversity initiative and Credit Suisse First Boston's Securities Women's Network. Diversity organizations like

Women on Wall Street and WOMEN Unlimited (The Women's Organization for Mentoring, Education, and Networking) are aimed at shattering the glass ceiling of male-dominated boardrooms and top-floor offices. Any traditionally marginalized group views political astuteness as a vital enabler to help turn the tide.

Corporate Turbulence and Change. Unhealthy politics are cultivated in the fertile soil of company instability and upheaval. The rate of restructuring, downsizing, mergers, and acquisitions is reflected in people's gallows humor: "So, who's your boss *this* week?" It's no secret that when companies grow through sprawling mergers, acquisitions, conglomeration, and alliances, so do pockets of concentrated power, turf lines, and hidden political brush fires.

Soul in Business. The above trends point to the dangers and frequency of overly political companies. Ironically, a simultaneous momentum of spirituality in business actually lowers tolerance for such destructive political climates. An explosion of books, tapes, organizations, conferences, seminars, and speakers spotlights the expanded role of faith in companies. For example, years ago, we didn't have Deepak Chopra's "The Soul of Leadership" at Kellogg School of Management, or spiritually rooted business-consulting firms like Attitudes That Work. Profit and prayer are no longer considered mutually exclusive. Positive, ethical approaches to politics and corporate influence may serve as a bridge between these historically separated aspirations.

Diagnosing Your Organization's Political Health

As steward for the political culture of your team, department, division, or company, you can gauge your organization's political health by tracking the presence of the following political symptoms. Some clues point to an Under Political (UP) style and others to an Overly Political (OP) style. The point is to realize that both mind-sets exist in your company and to diagnose whether there is too great an imbalance toward one political style or the other. While we do not offer a scientific way to quantify or score your company's political health, we believe that you'll be able to informally survey the lay of the land by checking for these specific organizational dynamics:

- *An Excess of Individual Politics Tip-Offs*. In our first chapter, you reviewed the tip-offs that someone has underestimated the role that politics have played in his career success. Obviously, if you've experienced or seen signals of politics at a personal level, it's also a message about the level of organizational susceptibility to dysfunctional politics. Just think of your organization as an aggregate of all of these individual political experiences.
- *Rampant Acts of Sabotage*. Similarly, the more that devious behavior occurs, the poorer the prognosis for your organization's political health.
- *A Company Reputation for Being Political*. An entire company casts a shadow about its politics, attracting or discouraging the most competent, ethical leaders. You probably have a sense of how your business is seen—by your employees, the public, and competitors.
- *Unhealthy Skirmishes, Turf Wars, and Battle Lines*. Conflict is inevitable and necessary in organizations. Conflicting priorities should be built into any company to ensure proper checks and balances. But when frictions escalate beyond a healthy level, wounds become scars and collaboration is doomed.
- *Isolated Teams and Silo Behavior*. Some company structures unintentionally promote isolated working conditions and reduced collaboration. The mere existence of insulated teams may simply signal a noncommunicative working style, not a political red flag. But a patchwork quilt of isolated teams can also indicate an Under Political (UP) mentality, with people averse to networking and self-promotion and managers uncomfortable with visibility and power.

- *An Array of "Corporate Siberia" Positions.* Team isolation may signal the second-class citizen status we've labeled corporate Siberia. Every company has an informal pecking order, but unhealthy politics rule if the caste system is endemic and divisive, or if targeted groups feel worthless after a merger.
- *Private Power Pockets*. In these Overly Political (OP) teams or departments, information flow is restricted, access to people is limited, and communication is guarded. This destructive, intentional insulation is fueled by self-interest, hidden agendas, or efforts to control information, resources, and power. In these moat-protected monarchies, power is so concentrated that certain managers get away with murder and may be hiding something. When unethical behavior is permitted and people are looking the other way, it's rarely an accident.
- *Relationship-Based Decisions That Ignore Competence*. The classic good-old-boy network leads to executives and vendors being selected because they're part of the "in" crowd. This inner-circle dynamic also decides promotions, raises, and bonuses when power networks take priority over performance.
- *Competent, High-Integrity People Aren't Elevated.* Besides selfish people being in power, political imbalance exists if managers with the most expertise and integrity *don't* advance.
- *Attrition Due to Politics*. Often people quit due to disgust about politics and feelings of helplessness, stress, or intimidation. Exit interviews reveal the disgruntlement, or you may anecdotally hear that the reasons involved politics.
- *Low Morale Due to Politics*. Watch for people who quit emotionally but stay physically, leading to an organizational disconnect. Does disillusionment drain time, energy, and performance? This victim mentality is contagious and saps hope. Cynicism about politics and management's tacit endorsement can bleed the organization of talent, productivity, and spirit.
- *CYA Mentality*. A "cover your ass" mentality may just signal poor management skills but could be rooted in an Overly Political

(OP) culture with tyrannical leaders setting a tone of fear. One mega–manufacturing company urged risk-taking but penalized mistakes. Since people protected their backsides by avoiding the risk of proposing new ideas, the corporation's innovations were delayed and it fell behind the competition.

- *Large Gaps between Public and Private Dialogue*. In hallways or closed offices people reveal true negative feelings about an idea, but in meetings a pall of silence grips the group. The more frequent these gaps are, the more this CYA cousin announces unhealthy politics and a history of punishment for speaking truth to power.
- *Self-Interest-Driven Agendas*. Being strategic or prudent is one thing, but overly political conditions reign when people keep their motives and goals so they can chase their own interests over the company's welfare.
- *Gossip and Negative Corporate Buzz Distraction*. Gossip about people is normal. But a political undertow douses performance when too much time and energy is spent spreading, affixing, and countering negative perceptions.
- *A Revolving Door and Unreasonable Turbulence*. Company equilibrium is tipped off-balance when top leaders continually disappear. They may resign, be fired, or become expendable due to politics. Turbulence at the top management level can indicate excessive power plays, ego conflicts, and turf politics.
- *No Leadership Models for Integrity*. Published company values that urge ethical behavior won't guarantee political health, but their absence spells danger. Do your written company guiding principles and leadership competencies include "integrity"? The omission can mean top management grants de facto permission for destructive politics.
- *Negative Publicity and Lawsuits.* Is your company currently a newspaper headline? Have top managers become greedy, released a false earnings report to influence analyst projections, or granted favors that are being questioned? Obviously, poisonous publicity

or a whopping lawsuit is a glaring red flag that your company culture has crossed the line to become destructively political.

A Call to Action

Hopefully, you now have a sense of the political winds within your organization. We've removed the elephant from under the table. Political imbalance is a spreading weed if left untended. When profits languish in a world of razor-thin margins, political turmoil can sink morale, shrink performance, and slash stock price. But an organization on solid political bedrock has resiliency against shock when financial earthquakes shake its foundation. Perhaps it is time for a revolution in business schools, leadership development programs, corporate training departments, and corporate universities to recognize an essential hidden dimension of leadership—*ethical political astuteness* to attain "impact with integrity."

Chapter 18

Expect Deception, Even (Especially) as a CEO

The Pressure to Deceive Leaders

That's where the money is.

—WILLIE SUTTON, BANK ROBBER

Someone once asked Willie Sutton, the famous bank robber, why he robbed banks. Willie replied, "That's where the money is." If we ask why CEOs are targets of deception, the answer is "That's where the money is"—in the form of salary, bonuses, options, pensions, and perks. People in power positions have the ability to make others rich or financially secure. So, to be seen by CEOs in the best possible light and to maintain that positive regard is often rewarding. Meanwhile, the forces of fear operate almost daily, with companies fluidly reorganizing and breaking apart, and competitive conditions shifting to change the fortunes of the winners and losers. Greed and fear, plus the stress of being measured monthly by one's company and quarterly by Wall Street, put enormous pressure on people to shade information or tell seniors what they want to hear.

A Wall Street maxim is "Fear and greed move markets." The same is true for people. Fear and greed move people—further right on the Organizational Savvy Continuum. They may do things that are overly political—more selfish and self-protective—and then rationalize it. It becomes tempting for people to bias information in their own favor and to avoid doing things that will upset a person with power. Does it work? Is it rewarded? Unfortunately, although it always hurts the company and individuals, our experience is that it can work and be rewarded for a long time. We have seen many people take kickbacks, set up dummy vendors, cheat on their travel expenses, and inflate numbers to get bonuses, stock options, and promotions before eventually leaving companies with lots of money and no jail time. So, if circumstances in your organization move in directions of fear and greed, you can expect some people to be less principled. With such temptation to deceive, and the potential rewards of deception, a good rule of thumb for CEOs and leaders is to expect deception. You might think that the higher you go, the less vulnerable you are to manipulation since you have power. In fact, the opposite is often the case, especially given (1) the advantages of overly political people and (2) the ease of deceiving CEOs and top leaders.

Advantages of Overly Political People

Overly Political (OP) individuals who deceive top leaders for personal gain are dangerous to company interests because they are knowledgeable about human nature and organizational behavior. They use this expertise to achieve an edge over others who are often more competent, ethical, and deserving. Even otherwise savvy CEOs underestimate OPs' advantage, and that leads to disastrous staying power of these corporate plagues. If the wrong person obtains and consolidates power, he can take control like the leader of a new democracy, where the dynamic is "one person, one vote, *one time*." The newly powerful person never leaves office and runs the country (or organization) for his own benefit. Here are the behaviors that give Overly Political people a strong chance of prevailing over others and even winning the CEO deception game.

Mastery of Words. Articulate individuals are persuasive and given credit for high intellect. If the manipulator has mastered the current jargon, key strategic concepts, and buzzwords, he can gain credibility in spite of his actual results.

Impression Management. Schemers know that what busy executives don't observe personally is often invisible and hardly registers, so it can be distorted. Therefore, they give impression management the highest priority during meetings, conferences, and field visits. By carefully managing impressions, they create an inflated perception of their talent and results.

Studying How Decisions Get Made. OPs study the gaps between the stated process for decision-making and what happens in reality. Who influences the leader? Do committees or task forces have any power? Are decisions made at meetings or before the meetings? The calculator uses this knowledge to get decisions to go his way.

Charting the Winner and Loser Projects and People. Spending considerable time swapping information, deceptive people are wired in about which projects will pay off and which will fall short or tank. They find ways to associate with winners or take credit for success. For projects that will disappoint, they distance themselves and can lay seeds of blame with others way in advance. Devious political players also follow the rising or falling stock of individuals. They monitor the corporate buzz and study the reactions of powerful seniors toward colleagues. Deceivers use this data to gauge what seniors like or dislike about people, to adjust their own behavior, and to decide whom to befriend and include in their network.

Networking and Corporate Buzz Prowess. The deceptive OP picks relationships based on her knowledge of shifting influence, power, and political stock. She tracks the power struggles, the rising or falling stars, and essential alliances. She gains access to the airwaves to take credit and create positive perceptions or to lay blame and damage someone's reputation. Relying upon her word mastery and a senior's susceptibility to blindly accepting comments, she plants sabotage seeds into the company airwaves:

- "Donna's done some good things but watch out. She's a real empire builder. Watch her during the next budget meeting. You'll see her asking for more and more."
- "Scott's made some progress. He's OK if you point him in the right direction, but the real strategist on the team is the guy I hired, John. Without him, Scott wouldn't have a clue about the long-term competitive trends."
- "Anybody would have hit these numbers given the macro trends. Don't confuse genius with a bull market. Actually, I think that Johanna left money on the table last year."

Calculated Attacks. Top leaders may overlook the Overly Political person's preoccupation with what he can get away with or what will stick versus what is true, fair, or right. A conniving ladder-climber will analyze his target: "Does he have the power to hurt me back? Is he under political enough to not see what's coming until it's too late? Can I say something that's plausible enough to be believed? Can I get other people with access to seniors to say the same things?" If the wily one decides there's little risk in attacking someone, he'll use his analysis and his mastery of words to say *anything* he thinks will work. We've seen naïve people dismiss the threat of such attacks because they know the *facts*. They can't believe the saboteur's attack can find an audience, but learn too late that it does.

Weapons of Mass Distraction. The OP is undaunted when his own poor performance or unethical behavior comes under fire because he has cunning distractions up his sleeves. He may start an informal self-promotion campaign about the results his team has achieved, become vocal about an exciting new customer he's wooing, or suddenly unearth some company "crisis" that he is heroically handling. This ploy of calling attention to inflated positive actions deflects scrutiny off him and is comparable to the auto mechanic saying, "I'm sorry I can't fix your brakes this week, but don't worry because I made your horn louder."

The irony is that some of the political aptitudes that Overly Political people possess are the exact qualities needed by Under Political people of higher competence and integrity but lower astuteness. Sadly, the unethical goals of deception compel the deceivers to pervert savvy into sleazy activities such as diverting resources to their budgets, playing the system or the boss's ego to climb the ladder, and preventing innovative ideas or crucial information from reaching senior management.

The Ease of Deceiving CEOs and Top Leaders

CEO vulnerability to deception partly stems from *self*-deception. Power leads to significant changes in some people, including increased narcissism and arrogance. Meanwhile, people around top executives have tremendous incentive to stay on their good side and to make them feel bright, right, and important. This translates into top leaders becoming the center of attention, receiving deference and agreement, and hearing little criticism or challenge. A caste system results, with the privileged few telling top brass what they want to hear while those who challenge ideas or bring bad news have diminished status. It doesn't take long for everyone to notice and shift their behavior toward what's being rewarded. It's easy to see how executives veer onto a path toward ego-driven blind spots, with these consequences:

- *CEO Disease*. Overly political manipulators know that success and power lead executives to greater hubris, leaving them vulnerable to false flattery, supportive body language (undivided attention, smiling, and so on), and feigned commonality with management's core values. We've already referenced CEO disease, whereby leaders believe all the compliments they receive, so we have to "cure them" by telling them, "You might not be as smart, funny, or good-looking as others are saying."

- *Out of Touch with Reality.* The conceited executive believes he can size up people and situations well, but if he has weeded out the people who speak the truth and is surrounded by people who give him self-serving or filtered information, he may be seriously out of touch with what is really going on inside and outside the company.
- *Susceptibility to Image-Based Persuasion.* Politickers know they can easily convince this type of CEO to take action based on comments like these: "If we do this, it'll put you in a very unfavorable light." "If we don't move forward, they will be able to criticize you." "Les is making you look bad. He's undermining the values you've stated. People are watching you to see if you are onto him and whether you'll take action."

Obviously, not all people in power succumb to such patterns. But, enough do for us to be skeptical when a newly promoted executive says "I'll never change. I know how to manage my ego. I don't want yes-men. I want people to challenge me since I'm not always right." These are great words, spoken by many leaders but practiced by few. It's hard to hear criticism, negative feedback, and disagreement. When you have power, you don't have to endure it. But such deafness to data is dangerous for a leader, hurting the organization and leading to further deception and distortion.

What comes with a CEO's territory is a great deal of complexity: multiple products and services, doing business in different countries and cultures, Wall Street concerns and board activities, changes in technology and regulations, and intense competition and marketplace challenges. All of these demands pull on a CEO's attention and time. These multiple plates to juggle are complicated by personal issues such as health, older parents, needs of children, a romantic relationship, and financial planning. The result is that CEOs may rely on the information they receive from relatively few people. So people who have regular access to a CEO have extraordinary influence. The CEO can't be everywhere at once and can't always verify facts, analyses, and recommendations that are presented. This leaves the door wide open to deception by political players.

You may not be a CEO, but this bleak picture that faces top-floor rulers is even darker for lower-tier managers. As a middle- or first-line leader, you are even more vulnerable, because your limited power makes you less foreboding to Overly Political individuals. Don't you wonder how they might be playing you, what deception has been going on right under your nose, and how you might feed it? What can a manager at *any* level do to prevent self-deception and deception by others? She can learn to detect it, manage her own perceptual screens and filters, spot "private power pockets," and weed out the Overly Political. Then the path is clear for more savvy teams and broader-based culture change, which you'll master in the pages ahead.

Chapter 19

Detect Deception and Catch Schemers Red-Handed

Mind Your Brat or Make Him Stay Home!

Recent corporate history teaches that leaders at any level should *expect* pockets of deception and self-serving people. If you allow it to continue, you're like the negligent parent in a grocery store who lets a screaming child knock down store displays, bump into other shoppers, and wreak havoc. The overwhelmed adult either pretends to be oblivious, helplessly picks up after the brat, yells angrily while escalating the misbehavior, or sheepishly shrugs at annoyed and shocked onlookers. In a sense, through nonaction and failure to set firm limits, the child is being trained to remain a tyrant.

Similarly, many top leaders are "too busy," look the other way, perform token damage control, or merely simmer about the destructive deception of self-serving people. But simply resenting and blaming the Overly Political few doesn't constitute sound or responsible leadership. As one client's Portuguese mother used to tell him, "Just remember that when you're pointing at other people, there are always three fingers pointing back at yourself." The ability to detect deception, distinguish it from innocent information distortion, and nab schemers red-handed are key savvy leadership skills.

In this book's introduction, you met Sondra, a real manager who learned of serious financial misrepresentations at the very top of her organization. Her story illustrates leadership's failure to recognize and halt deception, destructive politics, and selfish agendas. Sondra felt too vulnerable to correct a wrong that ultimately led the company to restate earnings, write off $100 million, and lose 15 percent of its stock value. Her organization's leadership immobilization cost the company dearly in terms of scandal, scorching fines, public reputation, and good people leaving. But it doesn't have to be that way.

Innocent Distortion of Information

Besides deliberate deception, two innocent human tendencies make it important to carefully screen information from people: "biased social accounting" coming from *others,* and the "halo effect" coming from *you*.

Biased Social Accounting. This term describes a distorted view of oneself or events that places us in a more favorable light. The tendency is far more innocent than calculated deception. A well-intentioned person might let biased social accounting skew his perception of how events occurred. This common slanting of information about deserved credit includes inflating one's own relative contribution and diminishing the impact of others. You may not even be aware you're doing this, sincerely believing the "objective facts." The savvy leader is aware of this forgivable bias in people, so he doesn't harshly judge it. However, he's prudent enough to factor this tendency into his screening of any information he receives.

The Halo Effect. This distortion is also innocent, and it originates with *you*. Guard against distorted positive perceptions you may have about others, especially potentially deceptive people. You have a blind spot if someone's negative behavior or performance is clear to others but not to you. This is a "double whammy." Not only does the Overly Political (OP) continue with deceptive practices and feed you self-serving information, but you also lose credibility with the rest of the organization. Why are we all vulnerable to such blind spots? Partly due to a phenomenon that social psychologists call the halo effect, the undeserved credit or benefit of the doubt that a leader may give someone on the team. The slack we cut people because of the halo effect can stem from "interpersonal chemistry," having things in common (schools, sports, religion, geography, or interests), working together for a long time, or loyalty. Studies show that the halo effect can be triggered by height, fitness, physical attractiveness, pleasant speaking voice, or a charismatic presentation style. Also, if you've hired someone, your mind has a way of justifying behavior you would not sanction in others. People may mutter, "Just watch Kyle get away with it. After all, he's Stanford's boy."

The halo effect surrounds people who possess some of the fortunate inside-track qualities, but also the clever people who are good at "managing up" in the negative sense. They know how to use their mastery of words, knowledge of the senior's agenda, and ability to play off of predictable ego and narcissism to leverage this halo effect and deceive people in high places. Then saboteurs' comments are trusted, undeserved credit for good results sticks, and accountability for bad results bounces off them. The rest of the team is demotivated and wondering, "This isn't fair. What's the real scorecard? What do you need to do to get ahead?"

Detect Deception and Screen Information

Just as it becomes a whole new ball game when you catch a child with his hand in the cookie jar, you can do lots to prevent and catch masters of deceit red-handed (and therefore, red-faced). Nothing in this chapter replaces proper policies, procedures, and corporate governance. It's crucial to have formal monitoring, control systems, and processes for tracking money and results. This includes management practices such as 360-degree feedback tools, climate surveys, suggestion boxes, channels for whistle-blowers to safely provide input, and other risk management safe-guards for *formal detection* of deception and graft. But this chapter is about *you yourself* becoming a walking *informal detection system*.

Screen Information Given to You. Because of purposeful deception, as well as biased social accounting and the halo effect, screen information and rarely accept it uncritically, especially if you suspect a colleague is Overly Political. Whether someone is unintentionally distorting data or purposely giving you self-serving or misleading information, learn to listen in a careful, discerning way. Without becoming cynical, refine your skills at picking up when you're the target of self-serving, shaded, partial, or misleading information. Here are some questions to ponder as you flush out deception:

- *Motives and Integrity.* What is this person trying to sell me? What is the overt issue and what underlying goal is being pushed here? Is she just making sure the results really work and help the company, or is she trying to change my view about a person or a project? Why? What's in it for her? Does she gain if I agree? How? What hidden agenda might she have? Is there a position, pet project, increased visibility, financial reward, ego protection, or other benefit to her by taking this stance, or can I trust what she's saying at face value?
- *Buzz Goals.* What impressions is she trying to create about herself? What perceptions is she trying to create about someone else? Is she trying to mudsling or to provide valid feedback out of concern for the team? What positive or negative traits is she generating?
- *History.* What is this person's track record? Is she usually a contributing and ethical person or have I previously suspected her

of pushing the envelope or crossing the integrity line? Is she usually fair and precise with evidence to back up claims about projects or people or prone to global inferences and exaggerated labels to describe people? Has she been accurate in the past when predicting what will happen?

- *Speaking Truth to Power.* Does she ever take a risk by disagreeing with me or telling me something I don't want to hear? Does she always side with me on issues during meetings? Does she ever take a stand or state her point of view before she knows which way I am leaning? Does she watch for my reactions to others before voicing an opinion?
- *Substantive Grounding.* Is there obvious depth or preparation in her knowledge and analysis when I ask follow-up questions or mere generalities that show she hasn't done her homework? Do others use her as a sounding board, coach, or mentor, or is she spending too much of her time politicking to develop true expertise or results?
- *Accommodating Behavior.* Do her body language and vocal tone sometimes strike me as being too eager or enthusiastic? Is she too quick to nod assent before I've even finished explaining my view? Is she really digesting my rationale, or prematurely supporting anything I say to stroke my ego? Does she laugh harder at my jokes than seems appropriate? Does she try to look, dress, talk, and act like me?
- *Sense of Trust.* Is her communication style open, direct, and responsive, or vague, indirect, and guarded? Does she seem to be hiding something, afraid I'll detect something?

Make Deception Transparent. Guarding against the halo effect and biased social accounting, as well as using more discriminating analysis screens to filter information coming your way, will protect you from misrepresentation and distorted information. In addition, you can implement several other detection-savvy practices to flush out manipulators.

- *Periodically Test People.* Ask people for their point of view before you reveal which way you are leaning on an issue. Force direct reports and peers to express their stance rather than play the usual game of follow-the-leader. Then change your position on an issue or decision. Now notice who changes with you and who holds his ground. This identifies the BS artists and the people you can trust. Of course, just because a person changes his viewpoint doesn't always mean he's trying to read and accommodate you. He may be genuinely flexible and open to being wrong, just as he attempts to be with all people. Watch for whether he's more rigid with less powerful people to gauge true intent.
- *Decode Global, Inferential Language.* Notice how often a person uses vague and inflammatory labels about other people that cannot easily be proven or countered. Check whether an OP is mudslinging by asking for further clarity about an inferential label. Just as conversational aikido included probing for details when someone trashes *you* with a vague negative label, now you push for specifics and actual behaviors to flesh out what the person means when he bad-mouths someone else. Tell the messenger that you believe in the "camera test." You need to understand what a video camera would see and hear when he says someone is "not a team player" or "dropped the ball." Now, whether the person backs off or has objective examples, you'll have greater clarity about *two* people—the person being *talked* about and, more important, the person doing the *talking*. Was he being devious and now is caught red-handed? Be careful here, though. Often, it's just sloppy language that fuels these unsubstantiated labels rather than calculated sabotage.
- *Reverse the Reward/Punishment Paradigm.* Instead of rewarding the yes-men and shooting the reality messengers, reverse this tendency. Start publicly thanking and rewarding people who point out your mistakes, prevent you from making them, and give you bad news. Disapprove of those who try to play it safe, straddle both sides of an issue, or avoid taking a stand. Come down hard

on someone who buffers you from problems, sternly explaining that she hasn't done anyone any favors, especially herself.

A Deception-Detection Pro

Ron Rittenmeyer went from Frito-Lay to Burlington Northern Santa Fe Railway and walked into the aftermath of an ugly power struggle at the top. He knew that many people believed the only survival choice they had had was to become very political, play it safe with seniors, filter information, and maneuver for favor. He had compassion for people's posture, but wanted to mold the corporate culture into a healthier range of political behavior. He needed to be able to trust what his reports were saying to him. Ron began screening information from people instead of blindly trusting it; he knew to expect deception given the fear permeating an organization in such flux. He scanned for clues for filtered or misrepresented information while double-checking his own halo effect tendencies and wondering whether skewed data was just the result of innocently biased social accounting or the product of deliberate deception. He had the mental game down cold, because he had a realistic understanding of human nature and his own vulnerability, particularly because he was a newly anointed power holder. This led to Ron's hearing about his own shortcomings and flawed strategies as opposed to suffering CEO disease symptoms of shaded truth and false flattery.

Ron also reversed conditions by rewarding risk-taking behavior and truth telling, but punishing sabotage or deceptive behavior. When somebody said something about someone else's performance, he didn't accept it at face value. He probed for specifics, forcing people to back up any negative claims. He stroked honesty and courage about bad news. His direct reports spread the word that Ron didn't want deadwood on his team, but that he would not stand for rampant bad-mouthing. People knew they had better have the facts and evidence if they were going to challenge a project or jockey for position ahead of a peer. Ultimately, Ron's savvy leadership strategies meant a shake-up on his team but had a positive transformational effect on the culture and performance. A bonus was that Matt Rose, an executive on his team with good interpersonal skills who forthrightly spoke his mind, emerged as a high-integrity political leader. Matt is now the CEO of Burlington Northern Santa Fe and widely respected throughout the company and industry. Turning around the political culture starts with a leader like Ron Rittenmeyer who understands the laws of human nature and takes bold steps to detect and discourage deception while encouraging honesty and straight talk.

Savvy Relationships, Savvy Teams

Decisions about romantic partners, friends, financial partners, salespeople, consultants, and politicians are "bets" we make on other people. Gloria Steinem said that more men than women gamble because "women satisfy their entire urge to gamble when they get married." People who have been burned in romance or finance, or sold a bill of goods by salespeople, often say that they ignored the signals that were there all along. There's an old management maxim: "Love everyone. Trust no one." Take off the blinders and use your "deception detector" to stack the deck in your favor in important relationships. By retaining your capacity to trust but detecting whom *not to trust,* you can dramatically cut down on deception. You'll still feel compassion for others, even if they have hidden motives and selfish interests. Along with their manipulative tendencies, deceptive people may also bring their own pain into your office, a sad reality conveyed in this quote:

> *Do not judge your brothers and sisters,*
> *for there are secrets in their hearts that would make you weep.*
>
> —ANONYMOUS, FROM A WORKSHOP PARTICIPANT

Chapter 20

Make "Private Power Pockets" Public

The most damaging impact of deception occurs when an Overly Political manager establishes a "private power pocket." In this situation, people live under fear of a tyrannical boss who rules with unethical behavior and a self-serving agenda. This controlling bully restricts access to team members and important information from people outside the team. The result is isolation and people fearfully refusing to answer questions before checking with their boss. To clear the air of this poisonous atmosphere, flush out these private power pockets and eliminate them.

The Cost of Private Power Pockets

The Bottom-Line Costs. The devastation to an organization when a private power pocket spins out of control and is exposed too late can include bankruptcy, job losses, a drop in shareholder value, pension losses, and reputation damage. When the discovered henchman is finally ousted from this kind of "closed shop," the cleanup costs can be enormous. Just as bad, sometimes no one discovers the problem until the culprit pilfers money and exits the company. We know of an executive who intimidated staff, drank and flagrantly socialized with women on the team, and then got a peer fired who was onto him. The president of the division had a blind spot for the guy, creating a halo effect that allowed continued outrageous behavior. After the oppressor left on his own terms, the organization discovered $25 million of unexpected losses.

Sondra, from our introduction, was trapped inside a private power pocket where a French division's financials were being fudged to line an executive's pockets. Her company's CEO said that he wanted "no bad news." The resulting financial scandal cost over $100 million and a stock price nosedive, all because people like Sondra were understandably too afraid to blow the whistle. Top management was to blame, not Sondra.

There are over eight thousand mutual funds that employ stock analysts and portfolio managers. These investment strategists study industry trends and macroeconomic data, but many times their recommendations are also based on their evaluation of a company's leadership. It is essential for these investment professionals to have the deception-detection skills to determine if CEOs, CFOs, and investor relations personnel in a company are giving partial or misleading information. Increasingly, investment professionals with better evaluation tools can bring greater honesty and transparency to open up such private power pockets.

The Cost to Employees. The disastrous impact from public exposure is obvious, but usually private power pockets never implode or explode into public scandals that bring company gutting, financial ruin, or trashed careers. More often, there is slower, but just as insidious, destruction. If you have ever worked for someone who ran a private power pocket, you know how devastating it can be. Employees face intimidation and punishment for speaking out. Many suffer erosion of their self-esteem as their integrity is challenged daily. They vacillate between hatred for the demagogue and self-loathing that they cannot bring themselves to confront the situation or blow the whistle, for fear of censure, job loss, or worse.

Enron whistle-blower Sherron Watkins testified that her internal memo to Chairman Ken Lay nearly got her fired by the CFO. Tobacco-industry whistle-blower Dr. Jeffrey Wigand clued *60 Minutes* onto Brown and Williamson Tobacco Company's documented ploys to hook smokers. Although he was eventually made a hero in the movie *The Insider,* his life was a living hell for a long time as his detractors went after him, his job, his finances, and his reputation.

The Cost to Top Leaders. As with general employees, just because a private power pocket doesn't destroy an organization doesn't mean that CEOs and other top executives are left unscathed. The political dry rot of fear-driven fiefdoms hurts people even in the highest places, whether they are in the dark or clued in but reluctantly tolerant of these insulated teams. Eventually, keen observers within the company's population question the awareness and credibility of senior management: "Don't they see what's going on?" And meanwhile, employees on the trapped team are asking, "Doesn't senior management care? Is my dictator boss somehow being protected? Is it safe to tell the truth?"

How Private Power Pockets Survive

Given the disastrous impact of private power pockets, their prevalence is amazing. They can only exist if one or both of the following conditions exist.

- *A Macro-Organizational Blind Spot.* You know that a deadly combination of skilled deception, the halo effect, and executive self-deception due to narcissism and arrogance creates vulnerability to false or filtered information. It's one thing to be duped by a highly skilled manipulator in a given moment, but when a CEO overlooks the many clues that a self-serving despot is injuring many people, the blind spot is pervasive and serious.
- *Protection by Senior Management.* Even worse, a guarded group with unethical motives may emerge through tolerance and collu-

sion rather than an accidental blind spot. If the group functions at the team level, a director or midlevel manager may be implicated. If the problem is with an entire division or function, a top executive or even the CEO may be supportive. If the secret society is the entire company itself, then the board of directors isn't providing enough scrutiny or accountability. Many of the worst corporate scandals in recent years involved people who knew what was going on but were intimidated by threats of being fired or transferred or were bribed in some fashion.

Private Power Pocket Signals

We've discussed how to recognize overly political behavior, various faces of sabotage, and clues for deceptive or distorted information. Here are other signals of private power pockets:

- *No Access.* The leader guards access to people and information. Direct reports are told not to communicate with others or answer questions from people outside the organization. When asked for information, they seem uncomfortable, saying, "I need to check with my boss."
- *Group Fascism.* Team meetings have little real conflict or debate. People don't take risks and they try to find out the leader's point of view before speaking. Few people challenge the leader, and those who do are put in the doghouse—fired or marginalized.
- *A Self-Protective Leader.* The leader guards his turf, becoming emotional about "intrusions." He only wants to work with consultants whom he knows or chooses. He avoids feedback surveys used by the company or, if he has to participate, rigs them in his favor.
- *Whistle-Blowing.* Exit interviews point to indiscretion and self-interest by the leader. Whistle-blowers later surface but may be severely punished.
- *Poor Morale.* Team members seem unmotivated, disillusioned, and resigned. Competent people with high integrity have left,

either by force or by choice, and the team seems to have an inordinate amount of attrition.

Sometimes the same qualities that characterize a private power pocket can also appear in more garden-variety "silo-structured" teams. Perhaps no one is erecting a moat around the team to hoard power or information for self-serving, financial, or scandalous motives. The insulation may just reflect a less communicative company norm or a rigid structure.

Weed Out Private Power Pockets

While you don't want to make a "false positive" diagnosis, you surely don't want to overlook a dangerously insulated private power pocket. You're left with several strategies you can install *before* you even see any symptoms.

Indirect Preventive Measures. Without calling attention to your additional goals of surfacing and detecting private power pockets, you can announce that for increased collaboration, leadership development, and organizational learning (notice that you *don't* mention corporate governance or risk management), you are installing any of these mechanisms:

- *Input Tools.* A 360-degree feedback instrument on all leaders is common. Also, many excellent anonymous climate surveys are available to improve the motivation and atmosphere in all teams. Install suggestion-box systems to encourage employee participation and cost-saving ideas. If, by chance, someone uses the vehicle for an anonymous tip-off about a private power pocket or suspicious behavior by a manager, so be it. These mechanisms give trapped employees an avenue for safely and anonymously blowing the whistle.
- *Forums.* Cross-organizational, interteam reports and town hall meetings give teams a chance to interact, learn each other's

businesses, and open up interdisciplinary communication for improved teamwork. Of course, teams that either don't show up or communicate guardedly provide clues that they may live in fear.

- *Visitations.* Consider periodically "managing by wandering around," so that you are accessible and connected. Who could fault such progressive management? Only the Overly Political control freak, since he's worried about what you'll discover. Get into the habit of actually sitting side by side with a task-level person to get the opportunity for reading her nonverbal signals and attitudes about her boss.
- *Strategic Reorganizations.* One client CEO populated cubicle pods with people from different parts of the company. Configurations changed every nine months. This practice promoted cross-organizational communication and lowered the likelihood of private power pockets. Team members couldn't be insulated physically for long periods. The frequency of change may have been too frenetic, but the strategy was ingenious.

Direct Preventive Measures. These are usually mandated once a private power pocket is actually exposed. You can also preventively initiate ongoing corporate governance and risk management measures. They aren't aimed at a particular team but instead send a message of rigor across the entire enterprise to ensure compliance with ethical and financial management norms. These measures include confidential interviews of randomly selected employees, exit interviews that double-check whether people's departure is due to Overly Political bosses, and risk management policies. Large banks require that an employee's two weeks of vacation be taken consecutively to foil embezzlement, since theft schemes require on-the-job presence. Consider implementing procedures that encourage whistle-blowers to surface unethical, illegal, or suspicious behavior. You must ensure their safety (think Witness Protection Program) and reward honesty. Prevent any personal vendettas or unfair fingering of tough but ethical managers by disgruntled employees. Make sure people understand that false accusations won't be tolerated. You're not trying to launch a witch hunt!

Spring into Action

In every instance where we have seen private power pockets, there was severe damage to the company. The longer a situation went without being addressed, the greater the fallout. Often, by the time an Overly Political person leaves, his organization has become a house of cards ready to topple. So once you detect and verify the symptoms, take immediate action to protect the people on the team, your company, and yourself. At the team level, weeding out untrustworthy people improves results, resources, and morale. At a companywide level, this cleansing improves morale and performance while protecting the corporation from scandal. Swift action defends *you* from potential sabotage, behind-the-scenes mutiny, or even liability. People are depending on you to do something.

Ongoing monitoring is essential. Depending on the circumstances, you might initiate the same kind of confidential interviews, audits, and independently administered surveys by outside consultants that you used to implement the preventive measures discussed above. Once wrongdoing is revealed, you may be required by law to take specific action to prevent further misdeeds, so work closely with your legal team.

Consider whether the person can change. If you have hiring and firing responsibility, consult closely with your human resources officers to decide whether the overly political ringleader of an exposed private power pocket can remain in the organization. If someone has run a closed shop, there's a good chance that she won't change. In most corporations, you can't fire someone without compiling an extensive paper trail and working in concert with human resources. In your decision-making, consider these tough questions:

- Did the person's hidden agenda just have to do with gaining power, or were legal and financial improprieties also committed?
- Was the person afraid of losing her job or in financial trouble that could explain her out-of-character behavior?
- Given human nature, how much deception are you comfortable allowing?
- What will be the impact on company morale if you do or do not remove the person? Who else is implicated and subject to discipline?
- Should you purposely keep the person on board but relegate her to a figurehead, or even put her in the "penalty box" as a message to others?

We're not telling you whether or not to fire someone, especially given the legal ramifications. We simply want you to see that private power pockets are a grave issue. If you decide to remove a person, how can you do it in a fashion that reinforces your norm of high-integrity politics and ethical leadership, without spreading paranoia or an air that "Big Brother is watching"? You don't want to be seen as an impulsive hatchet man or woman. Setting up mechanisms to thwart private power pockets will help to avoid ugly showdowns. But when you cannot prevent such situations, take into account how serious the problem is, what damage has occurred, the chances of repetition, the person's ethical track record and professed value system, and the impact on the company of your decision. Whatever you decide, you need to let it be known that *you are on it,* that you take deception and private power pockets seriously.

PART IV

LEADERSHIP SAVVY TACTICS TO BUILD A SAVVY TEAM AND COMPANY

Chapter 21

The Team Trust/Competence Grid

"Now *That's* a Tool I Can Use Immediately!"

We love it when people tell us they don't need to plan how to utilize our street-smart savvy tactics, since they are so practical. Here's another instantly applicable tool that helps managers and leaders at all levels—the Team Trust/Competence Grid. This grid sorts out people on key differences so that you can (1) size them up, (2) decide when to filter people's information and ideas, and (3) know what to do after detecting deception. The tool gradually transforms an organization by creating a critical mass of competent, high-integrity people who can be coached, trained, and managed into savvy performers. Savvy leaders assemble the best of three worlds—*competence, integrity, and political astuteness*—molding company culture by first getting "the right people on the bus," as Jim Collins describes in his road map to organizational transformation, *Good to Great*.

Constructing the Grid

On the Team Trust/Competence Grid, **Competence** is the vertical axis, ranging from low to high, and **Trust** is the horizontal axis, also ranging from low to high.

- *Competence* refers to a person's task-level credibility: How knowledgeable is she? What is the depth of her understanding? Does she add value in discussions? Do her ideas, concerns, and issues turn out to be valid? Is she good at what she does? If the answers are positive, she has high competence on the vertical scale.
- *Trust* refers to integrity, intention, and sincerity: Does she act in behalf of the company (high trust) or only her own selfish interests (low trust)? Does she purposely bias information, practice deception, sabotage, misrepresent data, tell you what you want to hear, or run a private power pocket? If you think she is an expert in a subject but you don't trust her motives or sincerity, you will be skeptical about the advice she provides.

On our grid, the horizontal scale of **Trust** (low or high) and the vertical scale of **Competence** (low or high) form four quadrants into which you can sort the people on your team and in your organization. Let's look at people who fall into each of the four quadrants and focus on the implications for how you might view and manage them.

The Team Trust / Competence Grid

	Low Trust	High Trust
High Competence	**High Competence / Low Trust** • Filter information given • Find private power pockets • Weigh strengths versus trust • Will feedback help?	**High Competence / High Trust** • Treat as a go-to team member • Elevate the person • Develop organizational savvy
Low Competence	**Low Competence / Low Trust** • Manage the person out? • Follow HR protocol	**Low Competence / High Trust** • Reassign to proper fit • Create a development plan for areas of low competence • Weigh strengths versus trust • Develop organizational savvy

Managerial Options for Each Quadrant

Low Competence/Low Trust. In evaluating competence, use the above questions to get a sense of someone's track record. To evaluate trust, rely on the many political style signals and ways of detecting deception you learned previously. If, based on your evaluation, someone belongs in the lower-left quadrant, there aren't many redeeming factors. The recommendation here is to decide whether to *manage out* the person from the organization, since there may have been a selection error. Of course, you must *follow human resources protocol,* and all due process from a legal and fairness standpoint is essential.

Low Competence/High Trust. This person has many of the values and behaviors that you want, but has shortfalls in key task-level competencies. What are your options? One possibility is to *reassign* him to a role more suited to his competencies and strengths, finding the right fit factor. A second option, if you feel he can grow and develop, is to invest in a *training or development plan* to raise his skills and knowledge to acceptable levels. If the areas in which he is weak are not amenable to training and development, you may need to make a tough call about this person, but this is a last resort after coaching, training, and redeployment. If he does survive, for him to thrive you may also need to ground him in political astuteness and *develop organizational savvy.*

High Competence/Low Trust. This person probably represents your biggest leadership challenge. She may be good and knowledgeable at what she does, but you've unearthed patterns where she can be deceptive or self-serving. You may not like how she treats others in the organization. You need to *watch for private power pockets* and *filter information* that she gives you, taking it with a grain of salt, reality-testing it, and using chapter 19's methods for catching her red-handed. We also recommend that you *evaluate the trade-offs.* Do her results and strengths add contributions that outweigh her BOP or Overly Political behavior? Are you able to filter what she tells you enough to separate out the useful information, or is it just too labor-intensive? How much damage is she doing to the team and the rest of the organization? What impact might her retention have on your reputation for sound stewardship of the organization?

As we suggested for weeding out the OP style, decide how much you believe she can change. Might feedback help? Some people who exhibit untrustworthy or manipulative behavior can improve if they receive feedback, combined with clear negative consequences for repeat offenses and ongoing monitoring. Sometimes, a political player doesn't realize how obvious and self-defeating her behavior is. The problem behavior may improve because of good-faith intentions to be more trustworthy, or due to the fear of consequences.

If you think this person is a reasonably contributing team member and might change with feedback, then it is probably worth a try. In this case, it is important that the feedback be specific ("You overstated your contribution to the Reynolds project and did not mention that Mary's analysis actually led to these consumer insights") and that the consequences for not changing are explicit. Also, emphasize that the person must absolutely refrain from retaliation against anyone on the team who provided feedback about her overly political behavior. Reassignment of a whistle-blower might be necessary (to a better job).

High Competence/High Trust. This person is worth his weight in gold to the team leader, so we call him a *go-to* person. He has a track record of being accurate in his predictions, knowledgeable in key areas, and valuable during discussions. In addition, he has demonstrated that he thinks about and acts in line with company core values and what's best for the organization. For example, he may make suggestions for changes in the organizational structure that actually reduce his own resources, head count, or turf. He may take a personal risk in telling you something you don't want to hear when he stands to gain nothing. If asked, he may take a role on the team that is not his first choice, because you need him to do it. Like anyone, he can falter at times, thinking of his own interest, but not in ways that hurt the company, and generally you can give what he says 100 percent credence. Since you want this go-to person around, you might want to *elevate* him and provide him with tools for avoiding his political blind spots, since he may have many Less Political Power of Ideas qualities. To make sure he is not Under Political (UP) or Borderline Under Political (BUP), you might decide to *develop his organizational savvy* through mentoring, coaching, and training.

Use the Grid as a Bridge to Savvy Team and Company Cultures

For the short term, use your savvy and detection skills to place your people on the Team Trust/Competence Grid, using separate pieces of paper or imagining where someone fits as she joins your team. With this new lens for viewing team members, you may notice behavior that you previously ignored. Naturally, shift people on the grid as you receive new data. You can use this tool to recruit, select, and gradually assemble a team and organization of high-competence/high-trust members. Using insights from the rest of this book, you can cultivate people's political awareness and skill, so that they aren't at a disadvantage when you elevate them to more powerful positions. You'll weed out the political cancers while ensuring that self-interest-driven individuals who remain lose their edge.

Chapter 22

Build a Savvy Team

One Small Step for Man, One Giant Leap for Your Team . . .

We hope you will use this book's ethical political strategies to achieve a position of positive power and influence. Beyond this, you may also lead a team, department, or division, if not an entire business. You can use the previous chapter's Team Trust/Competence Grid to understand your team's composition in terms of capability and integrity, so that you can assemble an optimal cadre of people. Now you're ready to increase your team's organizational savvy, visibility, and impact as you guide your people toward political astuteness. Ideally, you will reach even further, using the next chapter's principles to forge a high-integrity, high-influence organizational culture that is free from under political or overly political postures.

Assess Your Team's Political Health and Style Balance

Scan for Political Symptoms. We don't suggest mass distribution of the list of political health symptoms we revealed in chapter 17 for an open discussion of the group's political temperature. Such a bold move could be dangerous, especially without a skilled facilitator to handle potential volatility. Calling direct attention to political imbalance in a team wake-up-call meeting might feel too blaming and create uproar. It may be wiser to use a subtler approach to shape your team toward awareness and change. But we urge you to at least privately screen your organization's political health symptoms to take its political pulse. This will prevent your own denial and blind spots.

We know team leaders who so trust their teams and are so committed to developing "impact with integrity" that they conduct open forums, off-site retreats, or staff meetings about these issues. But most leaders prefer to informally diagnose their team's political health by scanning for the symptoms on their own and then reality-testing their assessments with one or two highly trusted team veterans. They strategize accordingly to implement some of the ideas in this chapter as they adjust their team's, department's, or division's political balance.

Build Political Style Knowledge. Every team is only as strong (and as savvy) as its weakest link. We recommend focusing your people on high-integrity politics as a potentially positive force in your company and inviting them to think about their own political style. You might want to personally teach our Power of Person and Power of Ideas mind-sets, informally coach them, lend them this book, send them to a workshop, or use language and concepts other than ours to get people to examine their own under political or overly political behavior. However, be careful, because if word leaks out to other groups that you're the only team discussing company politics, you run the risk of being perceived as Machiavellian or even as running a private power pocket yourself. So it's vital to monitor how people discuss this material and to emphasize the "high-integrity" dimension of your educational efforts—you're aiming for greater team influence in ethical ways that allow your team's expertise to benefit the company.

Focus on Positive Political Behaviors. Another approach is to avoid discussing what political style people possess (although people like such typologies and self-awareness). Instead, just identify the constructive political behaviors that you want people to hone and implement. Use assessment tools, feedback, coaching, appraisals, and training to help Under Political people learn savvy tactics and skills. Also, appeal to Overly Political individuals to rein in their excessive maneuvering traits that create distrust or alienation. You may find that the Organizational Savvy Skills Assessment offered at the end of this book is helpful to your team.

Discuss the Team's Political Style. Next, use your group's knowledge about political styles to reach consensus about the political style of your team as a whole. Do *not* ask people to identify one another's political styles or to slot individuals into the various quadrants on the last chapter's Team Trust/Competence Grid. These exercises would create unnecessary vulnerability and tension. However, open discussion about how various other organizations might view your team along the Organizational Savvy Continuum will be interesting, stimulating, and helpful for teambuilding. We often prompt intact teams to consider how they might be seen by the broader corporation in terms of political style. Then the teams can minimize their style-based risks or disadvantages and improve their team corporate buzz.

Strategies to Build Team Savvy and Correct Political Imbalance

Just as individuals can strategize actions to maximize political style strengths while minimizing predictable risks, a leader can implement teamwide practices to prevent her group from being either under political or too political. To illustrate managerial practices that will help your team as a whole manage its political style weaknesses, influence others, and protect itself, we'll revisit each of the six dimensions of political style. Our suggestions won't be exhaustive, but will illustrate how a savvy leader can help a team rebalance its political posture. As we move through the same style mind-sets introduced in chapter 2, the recommendations that are labeled "Be Less Political" are tactics that can be used for teams that are currently too political. The strategies that are designated "Be More Political" can be used to bolster a team's under political tendencies. Make sure that you guard against overcompensating for a trait, since this just creates a pendulum swing to new style flaws and risks.

Substance Power ↔ Position Power

Substance Power (Be Less Political). Demand task-level excellence to let your More Political team know that you don't overlook the power residing in the work itself. Schedule ongoing times for intact-team training sessions to guarantee that the team stays current technically and establishes a uniform set of technical standards and practices. The bumper sticker for this strategy reads, "A Family That Learns Together Earns Together!" If your team stays up to speed and achieves identified measures of excellence, it will be hard for outsiders to accuse the group of being overly involved in politics.

Position Power (Be More Political). But like individuals, entire teams can be too myopically focused on their functional competence, only to lose access to power networks. Help an insulated team by stressing the need to study formal and informal power within the company. There is plenty of information about management priorities, key relationships, and trends, so expect your people to devote a reasonable amount of time to understanding such agendas and to nourishing the team's critical interdependencies. The resulting power network will support your group's recommendations, provide warnings about conflicts with other teams, and tell your team its corporate buzz. At team meetings, ask your reports to provide networking updates about what they've learned about other teams or key people. Periodically invite outside managers and seniors to meetings for briefings or presentations, as long as this isn't a disingenuous or opportunistic move. Also, have your team discuss and assess other groups and individuals along the Organizational Savvy Continuum.

While savvy leaders and teams don't want a "turf tyrant" mentality, they need to be effective boundary monitors and advocates. Excessive role overlap or redundancy with other teams can breed conflict and threaten your team, so monitor boundaries and negotiate responsibilities with other executives. If overly political teams populate your company, especially deceptive private power pockets, train your team to detect sabotage and manipulation. You can also protect your team's turf from garden-variety maneuvering at interteam planning meetings about budgets and operating plans. Have team data-gathering and strategy sessions before cross-organizational planning meetings so that you have facts and analyses to support your requests. Anticipate and build a defense against other team leaders who might try to siphon away some of your resources and budget. Use input from your team to determine realistic stretch goals. You represent your team at planning meetings, so if you give away too much or overcommit, you will hurt your team.

Focus on Feedback and Learning ↔ Focus on Image and Perception

Focus on Feedback and Learning (Be Less Political). The Power of Ideas political style's openness to input and improvement is the cornerstone of a great team and company. Thomas J. Watson, former president of IBM, advised, "You can be discouraged by failure—or you can learn from it. So go ahead and make mistakes. Make all you can. Because remember, that's where you'll find success. On the far side of failure." This willingness to risk mistakes represents the spirit of inquiry essential to progress. Eleanor Roosevelt said, "I think that at a child's birth, if a mother could ask a fairy godmother to endow it with the most useful gift, that gift would be curiosity."

Yet, many ego-conscious Power of Person teams harm themselves and their organizations through their excessive "focus on image and perception." Confucius said, "A man who commits a mistake and doesn't admit it is committing another mistake." NASA's cocky team culture is partly blamed for the 2003 shuttle disaster, and some critics point to ego-sensitive complacency as a root cause of tragedies like the *Exxon Valdez* oil tanker spill or Three Mile Island. For overly political teams needing more of a "learner attitude," their savvy leaders can gradually cultivate a feedback-rich environment. Entire company transformation efforts can focus on building learning organizations as more and more corporations hire chief learning officers. You yourself can use the methods below to become the informal chief learning officer of your team.

- *Formalized Programs.* Savvy leaders institutionalize forums for learning and feedback, such as Jack Welch's famous GE Workout, where norms for feedback exchange were brutally honest. Climate surveys providing feedback about team functioning is the group analogue to individual 360-degree feedback tools used for leadership and professional development. Meet to discuss where the entire team can improve according to feedback.
- *Debriefing Mechanisms.* Install processes so that informal team feedback occurs regularly. One method is to end team meetings with a "debriefing session." At this time people share their reactions to the meeting, including feedback to one another about what worked well or what would be more effective for future meeting management and interaction.
- *Promoting the Learner Attitude*. More than anything, your own willingness to be an exemplar of receiving feedback nondefensively sparks a feedback-rich environment. We learn plenty about a company's climate simply by asking how mistakes are handled. If people live in fear of consequences for mistakes, they won't

take risks and the company is in trouble. Worse, they may protect their backsides, covering their tracks to hide their problems and weaknesses. Leaders don't find out about mistakes unless there is honest and safe dialogue about shortcomings. How should you handle mistakes? Let's say that a direct report comes to you and admits he was abusive to a peer from another team. Here are the steps to take to promote the learner attitude.

1. *Respond Nonpunitively.* Use empathic listening and reflect back the person's feelings instead of rolling your eyes and getting upset: "Jerry, it sounds like you're really disappointed in yourself for losing your cool with Sharon. You even seem worried about coming to me about this problem. Am I tracking you?"
2. *Appreciate the Person's Honesty.* Reinforce the person's integrity and urge future forthcoming communication: "Jerry, I have to be honest. I'm not thrilled this happened, just as you aren't. But I really appreciate that you trusted me enough to come and tell me. That to me says loads more about your professionalism than the fact you blew it with this one colleague. Thank you."
3. *Focus on Learning for the Future.* Discuss the root causes of the mistake and how it can be prevented in the future, probing for any warning signs: "What might have been the root causes? What can we learn from this? Could you have foreseen this happening and prevented it, and if so, how can we avoid this next time?"
4. *Work to Salvage the Situation.* Ask the employee to come up with ideas and suggest your own thoughts: "As far as the immediate situation, should I call back Sharon, should you, or shall we both write an apology e-mail? Would a humorous symbolic gift help?"
5. *Find Something to Reinforce.* This step might be tough to do genuinely, but if there's something positive, include this focus, even though overall the situation is not desirable: "From how

you describe the scenario, you did keep your cool when Sharon was criticizing your work, but you were triggered when she said something personal and unfair about your colleagues. It's admirable that you wanted to stick up for your peers."

6. *Acknowledge and Announce Your Own Mistakes.* You might make a general statement about only being human or give a personal example of a similar gaffe you've made: "Jerry, everyone loses it now and then. I haven't lately blown it with a colleague from another team, but remember last month? I was really ticked off in our team meeting and said some things that were out of line. So I've messed up, too, but what's important is to take responsibility for it the way you have, and to work on improving."

Focus on Image and Perception (Be More Political). BUP or UP teams need to think more about how they are perceived and do more to manage these impressions. Every team should know its reputation and influence stock, because such buzz affects access to management's ear, resources, and even a team's survival. The savvy leader prompts her team to think collectively about the positive, negative, and limiting labels used to describe its functional area. Work with your team to identify perceptions by other teams or powerful individuals, then develop concrete plans to alter problematic reputation descriptors. Even somewhat savvy teams can still benefit from this exercise, especially if they interact with even more politically active teams. When one political giant consumer bank merged with a large and even more aggressive investment firm, the retail bank's vice chairman told us he wanted us to help his top team to "better face off" with their counterpart's more combative style.

Do the Right Thing ↔ Do What Works

Do the Right Thing (Be Less Political). This political style dimension entails stretching the team to make sacrifices on the company's behalf. The team can become the corporate hero if it pitches in to help other groups. One Apple Computer engineering team made corporate history in the eighties when it shut itself in a building, hoisted a pirate's flag, and refused to leave until they had solved a major design challenge. But make sure the team isn't so self-*less* that it disintegrates into a dumping ground for unappealing projects. You don't want your team becoming "corporate Siberia" or the butt of jokes. Monitor for balance and properly document resources your team devotes to helping other teams. When interviewing other groups about how to improve your team's service, strive to go above and beyond, but don't let your team be abused or become a scapegoat.

If your team has had instances of self-interest or political greed, curb such activity by using mechanisms that ensure doing what's right. For example, in response to the accusations against Tyco of "granting unauthorized bonuses and using the company coffers as personal piggy banks," Senior Vice President of Human Resources Laurie Siegel became celebrated for masterminding groundbreaking bonus assessments based on behavior and values as well as results. Her China Council's charter helps Tyco's Asian business heads avoid competing with one another for common talent or physical resources.

Do What Works (Be More Political). Politically balanced managers encourage their people to elevate the team's status, power, and influence, but to do so with integrity. It is healthy and invigorating to encourage interdepartmental contests over organizational results, charity drives, and intramural sports. On the other hand, you don't want your team stepping over the "never say die" and "can-do attitude" line into negatively underhanded behavior. Therefore, invite your team to critique itself on its interteam communication, its treatment of others, and its integrity. Sober your team by explaining the disastrous results when Ford in 1973 decided to avoid fuel system corrections that would have prevented Pinto explosions when the car was hit from behind. Some top executives who wanted to get ahead financially almost wound up as obsolete as the Pinto did, with scores of lawsuits. The 1992 class action suit against Sears Auto Centers for allegedly overcharging customers provided further fuel for conversations about companies that may have taken shortcuts to profits while being ethically shortsighted. So grill your team about the level of competition it engenders within the organization and differentiate a positive "do what it takes" mind-set from naked self-interest to earn favored status on the corporate totem pole.

More Open Agendas ↔ More Private Agendas

More Open Agendas (Be Less Political). The tobacco industry brought scandal upon itself through an overly private agenda, so if you worry your team is too private and guarded with agendas, model honesty and urge group learning from examples like Tylenol and Saturn. The forthright, open handling of the famous Tylenol crisis was referenced early in the book. Saturn built a brand identity for friendly, down-to-earth relationships with its "family" of customers. So when a defective wire was suspected in 350,000 of its 1993 models, Saturn immediately sponsored a massive recall that featured free barbecues, tickets and transportation to baseball games, and theater trips for families while their vehicles were repaired. Saturn made lemonade out of lemons as up-front communication resulted in 50 percent of the cars being fixed within two weeks and customer loyalty that is legendary in the field.

Besides enhancing company-level open agendas, at the team level the savvy leader champions openly communicated progress reports, cross-unit visitations, job rotations, and open goal setting. "Open book management" is one way that leaders combat excessive secrecy norms. Some CEOs believe all financials are the property of the workforce. Anything you can do to reward honest and forthright communication corrects any tendency toward private power pockets, guarded mind-sets, or unethical business practices.

More Private Agendas (Be More Political). If your team is naïve about competition within the company, discuss what information is appropriate to share outside the team. Blind openness can expose your organization to unjust criticism, premature evaluation, or undue scrutiny that may disrupt team progress. If there are flawed data, safety dilemmas, or regulatory and compliance issues, the obvious step is to divulge status. However, a more private agenda may be appropriate to prevent a team from prematurely blabbing research glitches to people who don't comprehend scientific setbacks as part of normal experimentation. Similarly, a human resources team needs to make strategic timing choices concerning announcements about layoffs, mergers, and acquisitions. (We're *not* saying, "What they don't know won't hurt them," since this rationalization could lead to ethical breaches.)

Meritocracy-Based Decisions ↔ Relationship-Based Decisions

Meritocracy-Based Decisions (Be Less Political). The belief in rewards for performance regardless of political connections is an antidote to the good old boy network. You may not have the position power or Human Resources authority to determine how rewards and promotion decisions are made, but as a leader you can influence the right people to make eventual changes as you guide your own team or department toward a meritocracy. Companies like Intel, IBM, Genentech, and Hewlett-Packard have reduced cronyism and political behavior as the basis for rewards through clearer performance measures, "pay for performance" management systems, peer reviews, and objective discussion of results at appraisal time. Meritocracy-based decisions are also more likely when there is a database of people's skills, trumpeting that competence is the major criterion for advancement.

PepsiCo's Indra Nooyi, named *Fortune* magazine's eighth-most-powerful woman in corporate America, worked steadfastly with CEO Steve Reinemund to build a meritocracy based upon competence and results. Eric Foss and John Cahill at Pepsi Bottling Group consciously worked to eliminate promotion decisions based on schmoozing, relationships, or connections. Nektar CEO

Ajit Gill used peer reviews to ensure fairness and multiple checks and balances at appraisal time. GE's Jack Welch was the consummate meritocracy leader, not worrying about image, power, or telling the stockholders what they wanted to hear. His passion for GE's Six Sigma program gave him his own black belt. He held people accountable based on the number of defects in products and the cycle time it took to get them to market.

Promoting a meritocracy is compatible with an organization's commitment to diversity, since it's no longer what you look like that makes the grade. WellPoint's CEO, Leonard Schaeffer, named one of America's best CEOs by *Worth* magazine, built a diversity-driven organization that is lauded "for providing highly successful special assignments to help women reach the executive suite and for its strong representation of women on its board of directors." WellPoint has gained recognition on *Executive Female* magazine's "Top 25 Companies for Executive Women" three years in a row.

Relationship-Based Decisions (Be More Political). This dynamic gets back to networking, since some teams do not form enough relationships. While you don't want a team to spend all of its time schmoozing, under political teams may overemphasize due diligence in selecting contractors so that they waste time reinventing the wheel. Don't become so paranoid about ensuring a meritocracy to level the playing field that you overlook the importance of factoring in appropriate relationship-based considerations: loyalty, commitment by suppliers over the long haul through up and down cycles, and knowledge of the company's history. As long as complacency or deadwood haven't set in, teams can benefit from safeguarding some degree of relationship-based decisions.

Results and Ideas Speak for Themselves ↔ Self-Promotion

Results and Ideas Speak for Themselves (Be Less Political). For extremely image-oriented teams, adjustments along this dimension entail helping people to see the perils of the team's having a reputation for "strutting their stuff." You aren't adding complicated systems or programs, but simply inviting self-reflection and needed humility. An example is Art Levinson, CEO of Genentech, who expects companywide humbleness and a company culture that frowns upon excessive self-promotion. He exemplifies a corporatewide stance of humility and monitoring of promotion by not allowing the biotech giant to advertise on TV like its competitors. He commendably believes such advertisements in his lifesaving industry to be crass and inappropriate, stressing that he'd rather have physicians praise the company's impact on health care and lives.

Self-Promotion (Be More Political). On the other hand, is your team the best-kept secret within your organization, to a fault? Many groups err by leaning so far toward letting ideas and results speak for themselves that they become invisible or disrespected. Just as individual self-promotion is required to reverse a dangerously low profile that leads to being underestimated and marginalized, the savvy leader encourages his entire Under Political team to seek visibility and recognition for its ideas, results, and potential by establishing a stronger team identity. Think about charging your team with broadcasting its contribution through a team brand, perhaps with a logo, a tagline, or artifacts such as team T-shirts. Encourage team promotions through visitations to other teams to share learning (and accomplishments) or team newsletters to brief the rest of the company on achievements and progress.

We know of one managing director whose first action step upon taking the reins was to reduce the isolation of her team by asking for a monthly team newsletter to be put onto the company's intranet. Progressive division leaders sponsor team exposition days on which employees visit booths in an exhibition hall to learn about the accomplishments of other teams. This reinforces networking and a learner attitude, while achieving a balance between More Political and Less Political style values. We know of an uplifting company culture in which everyone from the CEO on down encouraged salespeople to announce whenever they landed a major new client by putting a brief customer welcoming message on the companywide voice mail under a practice called "Sell, Tell, Yell!" A savvy leader fosters discussion about how the team can put its handprint on its work throughout the broader enterprise, so that the group is ensured status as a valuable player and an integral business partner.

An E-mail Worth Saving

> A few years ago, at the Seattle Special Olympics, nine contestants, all physically or mentally disabled, assembled at the starting line for the 100-yard dash. At the gun, they all started out, not exactly in a dash, but with a relish to run the race to the finish and win. All, that is, except one little boy who stumbled on the asphalt, tumbled over a couple of times, and began to cry. The other eight heard the boy cry. They slowed down and looked back. Then they all turned around and went back. Every one of them. One girl with Down's syndrome bent down and kissed him and said, "This will make it better." Then all nine linked arms and walked together to the finish line. Everyone in the stadium stood, and the cheering went on for several minutes. People who were there are still telling the story. They say they'll never forget it. Why? Because, deep down we know this one thing. What matters in this life is more than winning for ourselves. What matters in this life is helping others win, even if it means slowing down and changing our course.
>
> —ANONYMOUS E-MAIL RECEIVED SEVERAL YEARS AGO

The savvy leader understands the power implicit in team spirit. A healthy team focus is more than the latest fad or buzzword in business. It's the heart of company morale, performance improvement, retention, organizational pride, motivation, and employee engagement. Typical team-building aims at expanding team cohesiveness and trust, but this chapter's contribution has been to view team-building under the umbrella of a team's political style. The high-integrity corporate politics leader shapes team values and behaviors according to which direction the team needs to gravitate along the Organizational Savvy Continuum. Progressive leadership includes mentoring and coaching your team to become politically well-balanced, astute, and savvy—operating within the Power of Savvy range. The Greek word for "coach" means to "bring one along," and this is part of your leadership charter, bringing your team along the road to "impact with integrity."

Chapter 23

Forge a High-Integrity Politics Culture

Passing the Soccer Game Test

The moment of truth has arrived. Does your company's political climate stand up to the "soccer game test"? Are people comfortable going to their kids' sporting events while wearing a T-shirt displaying the company name? Laurie Siegel, the senior vice president of human resources responsible for cleaning up Tyco International's politics-ravaged internal and external reputation, describes this level of company pride as the true litmus test for an organization's culture. You can't lead an individual or team to a healthy political mind-set and equilibrium unless you also forge overall culture transformation. Otherwise, any positive change at the individual or team level will fade, because the environment won't support ethical politics. It's like a surgical operation being successful, but the patient dying when he goes home to a germ-laden atmosphere.

We don't intend *Survival of the Savvy* to be a full-scale organizational transformation book, because volumes are needed to tackle a topic as all-encompassing as culture transformation. But our leadership savvy tool kit is incomplete without pondering enduring political climate change. You will first need to (1) set a high-integrity politics vision, explicitly making values-laden savvy a burning business platform. Then, you will gradually (2) weave savvy and integrity into your organization's fabric by reinforcing your ethical politics vision in your staffing, training, performance management, and corporate communication activities. Most important, you will (3) walk the talk so that your own moral compass is unwavering, preventing overly political behavior on your own part from turning the rest of your culture change efforts into a farce. While the slant of this climate-building chapter is toward company CEOs, bear in mind that you are the mini-CEO of your own division, department, or team.

Set a High-Integrity Politics Vision

> He that gives good advice builds with one hand.
> He that gives good counsel and example builds with both.
> But he that gives good admonition and bad examples
> Builds with one hand and pulls down with the other.
>
> —FRANCIS BACON

Tom Peters and R. H. Waterman carried what we call a "values vision torch" when they wrote the business epic *In Search of Excellence* because they defined excellent management as being values- and virtue-driven: "Every excellent company we studied is clear on what it stands for, and takes the process of value shaping seriously. In fact, we wonder whether it is possible to be an excellent company without clarity on values and without having the right sort of values . . . Virtually all of the better performing companies we looked at . . . had a well defined set of guiding beliefs." Two critical political polygraph questions are whether you've presented top management with a solid business rationale for ethical politics and whether you have properly installed an effective code of ethics and effective corporate governance.

Executive Team Business Rationale. Does your team of direct reports know that you mean business about high integrity? During the recording of pop music's number one hit "We Are the World," aimed at promoting world peace, producer Quincy Jones appealed to Stevie Wonder, Elton John, Dionne Warwick, Mick Jagger, and other superstar recording artists to "leave your egos at the door." Similarly, the savvy CEO has an explicit plan for selling ethical politics and demanding accountability at the highest level. The top management team, even ego-oriented seniors, must understand the political values vision torch by which the CEO intends to guide the organization. This might entail: an impassioned inspirational plea to do what's right; an invitation for the team to think about the symptoms of political poor health we've listed; straight talk conveying that the CEO understands and will detect deception, self-interest, and private power pockets; an invitation for each top executive to understand his own morals; or a bottom-line-oriented link between politics and finances. Based on your biases, choose your approach, but some sort of strong and clear high-integrity politics mission needs to be charted. That's the essence of leadership—conveying vision, expecting commitment to the vision, and steering the group toward your North Star vision.

Being business-minded people, your executive team will most likely respond to a financial leadership wake-up call like the one we sounded early in part 3, detailing the real costs of not snuffing out sabotage and deception or weeding out overly political people. The revolutionary news, though, is that there is now proof of the profitability of positive politics. You can go beyond instilling fear of negative consequences, because studies document that ethically oriented companies actually yield better financial results. Common sense dictates that employees are loyal and produce more when they're well treated, buyers repay suppliers who do not take advantage of a seller's market, competitors treat rivals more fairly when they are not trashed by them, and stocks rise when companies are forthcoming with shareholders.

But now, beyond intuition and what seems logical, research shows links between integrity and profit, as in Walker Information's 1997 survey of sixteen hundred employees correlating company ethics and company loyalty, and in the finding by *The Economist* that corporate performance is higher in organizations with strong ethics codes. Elsewhere, CEO Jerry Fleming's book, *Profit at Any Cost?: Why Business Ethics Makes Sense,* presents other compelling evidence tying moral leadership and financial gains:

- The Center for Economic Revitalization, an investment research firm, found that over a decade companies with support for public service and ethical philosophies rose 240 percent in their Dow Jones index versus a 55 percent average rise by others.
- The 1,082 corporations with directors and officers measuring highest on ethical standards also improved their competitive positions by 63 percent, demonstrating that "do the right thing" (a less political Power of Ideas trait) and "do what works" (a more political Power of Person trait) are not mutually exclusive.
- Fifteen Fortune 500 companies employing written ethical principles for over twenty years grew twice as quickly on average as Fortune 500 companies without written standards, pointing to the wisdom of the next section regarding a code of conduct.
- Fleming himself administered an ethics instrument to many business leaders and found that higher ethical judgments correlated positively with critical financial information in publicly held companies. His empirical link of company success to top management moral principles documents a business rationale as well as a values justification for behaving ethically.

A Code of Ethics and Corporate Governance. Conscientious leaders install a code of conduct, supported by ethics training and a robust system of corporate governance. They also know that a code becomes a token piece of paper unless it's well written, carries clear top-management endorsement, ties to the mission statement, is widely disseminated and explained, and is rigorously enforced by an ethics board or an ethics steering committee with zero tolerance for violations. An ethics code can be a living, breathing entity that is embodied in employees, but only if it's first modeled by top leaders and preferably supported by a full-time corporate ethics officer and newsletters that publish ethical standards and exemplars. Earlier, the handling of tainted Tylenol medicine was cited as a business-school case-study standard for ethical leadership. It wasn't magic that led to moral practices, since the parent company, Johnson & Johnson, had long cherished its high-integrity standards in the form of "The Credo."

Congress passed the Sarbanes-Oxley Act in 2002 to raise the ethics bar on CEOs and boards of directors by making independent directors responsible for audits of CEO pay and performance. Roger Lowenstein's *New York Times* article "A Boss for the Boss" cautions that there will always be some greedy CEOs and boards that permit them, exemplified by Dennis Kozlowski's demanding guaranteed severance from Tyco even if he committed a felony (and the board granted it!). Federal regulators will help, as will boards that are no longer reticent to raise questions about top management ethics. But Lowenstein warns that "regulators, investors, academics and even corporate directors are coming round to the idea that . . . Ira Millstein, the lawyer most active in the suddenly trendy field of corporate governance . . . has been championing for two decades: a better way must be found to govern the corporation from within."

This book is meant for managers at all levels, but if you *are* a CEO or top executive, our challenge to you is to contemplate the company legacy you'd like to leave. After all, these days your company balance sheet includes playing for your soul. You will derive great satisfaction if you can install systems that partner with legislation to extinguish greed and Overly Political behavior. Peter Drucker, management guru, captured the responsibility of the individual leader in setting the values vision: "The final proof of the sincerity and seriousness of leadership is uncompromising emphasis on integrity of character." In speaking of the employee population, he goes on, "They may forgive a man (or woman) a great deal, incompetence, ignorance . . . but they will not forgive his lack of integrity."

Weave Savvy and Integrity into the Organizational Fabric

Business schools traditionally define staffing, planning, organizing, delegating, budgeting, monitoring, and controlling as the core of management. Recent decades have added the functions of leading, motivating, developing people, and communicating as a liaison person. The manner in which each of these management responsibilities is executed colors the political canvas of the company and can convey a posture of high-integrity politics. So collaborate with others to manage your organization through systems and practices that are compatible with the balanced Power of Savvy style. Install management systems that satisfy and support the criterion of blending "impact with integrity":

- *Savvy Staffing*. The savvy manager seeks people with good ideas and competence who embrace integrity and the company's interests while wanting to be successful. Recruitment ad wording sends a message about the kind of values that companies seek, and interviewing protocol can include questions that ask candidates to describe how they'd act in hypothetical ethics and political situations.
- *Savvy People Development*. Coach, mentor, and train Under Political people to enter the political arena with integrity, competence, and savvy while guiding Overly Political individuals to understand the negative impact of crossing ethical lines on their careers and on company results.
- *Savvy Motivation and Performance Management.* We introduced the Team Trust/Competence Grid for sorting out team members. Savvy leaders reward, recognize, and elevate high-integrity, savvy people. They structure goal-setting and performance systems to

discourage destructive competition and encourage integrity. Many companies now base bonuses on more than just meeting goals, additionally including qualitative assessment of *how* results are achieved so that values and fair play are taken into account.

- *Savvy Compensation Practices.* A pay-for-performance system, otherwise known as "variable pay" or "at-risk compensation," doesn't guarantee a meritocracy. It can even fuel unhealthy competition and sabotage as people clamor to claim credit for results. Antidotes include clear performance measures so that relationship connections don't determine advancement. Also, 360-degree surveys can elicit feedback about people's treatment of colleagues. Naturally, the more that people are well paid and recognized, the less need they have for counterproductive political activity to gain access to wealth.
- *Savvy Corporate Communications.* Make all top-management presentations and speeches, Web site and intranet messages, sales and marketing standards, and other company literature and collateral resonate with the high-integrity-politics North Star vision that you set. Preach care in revenue projections and carefully monitor for stock price hyping and marketing releases that overpromise.

The business and moral imperative of managing your team and enterprise for an "impact with integrity" balance doesn't mean totally revamping management or human resources practices, but it does require examining systems and policies for their possible impact on people's mind-sets and actions. Is overly political or under political behavior the outgrowth of your management structures, compensation packages, or messages embedded in orientations, mission statements, and trainings? If so, you can tweak any problematic procedures and processes so that they're more compatible with your other savvy leadership efforts. Then your hard work to provide an ethical-politics vision, flush out deception or sabotage, weed out overly political individuals, and make private power pockets public won't end up going against the grain of your overall organizational culture.

Walk the Talk

> Those are my principles. If you don't like them, I have others.
>
> —GROUCHO MARX

CEO and Team Leadership. Finally, we invite your own personal soul-searching so that you are congruent with the politics vision you voice for others. After all, for you to set a high-integrity-politics company or team direction, you have to be straight on your personal ethics. Whether you call this getting your own house in order or modeling desired behavior, you know that this step is pivotal. Reminding you to "walk the talk" can sound like a sermon—a haughty appeal to look in the mirror. But the most profound changes often begin with simple, values-driven concepts. As Stephen Covey emphasizes in his self-improvement bibles *The Seven Habits of Highly Effective People* and *Principle-Centered Leadership*, we can only work from the inside out. Gandhi viewed broad culture change as starting from within when he advised, "Be the change you want to see."

The Moral Compass Meets the Slippery Slope of Integrity. A moral compass implies that a person has a set of clearly defined principles that guide her behavior—what she says yes or no to doing. She immediately feels out of integrity if she doesn't act in accord with these stated values. You might mistakenly associate a moral compass exclusively with the Power of Ideas political style due to its "do the right thing" mind-set, or because we described a "fall from grace" as a risk of the Power of Person style. However, it's only the extremes of the Overly Political (OP) or Borderline Overly Political (BOP) styles that are lured by what is self-serving—taking the "do what works" mind-set to the extreme.

Any Organizational Savvy Continuum position within the Power of Savvy style can operate with integrity. Yet, no matter how strong your moral compass, anyone can take a slide down the "slippery slope of integrity" which refers to compromising your values because of several forces: (1) pressure and fear, (2) power and status, or (3) temptation and conflict of interest.

- *Pressure and Fear.* We've already discussed the performance pressures and insecurities that threaten many people. Good, decent people succumb to fears, competition, and constant achievement demands by taking the easy way out or bending the rules, which gradually turns into plain old cheating. Most OPs once were good people who said to themselves, "I won't change," then let pressure, power, or temptations corrupt them. A key defendant in a current major corporate scandal, a lawyer who allegedly took millions in loan money from a corporation without having to pay it back, spent his career fighting the very kind of corruption for which he's being prosecuted.
- *Power and Status*. A high school athlete receives star treatment, beginning with the adoration of classmates and a coach who ignores poor grades to ensure his eligibility. He's later bribed to stay at a college with illegal gifts from the alumni club. Soon, he thinks he's above the law as a weak police officer forgives his reckless driving when asked, "Do you know who I am?" As a highly paid professional, he's arrested for drugs, firearms, or sexual assault, but he's acquitted. Tragically, what begins with some pocket money can end up as the sense of entitlement that led Rae Carruth, wide receiver of the NFL's Carolina Panthers, to be convicted of conspiracy to have his pregnant fiancée murdered. Similarly, a top executive can gradually fall prey to the same slippery slope when he gets away with things others do not. The pattern of being excused combined with the belief that he is the reason for the company's success leads him to feel entitled to unfair advantages, excessive perks, or freedom to mistreat oth-

ers. Some airline flight attendants say that the rudest passengers are the richest ones flying in and out of Palm Springs.

- *Temptation and Conflict of Interest.* The *Harvard Business Journal* article "How Ethical or Unethical Are You?" calls conflict of interest the root of all corporate scandals and is skeptical of readers who believe they'd never bend their morals. The following scenarios demand tremendous strength of character to avoid giving in to temptation.
  - Accounting firms auditing corporations stand to gain by pleasing clients with their reports. As Andersen allowed Enron to overstate profits by $600 million and understate debt by billions, they earned $25 million in auditing fees and $27 million in consulting fees.
  - A corporate board decides the CEO's compensation package but has vested interest in keeping the CEO happy since he selects those very same board members.
  - Compensation consultants make huge fees for recommending the pay of the same senior managers who will or won't rehire them the following year at a half million dollars per project. How objective would your recommendations remain?
  - Stock market analysts' ratings are for the very companies that do business with them, bringing great profits.
  - Mutual funds allow late trading for favored customers and are rewarded with more investment dollars being placed with the firm. This drains profits that would otherwise go to more people, but human nature rules.

Dostoyevsky wrote, "If a man lost his soul overnight, at least he would notice the loss and be desperate to restore. But men lose their souls so gradually that they don't notice it until it is too late." We believe Dostoyevsky's comments are relevant to the slippery slope of integrity. Perhaps the worst peril on the slippery slope is the first time that we get away with it. Then, the combination of no one finding out, no external negative consequences due to our power, the benefit derived from ignoring our principles, and our ability to rationalize can start an erosion of our moral compass. If we go too far down this path, we soon start tumbling down the slippery slope until our principles can resemble the ones in the Groucho Marx quip at the start of this section: "Those are my principles. If you don't like them, I have others."

Ride Herd on Yourself. Some of us are vulnerable to self-deception that may leave us maintaining, "That will never happen to me," only to later bend our values. Being savvy includes respecting the power of human nature enough to look for telltale signs of the snowball beginning to roll down the slippery slope. And yet, *The Economist* magazine found that "a sound ethical compass was Number One" on a Top Ten list of leadership qualities. So periodically scan your own behavior and thought patterns.

- *Behaviors.* Be sensitive to potentially questionable actions on your part—not keeping a confidence, gossiping, taking a bit more credit than you deserve, exaggerating or being "creative" on a résumé, flattering someone in power, making a snap judgment about someone and spreading negative buzz, overpromising and knowing you probably can't deliver, or slightly fudging expenses. All of these can seem small, but they may be harbingers of worse transgressions to come, so ride herd on yourself.
- *Rationalizing Thoughts.* Also, watch for the possibility that you might be self-justifying of borderline behaviors. Do you start accepting your own excuses and ignoring your own inconsistencies? Give yourself some solitude to do some serious thinking or work with a mentor, counselor, or coach if you notice these thought patterns:
  - "I need to cut some corners now so I can get into a position of power to do a lot of positive things."
  - "It would take me too long to do it the right way. Nobody is perfect."
  - "Everyone is doing these things. Most people are doing it way more than I am."
  - "I work so hard for this company that I deserve it."

— "I didn't really mean it that way. I probably could have handled it better but she is way too sensitive and has a big chip on her shoulder."

"Wanna Get Away?" Many corporate commanders in chief feel forced to gravitate toward increasingly political behaviors, such as keeping their agendas hidden because anytime they state a point of view it is interpreted as a "position." CEOs may feel less freedom to make mistakes, like any celebrity, and they encounter more ethical dilemmas. As the popular airline commercial teases, we've all been in embarrassing situations when we "wanna get away"—to slink out of the room. Many executives take a sabbatical, however brief it may be, to conduct a personal self-audit *before* there is a problem. We've asked you at various points throughout this book to challenge yourself and look in the mirror.

Increasingly, there are retreats for top leadership aimed at confronting the unique challenges of keeping one's bearings at the lonely top. CEO Camp and Top Talent are two firms that assist CEOs to retain their moral compass. But leaders at all levels of organizations face rapidly changing norms for success, new ground rules for corporate ethics, a hectic pace, and multiple tugging demands. Organization leaders must give themselves timeouts to focus and engage in self-reflection, if possible with outside guidance and structure. Bill George, former CEO and author, writes, "The test of leadership is ignoring those outside voices and learning to hear the one deep within. As a CEO, your attention ultimately has to be on the long run. The voices clamoring for your attention will be many. Your job is to find your own."

Epilogue

The Bigger Picture: A Societal Wake-Up Call

A "Work-Shop" Perspective

Your organizational politics journey has spanned a broad range. It started with a wake-up call about your own blind spots and political style, then dovetailed into savvy tactics that blend organizational impact, influence, and integrity. You then leveraged your own political savvy to become a steward for your organization—either at your team, department, division, or companywide level. We offered leadership ideas for building your group's political savvy and spearheading culture change. It doesn't matter whether you are a CEO, a top executive, a senior or midlevel manager, a supervisor, or a team leader—you can still impact your own group's political climate.

Weaving high-integrity politics into an already demanding life may put you on overload. We respect the limitations on your time and patience, and organizational constraints. You have enough on your plate just doing your "regular job." It's probably daunting to imagine how to fit organizational politics into the rest of your job if you are a Power of Ideas individual, and the thought of bolstering your substantive expertise may be foreboding if you have a Power of Person style. You're busy enough running a shipping department, managing a pharmaceutical research team, developing marketing or promotion plans, penetrating new vertical markets in financial services, or opening new outlets. But even if you try just a handful of tactics to protect yourself or more successfully influence your organization, you'll erase some of the bitter taste you may carry from past struggles with organizational politics.

You've learned these political skills through our book, rather than a workshop, but we invite you to adopt a "work-shop" mentality. We mean that it will take some "work" to implement high-integrity political tactics. It also means that we urge you to "shop" for the strategies that best fit your time constraints and corporate culture. We know that you won't "buy" all that we've said—but we hope you'll try our ideas on for size by actively sampling them, instead of just window-shopping or leaving them on the rack. Some of the leadership tactics may not apply to the level of your authority but many others are relevant to any sphere of influence. As Ken Kesey, the author of *One Flew over the Cuckoo's Nest*, once said, "Take what fits and let the rest go by."

One Candle Can Light the World

We hope your reading has led to new awareness and that you have gained insights from this book. If so, perhaps you believe in the folk wisdom that "one candle can light up an entire world of darkness." If you do, then we cannot resist posing a provocative next-step question: Would it be naïve or idealistic of us to suggest that you consider a grander vision? What might the impact on broader society be if individuals and organizations were to embrace the Power of Savvy balanced mind-set?

Those under political people and organizations who have sound values and substance might gain influence and power by becoming more politically sophisticated in a healthy, integrity-driven manner. Meanwhile, overly political individuals and companies might temper their self-interest, deception, and power obsession in an effort to develop greater concern for the common good. There's been such corporate, public, government, and educational outcry over power corruption and scandal in our society. Our dream is to extend the Organizational Savvy Continuum's recommended balance to every nonprofit, educational, government, and corporate organization. We hope you are inspired as well by this vision.

Hurricanes, Tornadoes, and Termites

Don't get us wrong. We're not peddling panaceas or quick-fix solutions to you, your company, or the world. We're not evangelizing or claiming that high-integrity political savvy is the answer to society's woes. We don't even believe that avoiding political blind spots is "the answer" in your own job. So we're certainly realistic about the challenge of rescuing your entire company, let alone broader society. These are mighty large changes! Still, we believe the return on your investment will be worth any time and energy you spend. We are optimists about your odds for success—at the individual, team, organizational, and even societal level, especially if you buy into the optimistic concept of one candle lighting up the world. It's been observed that hurricanes and tornadoes get all the publicity, but termites do more damage and create more change than all of the other catastrophes combined. And they only take small bites. Of course, termites create destructive forces of change and we're talking about making a positive impact. But the point is that perhaps it is really the tiny bites, the small changes that only each of us can make, that cumulatively add up to the spectacular, as the following parable suggests.

"The World Just Falls into Place"

A father was busy cooking his family a gourmet meal as a surprise for his work-weary wife when his five-year-old son tugged at his shirt asking him to play catch outside. Daddy, not wanting to be disturbed, told Johnny that he had dinner to make but had a game to give him until he was finished. The resourceful father ripped a page out of an old magazine, a page with a picture of planet Earth as seen from a satellite camera. The father tore up the picture into many pieces and gave them to the small boy. He said, "Here, honey. Put this jigsaw puzzle of the world together, and when you're finished, I'll play catch with you."

Johnny happily went off to work on his project, and Dad turned back to his creation with relief, confident that he'd bought himself an hour or two of peace and quiet. Ten minutes later, Johnny proudly handed Daddy the paper jigsaw puzzle all taped into place. The father was amazed and asked Johnny, "How'd you do it? Nobody can put together a puzzle of the world so quickly!" Little Johnny looked at his dad with the twinkle of wisdom beyond his years and said, "You're right, Daddy, I couldn't do what you asked. The page you gave me had a picture of the world. I couldn't figure that page out. No one can put together all of that. But I turned the puzzle pieces over, and on the other side was a picture of just one person. That was a lot easier to work on, and when I put that one person together, the world just fell into place!"

Even Saints Are Fallible

We invite you to be hopeful and patient about organizational and cultural change. Closer to home, we implore you to also be patient with yourself—with your own personal, professional, and career growth. No one is politically balanced, skilled, and savvy at all times. Everyone is only human, even Mother Teresa, an extraordinary person whose values, work ethic, and expertise elevated her to the brink of sainthood. Earlier, we applauded the Center for Attitudinal Healing, whose mission is to provide emotional strength and coping skills to children and adults with life-threatening illness. This nonprofit, nondenominational organization helps people in life crisis around the world, including Bosnia, Oklahoma City after the bombing of the federal building, and Scotland after a maniac killed fifteen kindergartners. Dr. Jerry Jampolsky and Dr. Diane Cirincione, who provide leadership for the Center, were in awe of Mother Teresa, the tiny woman who was on the path to sainthood. They felt honored when they met with her, and Dr. Cirincione asked her, "Mother Teresa, how is it that you can be like this all the time?" They had to lean forward to hear her meek, humble reply: "Dr. Diane, Dr. Jerry, no one is like this all the time."

Organizational Savvy Skills Assessment

If you would like to obtain a comprehensive, self-scoring assessment tool and interpretive guide, we invite you to contact the authors at the Web site www.survivalofthesavvy.com. Other tools and services will help you and your organization develop high-integrity political skills and savvy.

Acknowledgments

We are as excited about the publication of *Survival of the Savvy* as two composers might be about the debut performance of their first symphony. We're indebted to the many artists who shared their craft to help our composition reach you—our valued audience.

Through Mike Moser, we met our agent, John Willig, who gently managed our budding-musician expectations and patiently "arranged" our book proposal. He unveiled our work at the most revered "concert halls"—the publishing houses—and we were overjoyed when he landed the Carnegie Hall of the industry, Simon & Schuster's Free Press.

Our editor, Fred Hills, was a maestro as he helped us transpose our workshop-style delivery into a new key—the unique vehicle of a book—without losing the integrity of our original melody. As overall conductor, Fred helped each section of the Free Press orchestra to harmoniously blend their individual talents into a cohesive ensemble performance.

We appreciate the support of senior-level editors Martha Levin and Dominick Anfuso. Celia Knight's copyediting oversight and Steve Boldt's hieroglyphics sustained each note. Carisa Hays was our concertmaster of publicity, sharing wisdom on trumpeting the book's merits. Michele Jacob's virtuoso publicity vision and outreach have beautifully blended with Dave Hahn's extraordinary chorus at Planned Television and Arts. Kirsa Rein was the diva of detail behind the scenes, and Jennifer Weidman provided legal counsel. Suzanne Donahue and Brent Gallenberger staged our early promotion success.

Since packaging is everything, we're grateful for Cheryl Brandon's title and Bob Brandon's creative jacket-front concept. We apologize for not funneling all royalties to them as requested, but it would be unfair to scores of others who reviewed ideas: Ken Kahn, Madeleine Clark, Eric Brandon, Lori Brandon, Zack Brandon, John and Jan Seminario, Chuck and Linda Miller, Michael Lipson, Sandy Burnstein, Steve Birer, Terry Strauss, Naomi Kellar, and Joanne Kalp. We also greatly appreciate Ed Lederman's jacket photography.

Special "tedium trophies" were earned by early manuscript readers Jim Bolton, Cheryl Brandon, David Sander, and Susan Hirsch. Dr. Maurice Ghysels deserves special billing for scouring the manuscript, enriching our examples, and emboldening the book's reach and vision. Anne Palmer, Debra Dinnocenzo, and Brenda Besdansky were generous with their time and advice early in our journey. Marlo Brandon devoted days of tireless (and tiresome!) craftmanship to ensure copyediting quality.

We treasure the many colleagues and trainers who are sounding boards and loyal representatives of this material within corporations: Juan Mobili, David Sander, Karen Martz, John Futterknecht, Maryann Rettig-Zucchi, Lori Mazan, Alex Grimshaw, Jeff Dorman, Steven Giordano, Deborah Masters, Mimi Watson, Steven Milden, Harry Sloofman, Holly Peck, and Vivianne Thieberger.

Finally, we wish to acknowledge our enormous debt to Dr. Kelly Reineke. Many core concepts of the organizational savvy model stem from her dissertation on power, feedback, and deception. In addition, Kelly has provided ongoing guidance in the refinement of our seminars and coaching activities.

Rick Brandon's Personal Acknowledgments

In 1975 Bob and Dot Bolton hired me at Ridge Associates, one of the country's premier training firms specializing in corporate interpersonal performance. Their faith and mentoring formed the backbone of my professional life. No one has had a greater influence on my business ethics, competence, or professional success.

A midlife "career enlightenment" led me to seek more of my own personal handprint on my work, yet I didn't want an "exit lane" from Ridge Associates. I'm indebted to my friend and Ridge's CEO, Jim Bolton, for walking the talk so that I could forge a fulfilling "frontage road" alongside my ongoing Ridge work—Brandon Partners' seminars on corporate politics and motivation skills. This past year, Jim again extended his caring, patient flexibility in encouraging my writing of *Survival of the Savvy*.

For years Marty Seldman and I have been teachers and students of one another. His executive coaching gifts combined with my corporate training experience created the best-of-both-worlds fertile soil for this book. Marty dazzles me with his street smarts, wisdom, fairness, and precision with words.

I don't take much stock in gurus, but Jerry Judd taught me that discipline is "doing what you don't want to do when you don't want to do it," and Dr. Hugh Gunnison helped me remember that "there's a price to every dream." Recently, Dr. Jerry Jampolsky's practical model for altering attitudes has inspired me and countless others.

I'm honored by my scores of clients over a quarter century, especially those who entrusted me to build leadership bench strength with high-integrity politics: Citigroup, Genentech, WellPoint, Avon, FedEx Kinko's, Best Buy, Tyco, Autodesk, Pfizer, American Express, BNSF Railway, Trilegiant, Inhale Therapeutic Systems, McKesson, Credit Suisse First Boston, Deutsche Bank, Cadence Design Systems, and others. I greatly value having become a speaker for the Institute for Management Studies and am humbled by the distinguished faculty whose ranks I join.

I'm forever grateful to Laurie LeRoy for spearheading my first *Organizational Savvy* workshop. I also wish to thank Austin Zullo, Rob Gimbl, Genevieve Davy, Michael Dehoyos, Ingrid Giordano, Debbie Harrington, Nancy Stockbridge, Leslie Powell, Nora Brennan, Don Kraft, Meribeth Germino, Heather Cowan, Debbie Himsel, Paige Ross, Harriet Edelman, Bob Hurley, Wendy Bloom, Janis

Coco, Tom Rose, Joanne Kalp, John Scott, Paul Ulatoski, Lisa Welker-Finney, Ann Moreira, Jan Becker, Fred McAmis, Buck Linder, Denise Montana, Nisha Rau, Susan Avelluto, Bruce Wood, Mary Rusterholtz, Vivianne Thieberger, Greg Fox, Jim Arnold, Jim Henderson, Barbara Hurtig, Bill Tavenor, Annette Griffin, and Eileen Neill, whose advocacy first brought my seminars into organizations.

I believe that "you can't give from an empty bucket." I'm blessed with people who fill mine. My parents, siblings, and their families have extended loving support for a lifetime. You probably detect the legacy of my father Ralph's sense of humor and positive outlook woven into this book. My mother Lee's faith and drive instilled self-discipline, so essential while writing this book. My twin brother, Bob, has been my fan and my idol—literally at a cellular level.

I especially cherish my immediate family for their patience and support while I was in the "writer's hole" or "writer's haven" (depending on the day). I love and respect my son Eric, a truly "large man" in my life, and my daughter Carrie, who daily makes my life a joyous song. Finally, no words can ever adequately thank my wife, best friend, business colleague, and life partner, Cheryl. Her sacrifices before, during, and after the writing of *Survival of the Savvy* make her this book's quiet hero.

Marty Seldman's Personal Acknowledgments

My coaching career began in the mid-1980s because of the trust placed in me by an array of talented human resource executives: John Pearl, John Fulkerson, Mike Feiner, Hilary Eaton, Mike Peel, Ronnie Miller Hasaday, Dennis Zeleny, Ron Parker, Charlie Rogers, Pete Smith, Roman Santini, and Rolf Deusinger. I am forever grateful to them for those opportunities.

In the development of the *Organizational Savvy Model,* I have been privileged to work closely with many outstanding senior executives and their organizations. They have also provided feedback and guidance. Many thanks to Ed Bernard and Jim Kennedy of T. Rowe Price, Ed Ludwig of Becton Dickinson, George Boyer of MGM Grand Detroit Casino, Eric Foss of Pepsi Bottling Group, Peter Gibbons of ICI Paints, Mike Maroone of AutoNation, Ed Orzetti of Textron, Matt Rose of Burlington Northern Santa Fe Railroad, Peter Bassi and Sam Su of Yum International Restaurants, and Mike White of PepsiCo International.

Jovita Thomas-Williams has been a great role model of courage and conviction and a key partner, with Cathie Ruffner, in the development of *Organizational Savvy* as part of MGM Grand Casino Corporate University.

Ed Betof, Joe Toto, and Jeff Koeppel of Becton Dickinson were instrumental in highlighting *Organizational Savvy* as central to leadership development both in their leadership training and with the Conference Board through Jean McNulty. Their suggestions have been invaluable in refining the program.

David Kasiarz and Kevin Cox are great partners in the Pepsi Bottling Group Leadership Academy. Ralph Biggadike has been instrumental in bringing the model to the Columbia Graduate School of Business.

Jean Otte of Women Unlimited accelerated my learning about the specific challenges facing female executives, and Dr. Price Cobbs, author of *Cracking the Code*, has helped me understand many nuances of using organizational savvy to help African-American executives.

My work would not be possible without my many "internal" partners: human resource executives. I am grateful for my collaboration with Lucien Alziari, Neil Anthony, David Ayre, John Bronson, Joe Bosch, Maria Butz, Clare Chapman, Connie Colao, Freddy Cabrera, Brian Chitister, Daryl David, Gregg Dedrick, Bob Dees, Carol Dennis, Anil Dixit, Ken DiPietro, John Dowd, Bob Foreman, Sharon Fitzmorris, Jim Galovan, Ricci Gardner, Don Hamill, Rich Gros, Nancy Jagmin, Raquel Karls, Andy Kaslow, Steve Klug, Fred Khoury, Mary Kramer, Wayne L'Heureux, Melody Jones, Terry

Kirby, Olden Lee, Christabel Lo, Howard Marcus, Alan May, David Miller, Steve Milovich, Tom Mirgon, Pat Murtha, Maria Nalywayko, Dave Norton, Gretchen Park, Dave Pace, Addie Perkins, Kathy Plakatoris, Deborah Rowland, DiAnn Sanchez, Dave Sherb, Mannie Sousa, Julie Staub, Carol Surface, Michele Swanenburg, Jennifer Thomas, Mike Theilmann, Andy Weinberg, Scott Weisberg, Kevin Wilde, MaryLou Winchborne, and Staf Wouters.

Rick Brandon's energy, creativity, and stamina made the *Organizational Savvy* seminars a reality and a foundation for our book. It has been an exciting and rewarding collaboration, and Rick's dedication to making it happen despite many other responsibilities amazed all of us involved in this project.

Finally, I want to acknowledge the importance of the ongoing support and love of my family—Alli, Josh, Jyoti, and Kelly—and my assistant, John Futterknecht.

Index

Index

About the Authors

RICK BRANDON, PH.D., has trained tens of thousands of people in workshops and speeches and has thirty years of performance improvement experience. He has consulted, trained, and presented at companies worldwide, from start-up e-commerce to blue-chip companies. He owns Brandon Partners, offering workshops on corporate politics and managerial motivation through his flagship programs, Organizational Savvy and the Motivational Tool Kit. Brandon earned a Ph.D. in counseling at the University of Arizona.

MARTY SELDMAN'S thirty-five-year career includes expertise in group dynamics, clinical psychology, cross-cultural studies, training, and executive coaching. He is one of the country's most experienced coaches, working one-on-one with more than thirteen hundred executives since 1986. Seldman currently resides with his wife and daughter in Montclair, New Jersey.